Saving Haiti, Saving the World
Can Christianity Face the Challenge?

J.B.L. Charlot and Ruthy Charlot

Copyright © 2008 by J.B.L. Charlot and Ruthy Charlot.
All rights reserved.

Printed in the United States of America.

No part of this book may be reproduced in any manner whatsoever without written permission except in the case of brief quotations embodied in critical articles and reviews.

Contents

Prologue	v
Introduction	1
Chapter One	5
What Was Then, Is Also Now	
Chapter Two	21
God's Perceived Plan for Haiti, Haitians and the World	
Chapter Three	37
The Four Supports of the Haitian Culture of Violence	
Chapter Four	57
Perceptions of God and Religion	
Chapter Five	71
Of Religions and Spiritual Consciousness	
Chapter Six	85
There Are No Sinless Religions	
Chapter Seven	95
Timeliness, Truths and Thinking	
Chapter Eight	105
Religion, Selective Literalism and Brutality	
Chapter Nine	159
Salvation	
Chapter Ten	181
Conclusion	
Epilogue	189
Acknowledgements	191
References	195

Prologue

People will not look forward to posterity, who never look backward to their ancestors.
—Edmund Burke

The notion that mankind has progressed through a series of primitive stages of consciousness on his path to the present, and that these stages correspond to concrete forms of social organization, such as tribal, slave-owning, theocratic, and finally democratic-egalitarian societies, has become inseparable from the modern understanding of man...
For Hegel all human behavior in the material world, and hence all human history, is rooted in a prior state of consciousness...This consciousness may not be explicit and self-aware, as are modern political doctrines, but may rather take the form of religion or simple cultural or moral habits. And yet this realm of consciousness in the long run necessarily becomes manifest in the material world, indeed creates the material world in its own image.
—Francis Fukuyama

I certify to you that, with the help of God, we shall powerfully enter into your country and shall make war against you in all ways and manners that we can, and shall subject you to the yoke and obedience of the Church and Their Highnesses. We shall take you and your wives and your children, and shall make slaves of them, and as such shall sell and dispose of them as Their Highnesses may command. And we shall take your goods, and shall do you all the mischief and damage that we can, as to vassals who do not obey and refuse to receive their lord and resist and contradict him.

—From the *Requerimiento*

Haiti's birth as a nation owes a debt of gratitude to violence, and perhaps in the service of freedom, violence is legitimate. Legitimate violence, of course, belongs to the state, but the state, like the surgeon with the knife, should use legitimate violence only when it must, or, like in the Christian song, "Love lifted me when nothing else would help." However, the sad reality is that violence inevitably begets violence. Most of the violence that gave birth to the present civilization was unjust, ungodly, and unnecessary. This truth begs for affirmation, but until that comes, people will continue grappling with the rewards of institutionalized sin while stealthy consequences destroy what is most valuable. Generations will continue honoring mistakes of the past rather than working peacefully to resolve difficult problems. This book attempts to demonstrate that Haiti has reaped ruin from that legacy of violence, a legacy handed down by the enslavers and the would-be-civilizers of Haiti.

Should we care about the small country of Haiti because it was founded by the leaders of the Western world's only successful slave revolt? No. Because it was the world's first black republic? Still, no. Because it demonstrated to slave-owners that slavery had to be abolished or free people ran the risk of being devoured by enraged mobs of slaves who could not take it anymore? Yet again, no. Because it proved that people of African extraction have as much right to freedom, dignity, and prosperity as non-Africans? Not quite. If you care about right and wrong, the present and the past, republics, freedom, democracy and race, then commit yourself to caring about Haiti. Care about the Caribbean nation of Haiti because the challenge to decency, prosperity, and godliness posed by the enslavement of Africans - as a practice approved of by God - has yet to be overthrown. Care about the nation of Haiti because false charity haunts our world.

For example, the ravages visited upon the people of Darfur by their countrymen draws, in part, from the bad examples of the past. Hatred rages and the mayhem continues unfettered. People are being brutalized, partially in the name of God, partially because of interpretations of Holy Scriptures, and partially because of cynical foreign interests bent on enriching themselves at the expense of peace, prosperity, and human decency. In the past, Europeans robbed Africans and so-called Indians. The Europeans performed their heinous deeds in Africa - and in the Americas - and collectively they have yet to repent and make amends. There is hope when a leader of a powerful Western nation says, "My nation's journey toward justice has not been easy and is not over... The racial bigotry fed by slavery did not end with slavery or with segregation (Bush, 2003)." This is a brilliant start, but more is needed to dissuade the current band of oppressors. Drawing upon the legacies of the seventeenth, eighteenth, and nineteenth centuries, they rob, enslave, and annihilate people. Many modern-day enslavers, like the settlers of old, base their ideas regarding race, ethnicity, religion, privilege, and labor on their understanding of God and Scripture.

Care about Haiti because the Christian age is struggling to begin. Care about Haiti because those who care can help make Haiti into a true republic. Haiti can become a nation that protects and cares for all its citizenry and inspires the whole world to work for the advancement of the kingdom of God. Those who care about Haiti will become partners with God in the pursuit of justice, freedom, and honor for God and God's creation and shall be called "children of God," and "repairers of the breaches (2nd Kings 12:5-12)."

Saving Haiti, Saving The World represents a heartfelt appeal to mutual love and understanding in a genuine effort to share an understanding of God exemplified by the Word of God. By Word of God we mean the historical Jesus, not strictly the collection of writings known as the Bible as described by selective literalists, certain fundamentalists, and dogmatists.

At its founding in 1804, the Republic of Haiti held the attention of the most powerful nations on earth. America was not yet a major power, but its founders brought considerable influence to bear upon Haiti's development. Haitians, officially or unofficially, could not adopt or implement a policy or set a goal without coming under the scrutiny of the leaders of the nascent United States of America. Additionally,

Catholicism and Protestantism, as European/American imports, have been introduced, with qualified success, in an effort to shape Haitian society. The brutality, class stratification, superstition, and witchcraft in Haiti, for which the nation is rightfully criticized, are the consequences of the unwholesome aspects of these influences.

This book addresses the following question: What is the *real* message of God's love and truth and how does that relate to God-given common sense if there is indeed something like God-given common sense?

Historically, Christians do not get along well with one another. Many of us do not agree to disagree peaceably regarding thoughtful negotiation of the tension between God-given intelligence and common sense. At times, that mutual lack of respect drives violence. Even though sectarianism is in contradiction to writings in the New Testament and the spirit of God's love, it cannot be said that members of all the Christian sects have exemplified Christ's love for the Church, or even God's love for humanity, in their dealings with one another.

Saving Haiti, Saving The World proposes that selective biblical literalism leads many Christians to justify their support of war and their minimization of human suffering. In other words, it suggests that the church universal suffers from acute and misplaced biblical correctness. "Biblical correctness," in this writing, is defined as a *comfort zone where it is easier to go by the letter of the Sacred Book than its meaning.* Phrases and stories are taken out of context and used to create dogmas that excuse a variety of crimes.

If indeed everything in the Bible is the word of God to be followed to the last letter, how can anyone find fault with eighteenth century preachers for not feeling a duty for love and compassion toward the people of the First Nations (the so-called Indians)? Do not the words "For the evildoers shall be cut off, but those who wait for the Lord shall inherit the land (Psalm 37:9, 20, 38)" justify colonial clergymen who preached that Indians should be exterminated to the benefit of the righteous?

Believers must shake down the fear-inspired, blind biblical literalism that is so quick to find biblical correctness in flawed political platforms and in leaders who espouse convenient political ideals. *Saving Haiti, Saving the World* attempts to make space for the middle ground, where Christ's love can proactively be given a chance in political affairs.

Somewhere there is a middle ground. Somewhere in the midst of all this exists a place where Christ's love can be given a chance in political affairs proactively. Instead of playing politics the way Samson swung a donkey's jawbone, believers can submit themselves, like Abraham did, in intercessory prayer before God. It may be that the super-powers that claim to uphold the highest values of Christianity still have the opportunity to lead the faithful after the manner of God, rather than gloating over God's "enemies." That middle ground provides breathing space in which all Christians are allowed to look kindly upon other human beings with love. Given time, that breathing space gives Christians a chance to actively love those who are different instead of condemning them. That is a key element of gracious Christianity.

In pursuit of gracious, more "grace-full" Christianity, this book considers how all believers might benefit from religious leaders who have informed and shaped our beliefs, attitudes, and convictions. Extreme religious intolerance and sectarian bigotry must be relegated to the past. It is not enough for Christians to honor the Bible. Christians should honor one another for the love God has for them. The disobedience and arrogance reflected by the multiplicity of sects in the Church body cannot be nullified - but the God of Abraham, Isaac, and Jesus is a resourceful and redeeming God.

This book represents a call for the advancement of the kingdom of God, written with the goal that whatever bits of wisdom and insight found within these pages will enable any resident of the Americas to become part of an essential prescription for healing that will be applied in Haiti, across the Americas, and throughout the world.

Introduction

There is a common saying that is hurtful when heard or uttered by Haitians: "People get the government they deserve." Descriptions of Haiti focus on three things: poverty, corruption and disease, but saving Haiti and saving Haitians has been the dream of many over the centuries, even as many Haitians have given up on this possibility. Saving Haiti has been a concern of Haitian and American politicians, clergymen, laypeople, missionaries, and revolutionaries alike for over two hundred years. There have been many creative, informed, inspired, and revolutionary attempts to cure Haiti of its many ills and they have all failed. Even bad ideas can generate some success if implemented by people with positive attitudes. For even great ideas to benefit Haitians, something must change in the Haitian collective consciousness.

Though inspired by the great minds of the Enlightenment, and although it was powered by the energy and will of enslaved Africans, Haitian mulâtres, and white sons of the French Revolution, the Haitian Revolution nonetheless appears stillborn. Two hundred years after the European colonizers were beaten back from Haiti's shores, Haitians are still not free. A culture of violence, supported by the founding of the nation, religious ideologies - both Christian and traditional African - a disdain for human rights, and Darwinian individualism, manifesting as disconnection from concern for a common good, has been a blight on Haitian institutions. The hostility of Christians outside of Haiti, and the pressures they have applied from abroad have also stifled God's mandates for freedom in Haiti.

Saving Haiti requires a commitment from Haitians, Americans, and the world. In helping to save Haiti, the people who care and those who don't may come to see the glory of a nation of religiously and ethnically diverse people, bound by trial and tribulation. Saving Haiti needs those willing to actively shape their country while being committed to the idea of justice for all.

For those who believe there is a God who created the world and who is interested in our affairs, there is no avoiding the premise that everything in reality is interconnected. If it is wise to proclaim that God created this world for God's glory, and that God is the ultimate Lord of the nations, it isn't too much of a stretch to admit that God allowed the nation of Haiti to be created for a noble purpose.

John Dawson, in *Healing America's Wounds,* writes, "God rules sovereignly in the affairs of people and nations. He has not abdicated His Kingship over one square inch of this planet (1994). Dawson cites Acts 17:26-27:

> And He made from one every nation of mankind to live on all the face of the earth, having determined their appointed times, and the boundaries of their habitation, that they should seek God, if perhaps they might grope for Him, though He is not far from each one of us.

Taking cues from the many relevant stories in the Bible, one can argue that God does His great works through people, but human shortsightedness fogs God's miracles. Critical analysis can support the thesis that God allowed for the birth of Haiti but that the project failed because of leadership that embraces division instead of God-mandated unconditional brotherly compassion. Then the nation embraced politics of exclusion toward its own children. Such exclusionary politics have, along with other wages of the terrible legacy of slavery, fostered a culture of perpetual violence.

If there is any hope for Haiti to break away from the cycle of violence, its people must embrace God with all their might, their soul, and their thoughts. The cultural violence must be renounced. Not only must there be a break from those who lead in the spirit of classist and political vengeance, but there must also be a break with preachers of traditionally accepted, religion-inspired violence. The people of Haiti must listen to Jesus Christ and embrace his teachings of unconditional love.

Historical Christianity, as manifested in religious expression, seems to harbor a love affair with violence. As it is practiced, Christianity is a sect-ridden religion of intellectual divides that foments a culture of drift and discrimination as opposed to encouraging morally respectful peace, love, and harmony. As Christianity is interpreted and experienced by its supporters and its victims, it is often characterized by retribution and condemnation. When combined with Haiti's culture of violence and traditional disdain for human rights, the failures of Christianity appear even more vividly. This combination explains not only the vagaries of power consolidation, but it also accounts for the apparent powerlessness of the Gospel of God's love for the world.

What must be discarded is the packaging that obscures the strength and purity of the Golden Rule - do to others what you would have them do to you. The obscuring package subverts higher thoughts and aims and motives. Those who are misled by the packaging embrace behaviors and thinking that contravene God's plans for believers to "love one another."

This is a call to rethink what it means to be a Christian - to open oneself to the transformative power of forgiveness and to pursue excellence as individuals and as countrymen. Jesus came to set the world free, but people use Him as a whipping block, telling the faithful, "Hold onto this here Bible while I beat you for your own good." Jesus wanted His people to confound their oppressors and bless their enemies. The people of God, the "People of the Book" (those who worship in a religion based upon the religious texts of Genesis, Exodus, Leviticus, Numbers and Deuteronomy), are not doing that. It is past due for believers (individuals or nations) to tire of using Jesus as a marketing tool for financial gain and self-aggrandizement. Pyramid plan Christianity is not the best that God's children have to offer one another and the world.

These thoughts are shared in an effort to make sense of the disconnect between what is preached in pulpits and the misery inflicted upon - and by - professing Christians. This is a sincere testimony from the pews and a genuine effort to make what has been preached in churches compatible with common sense and operational in our daily lives. It is Christian duty to help change the sad realities of our time, for the Lord has said it Himself, "We are the salt of the earth." How useful is the salt when not mixed with the meal? What's it worth when stored in a jar, even if the jar is transparent? Shouldn't the adversaries of pluralism, the unrepentant maximalists, be reminded that there is such a thing as an over-salted meal? These words and ideas, as disrespectful as they may seem, come from hope that Christ-reoriented Christianity, rather than "Constantinian imperial Christianity" will pull Haiti and the world out of trouble (West, 2005).

Haiti is a traditional Christian country. When politically powerful professing Christians, such as Secretary of State Condoleeza Rice, declare Haiti a failed nation, it is fair to demonstrate that failure is as much political as it is religious. This too calls for a bold assessment of the history, the influences, the actions, and the attitudes of those who have contributed to the problem, yet today have chosen to stand idly by, like innocent bystanders, or even more ironically, have become the harshest critics. By those who were part of the problem in the past, and are some of Haiti's harshest critics at present, we mean those among America's leaders and servants rubberstamping policies. Even though many Americans have tried to save Haiti, many other Americans have impoverished Haiti to their profit (Damu, 2005).

1

What Was Then, Is Also Now

Catch the dream of beauty,
Fragile in the background of our shared history...
Breathe with it; let the possibility soak into your soul...
Grieve together...
And let yesterday's enemies lose their capacity for hate
As they consider lost love and missed opportunities...
                                             - Ruthy Charlot

Although the international press brands Haiti as one of the poorest, most backward countries in the world, it is a country destined for greatness. Haiti manifests a truth: that a people's greatest strength may also be its greatest weakness when exercised outside the wisdom and humility of God's love. The mission of the people of Haiti was, and perhaps is still, to destroy Western racism.

Haiti was the first black republic. It was also the first country in the Western Hemisphere to formerly abolish slavery, and it was the first to voluntarily reject exploitation at the hands of European settlers. Against great odds and reasonable expectations, the enslaved Africans and their part-European brethren (the mulâtres) threw off the shackles of slavery and colonialism - at least on paper.

In the early nineteenth century, when Haiti was emerging as a nation, Western racism was at its lowest low. Slavery, the saddest demonstration of people's willingness and ability to maim humankind, had been connected to skin color. God's children were being destroyed, body and soul, in His name. The excuse made for enslaving non-white men and women, first the indigenous peoples - and after their annihilation, black-African men and women - was that God had cursed them. According to the European political and religious authorities, God had supposedly established suffering-under-slavery as a way for people of African and aboriginal descent to be redeemed from their non-whiteness. In the case of Africans dying like rejected cattle, it was supposedly redemption from blackness. Not only did priests and pastors declare slavery good for the souls of black folks, but it was also believed to improve them physically, mentally, spiritually, and emotionally.

Maybe what happened in Haiti is that God wanted to prove that black people had not been enslaved for their own good. Through the actions of men and women of purely African, European, or aboriginal descent, and through the actions of those of mixed extraction, God demonstrated that skin was not more powerful than brain; that color has nothing to do with courage, merit, and competence; and that black people are not only people, but can accomplish great things. Through the people of Haiti, God sought to demonstrate that the concept of *miscegenation* (species-mixing) was the fabrication of sick minds, that the offspring of Africans and Europeans could equal and surpass the accomplishments of their white relatives. That's why, from Haiti's beginning, under the authority of Toussaint Louverture, the nation's founders offered evidence that blacks, whites, mulâtres, aboriginals, former slaves, former slave owners, Royalists, and Jacobins could create a society that the rest of the world would be wise to emulate. They maintained, therefore, that Haiti could lead the world in liberty, equality, and fellowship - that God did not make junk.

After gaining independence from France, Haitians appeared to embrace their vocation as apostles of freedom. The country opened its arms to welcome blacks and other oppressed peoples from everywhere, granting them citizenship when they set foot on Haitian soil. By volunteering for enrollment in Simon Bolivar's armies, Haitians contributed to his pursuit of freedom for all of Latin America. The subsequent emergence of a gallery of extraordinary men and women inside Haiti and abroad seemed to confirm that the miracle was still possible.

Sadly, nearly two hundred years after the Haitian revolution, the miracle of racial cooperation did not happen. Why? Because an original sin had been committed by the founders of the world's first black republic, a sin that gained a chokehold on Haitian society. Since the failure of total Haitian liberation, it has been a long and exhausting trudge in the desert.

The Historical Context

During the Haitian revolution, four types of leadership emerged to launch the nation's birth:

- Vengeful: as typified by Jeannot, the former slave, whose hatred of white men drove him to grotesque brutality and blood orgies.
- Sorcerous: represented by Jean-François, who had a habit of turning enemies, fellow warriors, and even old friends into zombies. According to the lore, zombies are made from humans who die after being poisoned by a bokor (a hougan who practices black magic) and who come back to life after three days and serve a "master" as very strong but obedient slave. Other lore maintains that zombies can be created from the astral bodies of dead people who have been dismantled, destroyed or cremated, or from the astral bodies of the living.
- Enslaving: like Biassou and Jean-François, who promised the whites that they would return the rebelling slaves to the fields in exchange for medals and recognition.
- Redemptive: exemplified by Toussaint Louverture, a devout Catholic and admirer of Jesus Christ, who abhorred crime and black magic. He got rid of Jeannot, outdistanced Jean-François and Biassou, and habitually transformed his foes into allies.

Under Louverture's administration and leadership, Haiti (then called Santo Domingo or Saint Domingue) prospered and enjoyed peace. Europeans and Africans worked together and built trust. Toussaint seemed to have muffled the mulâtre-black conflict. The leaders of the country opposed slavery. Class conflict had been put on pause and no longer appeared relevant to the day-to-day functioning of the colony. Fear and hopelessness had been removed.

While Louverture had been fighting - and winning - battles in Haiti, in France the French revolution was caught in self-destruction. The revolution's leaders, Robespierre and Danton for example, were killing one another. During the Reign of Terror, France languished in chaos. Everyone was in danger, regardless of class or station. The aristocrats and the members of the bourgeoisie had been killed or had gone into exile, leaving the leaders of the Revolution to send one another to their deaths courtesy of Madame Guillotine. People were equal in their terror, their confusion, and their deaths. Fear and hopelessness reigned.

The black neighborhood of Haiti was doing much better than the white neighborhood of France.

In the wake of the Reign of Terror, Napoléon Bonaparte stormed the French national scene. Like a thunderbolt, he struck down the excesses of the revolutionaries. Bonaparte may have thought he was saving the Revolution from itself, but he reversed it. France teetered on the brink of total financial collapse, but the colony of Santo Domingo was still amazingly rich. In the interest of stability, Napoléon sought to re-establish white colonial rule of Santo Domingo. Toward that end, Napoléon dispatched troops with his brother-in-law, Leclerc, at the helm.

At that time, four models of rational politics or democratic experiences were taking hold in the world: Corsica, with Paoli; the American Revolution; the French Revolution of 1789; and the Louverturian experience in Haiti. Napoléon rejected his father's politics along with his father's name, allying with France and choosing to be called Bonaparte rather than *Buonaparte*. His father, Charles Marie Buonaparte, and Paoli were not only fellow officers in the military but also friends. In addition to changing his name to Bonaparte because it "looked more French," Napoléon betrayed his father's revolution by allying with the French and co-opting the French revolution (Saul, 1992).

Had a victorious French presence existed in Haiti, Napoléon could have split or dominated North America, and had he not married the Martinique-born widow, Joséphine de Beauharnais (born Marie-Rose Josèphe Tascher de la Pagerie), he might have joined his armies to Toussaint Louverture's Haitian militias and gone on to dominate the "New World" (Bonaparte, 1986).

Perhaps Napoléon never joined forces with Louverture because his wife, Joséphine, advised him against yielding to "the ambition of a Negro," by whom she meant Toussaint Louverture (Bell, 1994; Bonaparte, 1986). Few heroes trigger as many mixed feelings as Bonaparte. In a way, his name deserves to be in the Temple of Reason. Napoléon supported the rights of people to worship God in their own way and he was probably the first to successfully challenge French anti-Semitism. Not only did he announce that the Jews of France should become full citizens of the Republic, but in July 1806 he called for the meeting of the Great Sanhedrin (Armstrong, 2001).

Napoléon also respected Islam. Upon entering Egypt with his troops, he proclaimed:

> I have come to restore your rights, which have been invaded by usurpers - that I adore God more than the Mamelukes and that I respect the Prophet Muhammad and the noble Koran. Tell them that all men are created equal before God - that intelligence, virtue, and science, are the only distinction between them (Armstrong, 2001).

Napoléon verbally adhered to the French Revolutionary motto, "Liberté, Egalité, Fraternité![1]" His views on humanity, life, God, and religion may not have diverged from those of Thomas Jefferson, but he did not demonstrate the humility of America's founding fathers. America's founding fathers modeled their new government from examples the world over. They even drew inspiration from cultures they deemed inferior. For example, representatives of the Iroquois Confederacy, purportedly the oldest living participatory democracy on earth, were guests of honor at the June 11, 1776 Continental Congress (Johansen, 1996).

Thomas Jefferson, whose fidelity to liberty and human rights were far from non-problematic, sat in judgment of Napoléon, when he stated:

> We believe no more in Napoléon fighting for the Liberty of the seas than in Great Britain fighting for the Liberty of mankind; the object is the same; to draw to themselves the power, the wealth and the resources of other nations (Chomsky, 2003).

As for Joséphine, if she were hostile to Toussaint Louverture, her public behavior toward him and his children did not betray this. The two had a cordial business correspondence (James, 1989). Joséphine's mother, Madame de Beauharnais, had a plantation in Léoganc, Haiti (then Santo Domingo) (James, 1989). After the British evacuated, Joséphine wrote to Toussaint about her mother's plantation, which had been left in ruins. Toussaint arranged for the repair and restoration of Madame de Beauharnais' property at the expense of Santo Domingo and sent the revenues to Joséphine Bonaparte. Joséphine had also entertained two of Louverture's children. Prior to Louverture's betrayal,

---
[1] Liberty, Equality, Fraternity (brotherhood).

kidnapping, and imprisonment by Napoléon's brother-in-law Leclerc, Louverture's sons, Placide and Isaac, often had lunch and dinner at Joséphine's house. She had befriended them while the two had been studying in France.

Many historians have explored the probable outcomes of an alliance between Napoléon and Louverture. When Louverture was making his overtures to Napoléon, Louisiana was already a French holding. What could Napoléon, with his pre-Louverture invincible army, and Toussaint Louverture, the self-taught general who had never lost a major battle, have accomplished had they decided to bring the revolutionary ideas of liberty and equality to the Americas?

From Napoléon's personal papers, it is clear that he considered allowing Louverture and the other self-freed slaves to dictate the terms of their relationship with France. In a letter never sent, Napoléon wrote:

> The time I hope will not be far when a division from San Domingo will be able to contribute in your part of the world to the glory and the possessions of the Republic (James, 1989).

Perhaps Napoléon chose not to send Louverture the letter when he realized that a Caribbean and North American offensive would preclude stealing India from the British.

Napoléon, the brilliant counterrevolutionary, may have recognized that the French revolution was a prolongation of the American Revolution. The French Revolutionary saying, "All men are born free and remain equal in the eyes of the Law," echoed Thomas Jefferson's "We hold these truths to be self evident: that all men are created equal and are endowed by their Creator of these inalienable rights to Life, liberty and the pursuit of happiness." Could it be that Napoléon, who did not balk at invading Russia in the winter, and who marched his troops into Egypt, hesitated to Napoléonize the American Revolution? Would Napoléon, who considered himself a son of the Revolution, have shied at mobilizing his troops against America in order to return the dreamers of 1776, America's founding fathers, to the light of Reason?

Emotion and prejudice dampened the flames of Napoléon's vision of personal grandeur. The commanding presence of Toussaint in Haiti, and the beatings inflicted on the French army by Dessalines, caused the French emperor to become so depressed that he sold the entire Louisiana Territory to Thomas Jefferson for the paltry sum of

$15,000,000. Intending to take advantage of Napoléon's need to finance his armies on the continent (Europe) and the Caribbean, Jefferson's emissary traveled to France with the intention of buying only New Orleans for $10,000,000. By selling the entire Louisiana territory so cheaply, Napoléon forever shattered his dream of mastering North America and the Caribbean. By opposing Louverture and the black Jacobins, perhaps Napoléon realized that at least in the Americas, it was not his business to master anybody.

As for Haiti and the United States of America, it has been said that the proximity of the United States to Haiti caused the small newborn nation's failure to thrive. America's foreign minister, Thomas Jefferson, led the world to boycott Haiti. This move thwarted the young republic's efforts to gain international recognition.

Much has been made of Jefferson's republican vision for the Americas and his commitment to human equality. Some consider him a God-loving liberal, an enlightened intellect who embodied the highest ideals of humanism while possessing the rarest of sensibilities, which allowed him to combine heavenly-mindedness with earthly efficiency. Others despise him as a hypocrite, highlighting the verbal insistence he made when questioned during one of his visits in France, that whites were not superior to blacks, and contrasting that with his record of slave ownership. No matter how thrilling his democratic and humanitarian ideas may be, his having written, "Blacks may be whites' mental inferiors" is as repugnant as his enslavement of the children his wife's half-sister, Sally Hemmings, bore him. If racism and democracy are mutually exclusive, then as a man, a scholar, a philosopher, and a statesman, Jefferson contradicted himself. For the people of the African Diaspora, Haitians in Haiti and abroad, and all people whose lives are devilled by race considerations, a pertinent question is this: how often was Jefferson right?

Jefferson's words and actions as a United States government official make it difficult to determine when he was right if at all. He failed to take a stand against slavery in crafting *The Declaration of Independence*. In regard to Haiti, he said that allowing Africans to govern themselves resulted in economic devastation. It was probably on Jefferson's recommendation that in 1806, formal trade between Haiti and the United States of America was suspended. His apparent personal and political acceptance of slavery have also been cause for his being named as the enemy of the world's first black Republic.

Jefferson supposedly said that sometimes it is necessary to water the tree of liberty with the blood of tyrants. Perhaps this belief served as common ground between Jefferson and Haiti's founders, but Jefferson and Louverture did not have similar attitudes toward government and temporal power. This, aside from Jefferson's attitudes toward Africans in general, may have had as much to do with the rockiness of the new republics' relations as did European racism. How could Toussaint, who concentrated as much power in his hands as he could, and Jefferson, a man in love with liberal democracy, have spontaneous chemistry, let alone agree on the business of statecraft and national administration?

After Louverture was tricked by the French, abandoned by the Haitians, and delivered to his death, Dessalines was free to rule. Unfortunately for Haiti, Dessalines was ruled by hatred of whites. However, through their sponsorship of the French Revolution, America's founding fathers had indirectly supported the Haitian Revolution. The first draft of the Haitian Declaration of Independence, penned by Charéron, drew from Thomas Jefferson's political philosophy and his Declaration of Independence. Quite regrettably, when Haiti's founders gathered to discuss the first draft of the Haitian Declaration of Independence, Boisrond Tonnerre unceremoniously interrupted the proceedings:

> Nothing so far in what has been said truly reflects our disposition. To write Haiti's Declaration of Independence, we need the skin of a white man for paper, his skull as an inkwell, his blood for ink, and a bayonet as a pen (Madiou, 1987).

Approving of these sentiments, Dessalines entrusted Tonnerre with the crafting of Haiti's first official document. Jubilant, he said, "Boisrond, I put you in charge to express my true feelings about white people."

It is rumored that after the Haitian revolution, Thomas Jefferson considered the new republic as a place to send rebellious slaves, but according to Carlos Wesley (1987) it was in the most vexing phraseology that Jefferson couched his proposition: "San Domingo would be a suitable receptacle in which to confine blacks transplanted to the Western Hemisphere who were no longer wanted in civilized society." Other than that, there is no official record of any real attempt to establish a relationship between Haitian officials and the American revolutionaries who had boldly carried the torch of freedom to Europe.

Toussaint Louverture may have tried to establish commercial relations with the United States of America, but he did not seek from the Americans what he wanted from the French: brotherhood (James, 1989). It might have been possible for Toussaint Louverture, and Haitians who were influenced by him, to find *philia* within the Western Hemisphere. Benjamin Franklin, Alexander Hamilton, and Thomas Jefferson had espoused the beliefs that had inspired tens of thousands of Haitians and Frenchmen to overthrow the shackles of slavery and prejudice. As for Alexander Hamilton, he is even credited for having spoken much in favor of the Haitian Revolution. He wanted the Haitian Experiment to succeed. He and Franklin abhorred slavery, truly believing in the equality of men. Hamilton drafted Haiti's first Constitution for Toussaint Louverture (Wesley, 2004). Strangely, Louverture and other Francophile Haitian leaders were so intent on uniting with what they mistakenly believed was truly revolutionary France that until Napoléon ordered Louverture kidnapped from Haiti, shredding the illusion of French-Haitian sympathy, the Haitians overlooked the possibility of finding Revolutionary brotherhood closer to home.

The godfathers of the French Revolution were American revolutionaries. Prior to the American, French, and Haitian revolutions, Thomas Jefferson visited the most exclusive social circles of Paris. He defended his convictions that all men were created equal. In France, Jefferson declared that no scientific evidence existed that a person was superior or inferior to another because of the color of the skin.

Benjamin Franklin is another of the French Revolution's better angels. When Franklin and Voltaire met for the first time at the French opera, they hugged each other to the thunderous applause of the huge audience. It was said that two great minds had at last met: that of Solon and Sophocles (Redman, 1977).

Like Jefferson, Hamilton, and Franklin, George Washington was another American who was ahead of his time. While not demanding that his young country follow his example, he freed all his slaves.

There was some receptivity among the American intellectuals of that era for the Haitian Revolution. In his book, *The American Evasion of Philosophy, A Genealogy of Pragmatism*, Cornel West writes that Ralph Waldo Emerson reconsidered his belief in the inferiority of black Africans, in light of the former slaves of Santo Domingo's successful rebellion. Emerson's racism was shaken by the triumphs of the Haitian rebels, and he began to support and sympathize with the Africans. Emerson saluted Toussaint Louverture as a genius:

> So now it seems to me that the arrival of such men as Toussaint (Louverture) if he is pure blood, or of Douglas if he is pure blood, outweighs all the English and American humanity. The Antislavery of the whole world is but dust in the balance, a poor squeamish and nervousness; the might and right is here. Here is the Antislave. Here is man; and if you have man, black or white is insignificance...I esteem the occasion of this jubilee to be that proud discovery that the black race can begin to contend with the white; that in the great anthem of the world which we call history, a piece of many parts and vast compass, after playing a long time a very low and subdued accompaniment they perceive the time has arrived when they can strike in with force and effect and take a master's part in the music. The civilization of the world has arrived at that pitch that their moral quality is becoming indispensable, and the genius of this race is to be honored for itself.

How likely it is that Washington, Franklin, and their like-minded contemporaries enjoyed killing the newborn Republic of Haiti in the crib?

Haiti's birth gave the world a glimpse of the beauty of cooperation among the races. Between the intellectual caliber, the wisdom of the founding fathers of the United States of America, the revolutionary fervor of the French Jacobins, the spirits of the Tainos and Arawaks who had gone ahead, and the glories of African diversity, Haitians opened the way for enormous opportunities.

God allowed for the birth of the Haitian mulâtre. Born of misery and exploitation but touched by grace, the privileged sons and daughters of kidnapped African women and white men, mulâtres were, by birthright, ambassadors of God's plan to eliminate racial prejudice - to make many people into one (James, 1989). By their education, their grasp of politics and government, by their industriousness and entrepreneurship, the mulâtres were an improvement over the *petit blancs* (the lower-class whites) and were ready to rival and surpass the *grand blancs* (the upper-class whites).

The mulâtre's black consciousness was first shaped by maternal love, rooted in African knowledge and traditions, while being given the opportunity to become further enlightened through European education and travel. The mulâtres thereby experienced the best and the worst European cultures had to offer. Some, like Alexandre Pétion (the son of Sabès, a petit blanc) may have never known discrimination in childhood. Why? Some petit blancs maintained lasting relationships with their black slave-consorts and many were monogamous. It was possible for their children to grow up in a family setting.

The Haitian mulâtres were in an extraordinary position of strength and strategy. They were born to bridge the gap between African wisdom and European opportunism. They were to be the apostles of the gospel of equality between the races. In words, and by their success in life, in many of their actions, the mulâtres, along with their black siblings, demonstrated the falseness of the white man's claim to superiority (James, 1989).

While in France, 24-year-old Alexandre Pétion caught the attention of a French observer. Said the observer, "If I were the right Authority, I would hesitate to let this quiet and meditative man return to his country and his people (Madiou, 1987)." Indeed, Pétion returned to Haiti, and along with Dessalines, catalyzed Haiti's independence from France.

Mulâtres could synthesize the best aspects of their parentage. Is it so surprising that a Haitian, Jean-Baptiste Point du Sable, founded one of the greatest of America's cities, Chicago? That Alexandre Dumas de la Pailleterie was a general in the French Army when Napoléon was only a major, and that only by an extraordinary twist of fate did Napoléon succeed him as Commander-in-chief, and then that Dumas's son and grandson became two of the world's great novelists (Rogers, 2004)? Or that John James Audubon was one of the West's great naturalists?

Haitians seemed bent on taking the international scene by storm. They presented themselves as people of great learning - intellectual shining stars that stunned the world: Louis Joseph Janvier, Anténor Firmin, Emile St. Lot, and Louis Déjoie, Sr. The people of Haiti have been professors in the great universities of Europe, North America, Latin America, and the Caribbean.

Today, Haitians are known primarily by the slur "Boat People," but in the pursuit of excellence, they rise like the quiet tide. They number among the best engineers, health care professionals, and experts in their respective fields and trades. They are productive members of the American and Canadian armed forces. They work for NASA and are among the administrative brains for the United Nations. Haitian children and grandchildren of the Diaspora shine at school and pursue great dreams while expressing their Haitian identity, evidence that some well-advised Haitian parents have kept the faith.

When the Federal Drug Administration (FDA), out of soft reasoning, labeled Haitians as being infested with AIDS, this statement was met with a barrage of protests from a rainbow of people. Consequently, the FDA eventually recanted their defamation of all Haitians. The statement that Haitians were congenital carriers of AIDS met with an avalanche of protest from people who did not meet the FDA's policymakers definition of what or who Haitians are. In addition to not being HIV positive, the protestors were polyglots of every skin hue and eye color. Brown, black, blue, green and hazel-eyed people whose skin ranged from black-red to sunburned pink, they identified themselves as Haitian in defense of Haitians. It was a slander against Haitians and Haiti, which Haitians, overt and otherwise, did not allow to stand. Before lecture halls in front of large and small audiences, Haitian professionals challenged ill-advised university professors, who had come to some unfortunate and unsubstantiated conclusions. Confronted by scores of Haitians who were not HIV positive, these scientists were forced to reconsider their so-called facts. Recant, they did; and apologize, they did. Scientific articles published in respected journals were retracted.

Haiti's Original Sin

In the collection of ancient writings known as the Bible (called by some The Tanakh, and others The Books of Moses, and others still, the Novels of J) there are stories regarding a man called Moishe (or Moses). In some ways, Moses is the prototypical Haitian mulâtre. Born in Egypt as the son of a slave, through a variety of circumstances, Moses became a member of the household of that land's ruler. Pharaoh's daughter adopted him as her son. As the son of Pharaoh's daughter, Moses was placed in the highest social and political station in Egypt. Interestingly enough, his biological mother had a hand in his upbringing, as she, through luck or blessing, became his wet-nurse. He was born to misery but raised to glory.

He grew up as the greatest of Egyptians, yet had ties to some of the lowliest people in that land. He was similar to the Haitian mulâtre who drew his ancestry from the oppressors and the oppressed. His schooling was Egyptian, his privileges, for the most part, were Egyptian, but his mother tongue - his heart - was Hebrew. He did not know physical hardship, but that doesn't mean he escaped it altogether.

As a member of Pharaoh's household, Moses was in a position where he could have become Pharaoh's successor. Even if he did not become Pharaoh, he would have power and influence in Egypt. From his position of power and influence, he could have improved the circumstances of the Jews in Egypt.

Moses was not the only person in Egypt who had risen from a position of no importance to a position of great importance. His ancestor, Joseph, had lived similar circumstances. Unlike Moses, Joseph had been born free. His envious brothers had sold him as a slave into Egypt. In Egypt, through God's blessing, Joseph rose in power and responsibility until, eventually, he was greater than the brothers who'd betrayed him. Joseph climbed so high that eventually he became second only to Pharaoh.

Moses saved his family and his people, and rescued them from Egyptian slavery, but did he have to take them out of Egypt to do it?

According to scriptures, the story of how Moses came to be exiled from Egypt goes like this: Moses reacted with wrath to injustice happening right in his face. One day, Moses witnessed an argument between a fellow Hebrew and an abusive Egyptian. Enraged, Moses killed the abusive Egyptian and then hid the body. After that murder, Moses came upon two fighting Hebrews. He tried to intervene and was rebuked by them for being a hypocrite, as he himself was a murderer. Fleeing further condemnation, Moses left Egypt.

Before Moses ran off, one of the enslaved people he'd rebuked asked him, "Who appointed you judge and ruler over us?" Perhaps God, through an extraordinary chain of circumstances, had intended to create that opportunity. Unfortunately, a murderous rage caused Moses to lose face before the Hebrews and his perceived authority over the enslaved.

Moses was correct in defending the Hebrew who was being beaten by the Egyptian, but he had a responsibility to both men - and in killing the Egyptian he did the one thing that would make it impossible for him to help Hebrews as residents of Egypt. Moses went into exile for nearly forty years. How many Hebrews died because Moses was not in Egypt to intercede for them? When he murdered the Egyptian, he lost his standing, power, and influence in Egyptian society.

Moses made one bad move: committing murder. The murdered Egyptian may have earned his death, and the killing may have been just, but because of that action, Moses fled to Midian. Following his return from Midian, he spent forty years wandering in the desert, along with the nation of Israel. There was a happy ending to their story because God always has a contingency plan to compensate for human misdeed.

When Moses returned to Egypt, there was a different Pharaoh. This Pharaoh had come of age with Moses in the previous Pharaoh's household. Whatever their relationship had been before Moses went into exile, when Moses returned they were adversaries. Working together, those two men might have managed to save the Hebrews from slavery in a way that allowed Egyptians and Hebrews to live in harmony. Maybe the Egyptians did not need to be cursed and to lose all of their firstborn children. Maybe the Hebrews did not have to wander the desert for forty years and dedicate themselves to war.

In Haitian history, two of the nation's founding fathers committed an original sin, which set the depressing tone for Haitian relations inside the country and abroad. Rigaud and Louverture were two great men in an age of great men. Rigaud was a mulâtre and Toussaint had been a slave for most of his life. Rigaud had been born to great, if constrained, privilege. He had wealth and education that many whites did not enjoy. Louverture was intended to be lower than a servant, a slave. Both had been denied the God-given rights of men and women. Despite their different backgrounds and life experiences, they could have worked together to liberate Haiti because they shared that history.

In the course of the revolution, Rigaud kept to the south of Saint Domingue while Louverture subdued the rest of the country. Before they ever met face to face, they had grown into admirers of each other (James, 1989). They were building a nation together: if not as equals, as free men. Both believed that they needed to come to an understanding with France and the Revolution. They might have been able to create a beautiful Haiti together, as equals: Rigaud taking direction from Louverture even though in the forces under his direct control, no black man ranked higher than a captain. Rigaud and Louverture might have turned mutual admiration into sincere friendship if not for Hédouville. Hédouville had been sent by the Revolutionary government of France to regain control of Haiti. Hédouville sprung a trap on Rigaud and Louverture - and Haiti itself. The temptation Hédouville offered was the opportunity for Rigaud and Louverture to eavesdrop on each other.

Hédouville was not the only European representative who wanted to divide Louverture and Rigaud's loyalties. The British Crown, which had long lusted after the former French colony, had been courting Rigaud and Louverture separately. Both Rigaud and Louverture were hard-pressed to defect to the English Crown. Their fledgling friendship was strained and Hédouville found opportunity to destroy not only that growing relationship but also their sense of mutual benefit.

Hédouville had been sent to Haiti to cut a deal with the Haitian rebels and to make sure that the deal favored France. Toussaint believed in the French Revolution, but he did not believe in the sincerity of the French. Rigaud recognized the race prejudice of French ambassadors, as did Louverture. Louverture knew that Rigaud was not entirely free of race bias himself.

All the opportunities were there to make it easy for Hédouville to inject his venom. Hédouville, a Frenchman, was a snake. (This is not to say that pro-colonial Frenchmen of that time were, in general, untrustworthy, destructive, malignant and hypocritical creatures. Snakes have always been good for agriculture and they trouble no one unless their lives are threatened.) Rigaud and Louverture were traveling to meet Hédouville in the same horse-drawn carriage. Hédouville had been working on Louverture and Rigaud separately. Hédouville created an opportunity for Louverture and Rigaud to listen while one spoke about the other. Rigaud and Louverture missed their high calling, ate the bitter fruit of eavesdropping, and became antagonists. Hédouville convinced Rigaud that as a mulâtre, Rigaud was more important to the cause of France than Louverture, a black.

That was the beginning of the irreconcilable differences between blacks and mulâtres in Haiti. Like all original sins, this failure had a domino effect. The cascade of events falling from this petty betrayal led to the War of the South[2]. Relations were so bad between blacks and mulâtres in Haiti that the nearest it came to resolution was with Dessalines apologizing for the atrocities committed on both sides of the fighting. Sadly, if not atypically, even while apologizing for the atrocities, Dessalines blamed the whole affair on Louverture.

Rigaud and Louverture were great leaders, but they should have known better and held onto their mutual understanding. They also allowed the wrong people to speak into their lives and thus the culture

---

[2] La Guerre du Sud.

of Haiti. They should have considered the counsel of white men such as Laveaux, Sonthonax, Roume, Vincent, and Polvérel rather than side with the neo-imperialists and others who would reverse the gains of the French Revolution or apply them selectively (like Hédouville and Napoléon), which left Haiti vulnerable. These vulnerabilities in statecraft set the tone for negative internal relations. Hédouville provided the temptation, and subsequently Haitians were blinded by poor perspective brought on by their failure to hope and trust. Hédouville's duplicity brought out the worst in Haitians as a people. In the wake of his trick, Haitians dropped the tri-colored ball of liberty, equality, and fellowship. Rather than focusing on building themselves up as a people as well as individuals, rather than embracing the best of Europe and Africa, philosophically, spiritually and materially, they found their worst enemies in one another.

2

God's Perceived Plan for Haiti, Haitians, and The World

History suggests that Haiti was intended to be a place where God would be celebrated in the unity of black, white, former slave and slave owner, woman and man, but strangely enough, the men and women who fought free of the brutal plantation system appear never to have gained freedom from violence and brutality. The country they founded is one characterized by violence at every level of society. While individual Haitians are successful, moneyed, hard-working, innovative people, the country itself is a byword for wretched poverty, blanket injustice, social Darwinism, and creative brutality. Haitian-to-Haitian interactions are distorted by mistrust, envy, and individualism. The resulting dichotomy has given rise to three demons that Haitians are forever wrestling: misperception of country, a culture of violence, and religious perversion.

There is a story of a jockey that painfully illustrates the very Haitian dilemma. A celebrated jockey began a race mounted on the best of all possible horses. He pulled ahead of the other racing steeds. While ahead, he tripped his own horse with the crop and tumbled to the ground but jumped to his feet and remounted. He continued the race, beating all the other jockeys across the finish line - where he was declared the loser.

He'd jumped on the wrong horse. Somebody else's horse.

Early on, Haiti's founders were like brilliant jockeys, racing ahead of everyone else in pursuit of the highest goals of the Enlightenment: equality, liberty, and fellowship. They fell off the horse: maybe because of the roaring of the crowd (the competing interests of France, Great Britain, and the United States) or maybe from disorientation brought on from the vigor with which they galloped. They remounted, but they've been riding the wrong horse for nearly two hundred years.

As if blinded by experience, the leaders of the newborn Republic of Haiti made no valuable official effort to establish relations between Haiti and the nascent United States of America. Connecting Haiti's emergence as a Republic with the American Enlightenment might have made for a better Haiti (and America, and consequently, the world). This is not to say that it would have been easy for the people of Haiti, under Toussaint and Rigaud, to resolve the apparent contradictions of the Enlightenment and the destruction of people and cultures it entailed in the "New World", but it would have made for a better founding of Haiti.

Yes, there were political and economic constraints imposed on Haiti from the outside, and yes, the United States of America imposed many of those external constraints upon Haiti. Year after year after year, the pressure continued. In 1820, South Carolina Senator Robert V. Hayne, defending the point of view that acknowledging Haiti's independence would have thrown slavery, the foundation of the American South's economy and prosperity into question, stated: "Our policy with regard to Haiti is plain; we can never acknowledge her independence (Dunkel, 2004)." George Washington as President (1789-1797) and Thomas Jefferson as Vice-President (1797-1801) and as President (1801-1809), did not appear to go out of their way to help Haiti achieve economic autonomy and recognition from the rest of the world. However, analysis of the personal papers of Thomas Jefferson, Benjamin Franklin, George Washington, and John and Abigail Adams doesn't disallow the possibility that had Rigaud and Louverture been united in nurturing the most egalitarian of the principles of the French Revolution in Haiti, Haiti might have found some support with some of the most powerful and influential people in the United States. Arguing this possibility doesn't mean that the active role France played in the American Revolution might not have led to the American government helping France retain control over Haiti. Nevertheless, it wasn't the government of Revolutionary France that had helped fund the American Revolution but the French Crown seeking revenge against the British Crown.

The leaders of the Haitian and American revolutions failed to tie their countries to each other. In part, America's refusal to abolish slavery precluded that. Haiti's disdain for America might also have been an echo of the French contempt for the British. It's hard for children not to grow up to embody the worst (as well as the best) of their parents. Ironically, children often manifest the vices and weaknesses of the rejected parent.

Among the founders of America were men and women whose choices sometimes coincided with the best and broadest aims of the Enlightenment. Abigail Smith Adams wrote to John Adams in September 1774 upon learning about a conspiracy of *negroes* in Boston who would fight for the British if promised liberation: "I wish most sincerely there was not a slave in the province. It always appeared a most iniquitous scheme to me - fight ourselves for what we are daily robbing and plundering from those who have as good a right to freedom as we have. You know my mind upon this subject." Later, upon learning that the British had bombarded the town of Falmouth, she exclaimed, "We have done evil or our enemies would be at peace with us. The sin of slavery as well as many others is not washed away (Roberts, 2004)." If it is true that one woman's prejudice impacted the political relationship between Napoléon Bonaparte and Toussaint Louverture, why is it unthinkable that the formidable intellect of Abigail Adams might have made a major difference in the relationship between "embryonic Haiti" and "emerging United States of America" had the proper channel of communication been established?

John Adams was one man not to have lost sight of that truth. Did he not write to his daughter Nabby that "it is by the female world that the greatest and best characters among men are formed (Roberts)?" Those who opposed slavery and believed that all men were created equal might have become secret friends of the Haitian Republic had Louverture and Rigaud remained friends themselves. Personal philosophies and preferences, especially in politics, cleverly forge the last word in official and unofficial historical narratives. Remember George Washington who, while he would not demand that his young nation do the same, willed that all his slaves be set free following his death.

What Haitians Did To Themselves

Blinded by bitter experience, black Christophe and mulâtre Pétion waged war on each other. Rather than negotiate a political transition through dialogue, they slashed at each other's throats. Had respect prevailed between those two great men, perhaps mutual understanding and even love would have ruled in the debates, and then Haiti would have been forever launched into greatness. Life today for Haitians would be so much more beautiful.

Haiti's founding fathers banded together to kick the oppressor out but showed contempt for one another's lives and well-being. What a dreadful display of disloyalty and ungratefulness! Pétion saved Christophe's skin from Petit-Noel Prieur and Sans-Souci only to later find himself Christophe's archenemy. Vertières's hero, Capoix-La-Mort, fared better with the Frenchman Donatien Rochambeau, who, in admiration for the courage Capoix demonstrated in combat, ordered a few minutes ceasefire to salute Capoix's valor. Christophe found Capoix too stiff and too proud (Madiou, 1987). Capoix did not stand up to salute Christophe. Instead, Capoix was resting under a tree when Christophe showed up to visit, and he remained seated with his hat on his head. Christophe, because of this, hated Capoix "to death" and this great hero of Haiti's war of independence, Christophe's comrade-in-arms, was subsequently murdered because of Christophe's plotting (Madiou). Yayou rescued Pétion from being annihilated by Christophe, only to later be eliminated by Pétion. No dialogue was possible with Gérin. Magloire Ambroise did not ask for dialogue nor was he given the chance to discuss his concerns with Pétion. Magloire Ambroise was compelled to commit suicide under the first democracy-minded President Haiti ever had.

Freedom-hating authority figures in Haiti are typically known for their superiority complexes. The divisions, discord, and internecine fights that are common in Haitian politics are the legacy of Haiti's feuding forefathers. For example, Haiti's first head of state, Dessalines, was flattered into his dictatorship and then gunned down in an ambush. It was Christophe who, at Haiti's first great military parade, ordered the same soldiers who had defeated the greatest army on earth, Napoléon's, to kneel down and swear blind allegiance to Dessalines (Madiou, 1987).

This was uncalled for because these soldiers were loyal to Haiti and Dessalines. Those soldiers, Haiti's other forefathers, had driven the French and the English from Haiti's shores through personal courage and sacrifice. Even though Dessalines was their ranking superior, they were equal to him in glory. Therefore, they should not have been made to bow down to him. A salute had been sufficient in the greatest armies of the world, so why not in Haiti? In ordering those soldiers to abase themselves before Dessalines, Christophe set up Dessalines for a fall.

Some critics believe that Haitians are warped by the ambition of becoming absolute rulers of Haiti. Whether emperor, king, or president, complete control is the goal. Consequently, once Haitian independence was proclaimed, competing strongmen and two presidents divided Haiti. They were Christophe, in the North; Pétion, in the West; Rigaud, in the South; and Goman and Acaau, in the Southwest peninsula.

This "superior than thou" attitude of authorities in Haiti has been the norm. Haitian public servants do not serve: they rule. The desire to rule embodies a huge flaw in Haiti's leadership: pride. There is an absence of humility - a belief that a ruler need never answer to anyone. Almost every soul aims at attaining the highest position: the presidency.

This desire to be president is paradoxical because in striving to be superior to all other Haitians, would-be absolute rulers advertise their belief in their own inferiority. While a few Haitians have demystified the presidential mystique, it is not unusual for a Haitian president to be stiff and thin-skinned.

For example, Léon Laleau and President Elie Lescot were old friends, but they became foes as a result of a jest Laleau made about Lescot. Lescot had been dressed completely in gray. When Laleau saw Lescot he joked, "Take a look at his Excellence: everything about him is gray except for the gray matter." (*Regardez son Excellence, tout est gris excepté la matière.*)

The same Lescot had a falling out with one of the Légers because the man had poked fun at a spelling error President Lescot had made. Léger had been reading one of President Lescot's letters to some friends. President Lescot had forgotten to add an "r" to the verb "manger" (to eat). Instead of writing, "Te souviens-tu de ce restaurant au bord du Potomac où nous avons été manger?" Lescot had written, "Te souviens-tu de ce restaurant au bord du Potomac où nous avons été mangé." This meant "Do you remember the restaurant near the Potomac River where we went to eat?" instead of, "Do you remember the restaurant near the Potomac River where we were eaten?" Léger paused in his reading and said to his audience, "Listen to this bit of news; the President is dead: he's been eaten." That incident was supposedly enough to end Lescot and Léger's friendship. A lesser known story is of two men who were active in Haitian exile politics during the 1980s. One of them, a presidential hopeful, was incensed when the other implied that all presidential candidates had something of social conspirators in them.

Race Bashing

The Republic of Haiti's origins supported Pan Americanism. Haitians armed Simon Bolivar in his campaign to rid Latin America of colonial powers. Haitians advised and fought alongside Bolivar and his officers, embracing their destiny as liberators. But when it came to respecting and embracing diversity within Haiti, Haitians missed the mark.

Basing too much on the saying "Dessalines doesn't want to see any more white people up in here!" (Dessalines pa vlé wè Blan ankò), Haitians refused people who were not members of the African Diaspora from legitimate participation in politics. Denying Lebanese, Syrians, Jews, Chinese, French, and white American residents of Haiti the right to official participation in politics while allowing them to own businesses worked against Haitian interests. Feeding into Haitian classism and colorism, it created a sort of disenfranchisement that targeted the well-to-do. This Haitian variation of exclusivity traded against community interest. Non-black residents of Haiti were alienated. How different was this from keeping power and influence out of the hands of the masses? The alienation of well-to-do non-blacks gave them tacit permission to milk the country and hide or invest their riches abroad. This bears some similarity to how American special interests form corporations, register them abroad, and use them to influence domestic policies while maximizing profits at the expense of their neighbors. In Haiti, the alienation of the well-to-do non-blacks made the sense of belonging essential for cordial life and common comfort difficult. That sentiment of belonging is the secret for genuine commitment to common good. Kill it and everyone in the community suffers for it.

Mulâtres in Haiti and abroad practiced racism and classism extensively. The mulâtres who revered their fathers' whiteness, putting that on a pedestal while despising their mother's skin color and "her kind," they dropped the ball. CLR James wrote in his Haitian history, *The Black Jacobins*, "Yet, The man of colour who was nearly white despised the man of colour who was half white, who in turn despised the man of colour who was only quarter white, and so on through all the shades." Jean-Baptiste Point du Sable is another Haitian mulâtre who failed the highest calling of the French Revolution and the Enlightenment, even while founding the city of Chicago alongside his "Indian" wife. Although Point du Sable was married to a woman of the Potawatomi - someone who was despised as a red Indian by American colonists and Europeans in general - he made no overture toward his fellow blacks or mulâtres. He may not have seen them as his fellows. Point du Sable had no use for them and did not welcome them at his outpost. He was an elitist where other people of color were concerned. In his discrimination, he dropped the ball. Eventually, he was driven from the community he'd founded and died a near non-entity in the Mississippi (Graham, 1999).

Haitian Misperception of Country

The relationship between the people of Haiti and their governments has been characterized by mistrust and contests of will. Haitians conceive of country and nation as a way of enriching themselves and their families without giving of themselves and their families. Too many Americans, Christians among them, seem to have fallen for this way of life.

The first form of government used in Haiti was militarism. After Dessalines beat back the French, the former colony's war footing was deemed the best way to run the country. Officers of the army were given control of vast sections of land. Their primary aim was to keep an eye out for invading whites. The white invaders never came. Over time, as the ways and means of power consolidation and appropriation were developed in Haiti, the pettiest kind of duplicity occurred: the mulâtres of the so-called educated elite created a political fiction they called *la politique de doublure*. An ignorant black, specially selected by that privileged minority, was made president while actual control of the government remained in the hands of a mulâtre oligarchy. This oligarchy exercised its power with an iron fist. The members of this secret organization had a limited idea of *common good*. It was centered on their collective needs and desires. Not unlike certain political families ascendant in American politics, noblesse oblige and political legacies were given short weight. Enriching themselves and their friends and allies, whether within the borders of their country or abroad, was indicative of their passionate pursuit of excellence.

La politique de doublure's investors and creators were blinded by their desire to enjoy the privileges of white colonists. Blinded by colorism, they underestimated the intellectual alertness of the masses they attempted to dupe. As straw-president after straw-president was given the appearance of authority, the masses' alienation grew. They were the majority and they perceived that their country's government despised them.

In *The Revolt of the Masses* (1932), Jose Ortega y Gasset posited that for the elite of a country to be worth anything, its members ought to think and work for the common good or risk being dismissed as encumbrances. He redefined the term aristocrat to refer to a member of a small group of people who possess a keen sense of the common good, and who commit themselves to achieving their worthwhile goals. "A society is not really a society unless aristocratic," he said.

World leaders of today appear to at least give lip service to this idea. The elite of Haiti are an exception, and their long tradition of opulence and comfort in the face of misery has set a dangerous example, one that appears distressingly attractive to Americans enamoured of privatization and looting of the public trusts.

The Haitian majority has long regarded the Haitian elite as an encumbrance. Like the worst European aristocrats of old, they enrich themselves, in terms of experience, personal time, and disposable wealth, at the expense of the rest of the nation, which they only view as a necessary subservient bunch, a mere disposable commodity. Such an example of political blindness suggests that Haitians are more interested in having servants than in being free.

Haitian leadership has failed to realize that one of worst things that may befall a country is for large groups of downtrodden people to believe they have nothing to loose. It is believed that the poorest people of Haiti appear bent on destroying and burning property because they have no sense of belonging and no hope. Haitian nationalism is martial, uncaring, and dry. Haiti prides itself for being the first black republic in the world, but it fails to give men and women what matters most: a sense of their collective and individual importance. The Haitian concept of national sovereignty derives from the conceit that Haitians were the first enslaved blacks to rout their oppressors while failing to address the need, the unspoken wish, for every black to belong.

Too many of Haiti's many constitutions read as exercises in the stupidity of exclusivity. Some laws are paradoxical. Haitians pride themselves on using the code of Napoléon, but that emperor never gave a damn for Haitians or for Haiti. Neither Napoléon, the members of the bourgeoisie who hailed him as savior, nor the bonafide aristocrats whom he modeled himself after had love or time for the masses. Napoléon is a key reason why the Haitian experiment in republicanism failed. Few Haitian leaders saw the disenfranchised, the poor and illiterate, the majority of Haitians, as relevant to Haitian politics. They failed to understand the real issue: that when large groups of people live without access to clean water, sanitation, food, and shelter, they become a danger to others and to themselves.

Magloire, for instance, dismissed the teeming slum of La Fossette as trash while touring the northern capital of Cap Haïtian. According to a high-ranking, military friend of the General-president, while visiting the opulent and cozy neighborhoods of Haut-du-cap and Carénage he said to his Minister of Finance, Clément Jumelle, "If we are to do something worthwhile, these are the people that count."

According to some historical accounts, only one Haitian President, Dumarsais Estimé, asked the right question when he came to power: "What can be done to improve the lot of the People?" It is detrimental to dispossess the wealthy in favor of the masses, and it's potentially worse for the leadership to mistreat those who have nothing.

Haitians have witnessed what comes from anger, resentment, and envy: a nation of individual overachievers but collective narcissists. It has infested their army, which grew to be an expensive, introverted, white elephant of an institution: at times, dangerous and ferocious but also socially and politically reactionary. The elitism is less about the pursuit of excellence and more about narcissistic exchange of social and material capital devoid of general social context (some might call it social conscience).

President Stenio Vincent typified this line of thought. A staunch nationalist, he fought the American occupation of 1915 with all his might, yet he despised Haitian peasants with a specific and detailed passion. Vincent did nothing to improve their lot. His negligence and his irresponsibility allowed President Trujillo of the Dominican Republic the opportunity to slaughter thousands upon thousands of Haitian migrant workers.

Duvalierism, a noiriste construction, presented itself as a pro-black movement. Unfortunately, its adherents confused retroactive justice with ethnic mass murder. To compound their stupidity, the Duvalierists, like the Lescotists, clearly aligned themselves with one class and color. Commendably, the Duvalierists made it possible for dark-skinned people to enter universities and become professionals. Damnably, the Duvalierists also attempted to repair past injustice with brutal, unjust methods bordering on genocide (e.g., the mass killing of mulâtres in Jérémie). The problem with noirism, as it existed under Duvalier, was the commitment to extract repayment for white supremacy, with interest. In blood. Even from blacks. In the 1990s came the

Lavalasse phenomenon: ugly, deceptive, petty, and unproductive. They, the social activists who wanted to have the last word, sank the country deeper into the mire.

Militarism, Lescotism, Duvalierism, and Lavalasse have all contributed to the violence, exclusivity, and vengeance that has shaped a harsh reality for Haiti as a nation. These are the bullet points of Haiti's curriculum vitae thus far. Yet, there is a hope that where anger, resentment, and envy have long prevailed, all believers will one day witness mutual and genuine compassion. That is true human nature and that's what works in the eyes of God, not the "Homo lupus homini" (man is the wolf of his fellow man) sanctioned by greed and our fascination with violence as an easier way. Otherwise, people grow resentful and alienated. And as a result nothing, thus far, has worked. Because of this oversight, anger, resentment and envy are the people's claim to fame. Accommodation is better than revolution. The people need to know that those running their country are truly committed to achieving the common good. The leaders should allow their policies to be inspired by the writings of Yves R. Simon in his *Philosophy of Democratic Government*. They should demonstrate genuine concern; keep hope alive; and adopt collective beneficial interests. If the leaders adopt such policies, the people will be slower to riot.

Violence in Haiti

A nation whose fame should have been unity and concord instead embraced violence. Violence in Haiti is a culture. It's everywhere: in family, in society, in politics. Verbal violence and religious violence are praised and taught in the school system. Violence has even colored the way of dispensing healthcare. Yes, violence, violence, and violence: against the poor, against women, against children, against the beautiful nature of Haiti - her soil, the plants, and the animals. It's been said that if the animals living in Haiti could get exit visas, almost all of them would have left the country long ago, because they are so mistreated there.

The Haitian propensity for violence must be studied in depth. Its root causes must be brought to light, exorcised, and removed. Though a nation that should preach unity, harmony and compassion, it is a place where the citizens say, "Better that the cross be on the back of my neighbor than on mine." (Pito la Kwa al sou do vwazin pacé-l al lakay mwin). The truth is, when the cross is on my neighbor's back, it's too close to mine; therefore I must help my neighbor remove it and destroy it.

Violence was inevitable with the revolt of the enslaved. Escape from the French thieves was pursued by any and all means. This was absolutely necessary as the French colonists and soldiers were not about to give the rebelling blacks and mulâtres any chance at freedom or equality. Haitians had learned violence from French colonials such as Caradeu, Praloto, and Donatien Rochambeau. These men and their contemporaries organized systemic violations and abuses that were too much for anyone to endure. Mass hangings, drownings, and shootings were some of the ways these men amused themselves by instilling terror in the African populace. Rochambeau was particularly vile. He imported bulldogs from Cuba that had been bred and trained to eat men alive.

After wrestling control of the colony from the callous grand-blancs and kicking out the venal petit-blancs, many Haitians were still willing to give the French the benefit of the doubt and deal with them as if they were civilized persons. Louverture understood the aims of the French Revolution. He wanted the glorious hope embodied by that document to seize the minds and hearts of every man, woman, and child living in Haiti. But Napoléon torched that dream in the flames of his greed and ambition.

Napoléon had no intention of letting the French Revolution and its slogan "Liberty, Equality, and Fraternity" benefit blacks and mulâtres in Haiti. Napoléon gave his brother-in-law, General Leclerc, clear instructions on how to handle Saint Domingue. Louverture and the other rebel leaders were to be neutralized (that is, sent into exile or killed) and slavery reinstated. After Toussaint Louverture was tricked into surrendering to the French, Leclerc mobilized his forces to return the colony to a slave system. Leclerc did his best to put the blacks back in chains and under the overseers' whips, all in addition to stripping the mulâtres of all privileges. Leclerc planned to return the blacks to the fields or kill them. The leaders of the rebellion, those who had beaten back the colonizers and administrated the colony as ably as the white men before them, were to be deported or drowned.

Haitians were not returning to the plantation fields on any terms but their own. They would not be exiled from a land haunted by the people the whites had annihilated before transporting Africans to it, and they would not leave the soil that had absorbed their copious blood and tears, and sweat. Under Leclerc, Haiti's forefathers were given the choice of leaving Haiti, being killed, returning to slavery, or removing the threat of French martial influence from the country. It was either destroy the assassins or be exterminated. Despite losing the general who had led them through victory in war and in peacetime, Louverture, under General Dessalines, the Haitians banded together to drive the honorless French from their borders.

After the Haitians were indisputably victorious, the violence should have ended, but it did not. This is not to condemn Haiti's African and mulâtre ancestors. They stood on nobody's shoulders and had few role models who weren't vicious monsters and hypocrites themselves. These were men and women who had survived organized violence, and backbreaking, mind-numbing physical labor. Most of these people were illiterate. Somehow, the brutality that was visited upon the majority of Haiti's founding fathers - the blacks, when the French held the island - had been passed down through the generations. Haiti has born a bitter fruit: brutality is almost a cherished and cultivated heritage.

With hindsight's perspective, we can evaluate Haiti's failure to become a country where men, women, and children live out God's wish for His children to prosper in harmony. Thank goodness this book is not an autopsy report. Haiti is still alive; the comatose patient is showing reflexes. There is hope for a miraculous recovery. But the people of Haiti must acknowledge their problem in order to understand it, and through understanding, solve it. They cannot bury their heads in the sand and ignore that violence is a way of life for Haitians.

In the late '70s in the *Pentagon Papers* there was an account about the late Sylvio Claude. Claude had been tortured and beaten by the Haitian police and military for standing up to the dictatorial Duvalier regime. "That's all right," read the account. "Beating has always been the Haitian way of life." Yes, the country that inspired the sweet melody of the song *Yellow Bird* is a place where, not too long ago, people knowingly dined, laughed, and danced in the vicinity of torture chambers (legalities and actual practice not always being mutually exclusive). Even among educated people, threats like "I'll have you flayed if you don't stop bothering me" (in Kréyol: M-ap fè kalé-w si ou emmerdé-m) were commonplace and literal. In the population at large, skulls were broken over stolen bottles of rum or pieces of cheap jewelry. The sight of blood did not disturb many. Any government official, police officer, or armed civilian, could kick, smack, and kill with impunity and a smile. The clergy, Protestant and Catholic - and also Voodooist - and government officials, not too long ago, appeared to sanction physical brutality against women and children. Consequently, when Haitians get together, they can - and do - exchange stories of what they have experienced and witnessed whether in religious, political, or domestic contexts. Consider the following:

It is 9 a.m. on May 17, 1956 at Lycée Toussaint Louverture, Port-au-Prince, Haiti. Everybody is already inside the classrooms. Something is in the air. The students, children between eleven and fourteen years of age, look into the eyes of their teachers and glimpse anxiety. Soon, the reason for that anxiety will become all too clear.

There's a signal! In protest against the sitting president, the students dance while chanting, "Down with Magloire! Down with Magloire! He's no good! He must go!" (A bas Magloire! A bas Magloire!) "He's no good; he must go! He's no good; he must go!"

At first, the teachers insist on silence from the students. But their vehemence grows more and more subdued, for the children are hot. For days and months, they have been subjected to speeches on the radio about anti-people, anti-peasant, anti-proletarian, pro-mulâtre President, General Paul Magloire. The uncaring general Magloire, already sitting in office, cannot - must not - be re-elected. All the students cry out for his dismissal. They want to be little heroes.

By eleven-thirty in the morning, the school is surrounded by military personnel. Military police and officers, in khaki uniforms and toting guns, stroll around the building. "Will they get in?" the students wonder. The students don't think so (according to their sources, all the doors have been locked). The dancing and the chanting of anti-Magloire slogans continue. Suddenly, military personal and police officers appear in the classrooms. They indiscriminately use nightsticks and rifle butts on the faces, buttocks, backs, and heads of students and teachers. There are screams and yells from every room. Desks and benches are overturned. Students run behind teachers for protection: teachers retreat behind students, shouting their credentials.

Blood covers the school uniforms and the floor. "Mon Dieu," says a French teacher. "En tout cas je meurs chrétien." (Dear God! At least I die a Christian.) The beatings continue interminably. "Dear Lord, will they ever stop?!" Adding to the insult, the soldiers are laughing.

One student has taken refuge inside a window casement on the second floor. A soldier spots the cornered boy. Grinning, he closes on the boy, his nightstick swinging. The boy, who has already taken a blow, believes he is going to be hit again, perhaps in the same shoulder that had been injured in the mêlée. The boy's arm is locked over a huge schoolbook, *The Gallus Dicens*, which he was carrying when he took the first hit on the shoulder. As the soldier approaches, the boy decides that he will not be killed inside a window. He jumps, landing on his two feet, but more policemen surround him and beat on him. He manages to wriggle free and run away. Though he is quick, a particularly determined law enforcer is gaining on him, gun in hand. The kid is moving as fast as he can toward St. Ann's Square across the street from the school. A barbed wire fence separates the square from the sidewalk. The boy thinks, "Let's jump." He does so, but the fence looms high above him. There are two or three more lines of wire that he hadn't seen. The barbs bite into his flesh. Blood flies. The kid falls on his back and rolls to avoid more blows from the policeman who is even angrier now because his nightstick missed. The policeman pulls his gun out again. The kid is now up and resumes running. The police officer, trying to shoot the child, is still in pursuit. Of the crowd of bystanders, some position themselves between the police officer and the fleeing student. Soon, the student is on the sidewalk. He realizes he is on Rue St. Honoré and that acquaintances of his father live on that street. Leaving the sidewalk, he runs to their door. Before he even knocks, the door swings open and it is locked behind him, leaving the mad policeman outside. There the kid receives care for his injuries. As he recounts this story, he wants to remain convinced that even in hell there are God's good angels.

Another student in that school was not so lucky.

I too jumped from the second floor window but fell in the back yard, and the policemen were ready for me. They beat on me repeatedly. (In Kréyol: Baton jété'm, baton ranmassé-m.) And I was also repeatedly hit with their rifle butts. I managed to escape, and I tried to climb over the wall that circled the school, but someone ordered, "Fire!" I felt a sharp pain: I was hit. Covered with blood, I fell down. They pulled me up, forced me to stand on my feet, hit me, and then dragged me away by my injured shoulder, while blood poured out, toward a waiting pickup truck. On the way to the truck, another soldier ran to me and hit me in the head with his nightstick, leaving me to this day with a perpetual headache. Then, I was thrown inside that truck with other bleeding students and our seriously wounded English teacher.

Fifty years later, that student, now a grown man living in Miami, still carries the bullet near his jaw as a reminder of that day.

The soldiers and police officers who beat women and children that day were not only low- ranking members. The chief of police, a position of prestige, was in attendance. He came toward the end of the assault, supposedly for the purposes of quality control. He said, "Wherever you shall see the police there must be carnage: there must be blood."

There was an English teacher in the truck with the man who'd taken a bullet near his mouth. That teacher had not been demonstrating against Magloire, but was the ex-girlfriend of one of the police officers sent to subdue the student uprising. After he'd beaten up some students in their classroom, he sought her classroom. Upon finding her, he beat her so severely that she lost a breast from her injuries.

Where is the military code of honor? Where is the respect for the uniform? What lesson did the military teach that and future generations? Why should any child's memory be littered with impeccably dressed, grinning, high-ranking officers administering the *coup de grace* to dying men fresh from the firing squad? Why must children witness such carnage?

3

The Four Supports of the Haitian Culture of Violence

Four factors have contributed to Haitian's affinity for violence: the legacy of slavery; the effect slavery had on the subconscious of the founders of Haiti; how that violence and those effects were passed on to the descendants of the founders of Haiti disguised as parental discipline; and how religious fundamentalism supported and continues to support violence in family life, politics, and government.

To many, the subject of slavery is unpalatable and even annoying. People shut their ears, their minds, and their hearts when slavery is mentioned. Those who do not want to discuss it tend to fall into one of two camps: either they believe that they understand it completely, or they believe that too much emphasis is placed upon it. Either belief draws upon the idea that exploring the past and how it relates to the present is impractical. The past is considered irrelevant. People who dismiss slavery as a valid point of discussion when analyzing the current condition of blacks in general, and Haitians in particular, detract from problem solving. A reluctance to discuss slavery or to consider it relevant to current problems stems, in part, from the fear that the wronged would demand monetary reparation - or that whites would feel shame.

Slavery was invariably catastrophic, one of the harshest injustices people can commit against other people. In Haiti, as in America, enslaved Blacks, through white-on-black violence were kept from providing for themselves and their children. The net effect is that black households lag behind white households in terms of wealth.

Free members of slave societies, their families, and their ancestors benefited from the labor extorted from the enslaved. Meanwhile, the slaves - these black men, women, and children - could have used this time, which was stolen from them, to better themselves and their families. Instead they were chained to the bottom rungs of the socioeconomic ladder, where they were prevented from amassing wealth and investing in their present, let alone their futures.

In America, most discussions of slavery and its legacies are unwelcome. Participants in such discussions opine that the impact of slavery is overemphasized. Some say, "I can't be held responsible for what someone else did." But for many, it was their forefathers who did wrong, or their forefathers' friends, acquaintances, colleagues, and partners. Regardless of the challenges of life white people might find themselves experiencing now, they are building upon someone else's work, forced by misery at the behest of another, exploited and sacrificed. The wrongs permitted by these people's ancestors resulted in material wealth and resources, and these resources constitute a trust that has been passed on through society and favored families.

Authors like CLR James (1963), Don Ohadike (2002), and Gail Elizabeth Wyatt (1997), offer perspectives that explain how the present is related to the past.

> The kidnappers relied on brutality to break the spirits and stunt the imaginations of their victims. The people kidnapped from the interior of the African continent, endured long marches while chained to one another and weighted down with stones. The kidnapped who traveled to the slave ships by river, lay in boats for days on end, rotting from bilge water below and burning from sunlight from above. In the holding pens at the slave ports, no brute could endure the stench without fainting yet the people in chains had to suffer the stench and the filth. The slavers packed their victims on top of one another. The cramped conditions prevented the kidnapped from lying down or sitting upright. Despite the weakened condition in which the slavers kept their captives, the victims habitually revolted at the ports of embarkation and aboard the ships. The slavers kept them chained to each other and to iron bonds. The close proximity of so many naked human be-

ings, their bruised and festering flesh, the foetid air, the prevailing dysentery, the accumulation of filth turned these holds into a hell...A captain held up by calms or adverse winds was known to have poisoned his cargo. Another killed some of his slaves to feed the others with the flesh. The enslaved died not only from the abuse but also from grief and rage and despair. They undertook vast hunger strikes; undid their chains and hurled themselves on the crew in futile attempts at insurrection...it became the custom to have them upon deck, once a day, and force them to dance. Some took the opportunity to jump overboard... (James, 1965)

These were just some of the horrors imposed upon men, women and children by Christian slave traders. The enslaved were forced into submission by sheer wickedness. In order to control these men and women, white slave traffickers and owners had to subdue and sear their own consciences. C.L.R. James (1965) put it well in describing the mental acrobatics and twisted resourcefulness that slavers employed in securing the lasting submission of the enslaved:

The difficulty was that, though one could trap them like animals, transport them in pens, work them alongside an ass or a horse and beat them both with the same stick, stable them and starve them, they remained, despite their black skins and curly hair, quite invincibly human beings; with the intelligence and resentments of human beings.

As James, Ohadike, and others have explained, the white slavers used calculated brutality to cow the enslaved into docility. This cold pragmatism made it look like the white slavers didn't care about protecting their investment. But first and foremost, the white enslavers wanted to terrorize the Africans into submission as to preserve their own skin.

Some of these slave traders and owners identified themselves as Christians. Religious practices, religious texts (both the Old and New Testaments of the Bible), and cultural traditions, both European and African, were readjusted to justify the slave trade and attendant brutalities. For example the author of some of Christianity's most cherished English hymns owned and captained slave ships.

While being at the same time mastermind, active participant, enforcer, and supervisor of the level of hell that was the slave trade, this man composed sacred hymns as a member of historical Christianity. His "How Sweet the Name of Jesus Sounds" and "Amazing Grace" are beloved by Christians to this day. One question to ask, no matter their level of interest in spiritual matters, is where in the midst of his evil acts did this man find inspiration for these hymns?

The wickedness of some of Haiti's founders - including but not limited to murderous witchcraft, zombification, and the barbarities of Jeannot - are denounced in this book and elsewhere. Jeannot was a particularly bloodthirsty rival of Toussaint Louverture. He skinned white people alive, drank and ate from their emptied skulls, and ordered the legs of white men he thought too tall to be cut shorter. Let no one say that men like him deserved to be enslaved because they were uncivilized and needed to become Christians. Sadly, being bloodthirsty and being Christian are not mutually exclusive. Jeannot was no worse a cannibal than his white European Christian contemporaries. Unlike some of those people, he never wrote a hymn that became popular across denominations, like his would-be mentor on the slave ship. With Jeannot's white-focused cruelty, one can claim, "The chickens had come home to roost."

Ironically, the system did not spare the slave traffickers and buyers. All of the Americas and the West Indies took slaves (James, 1965). Every year, about one-fifth of all who participated in the African trade died - and they believed themselves to living their lives and conducting their business affairs according to God's will.

> The purchasers examined them for defects, looked at the teeth, pinched the skin, sometimes tasted the perspiration to see if the slave's blood was pure and his health as good as his appearance...Having become the property of the owner, he was branded on both sides of the breast with a hot iron. An interpreter explained his duties to him, and a priest instructed him in the first principles of Christianity (James, 1989).

Yes, reparation is in order unless one is the kind of believer who thinks blacks are the devil and that like Michael Moore wrote in *Stupid White Men*, "Give the devil a bone he'll want the whole leg." And this is where a positive attitude toward people of color in America will foster a positive attitude toward blacks in general and Haitians in particular.

Perhaps it will serve as an eye-opener for racist Christians throughout the world to do their part in bringing to reality Jesus' dream and prayer: "Father, make them one in you." Let people in the Americas understand that what is owed black men and women is such a big debt that no amount of money can repay it. The necessary reparation is not monetary but mental. Recompense must be offered through attitude change, with attitude being defined as a small thing that makes a huge difference. Between Michael Moore, who might justify reparation and John McWorther, author of *Losing The Race,* who deplores what he calls black indulgence in "victimology," there is a more constructive and user-friendly middle ground.

One: When looking at a non-white person, let the beholder understand that God loves this child as dearly as He loves any other. Let the beholder believe that every person they encounter is God's dearly beloved child.

Two: Get out of the racism closet. Go beyond paying public lip service to the idea that Blacks and other people of color are the equals of whites. Teach children that God doesn't discriminate between the races and ethnicities and that white people are not God's favored over all other people in the world.

Three: Understand that were it not for the injustices committed against their ancestors by those who willed their descendants fortune and opportunities, most people of color would help improve life, not destroy it. (Does the well-meaning individual really believe that given a chance, blacks want to destroy white lives?) Geniuses too can be black. Refrain from making Napoléon Bonaparte's mistake. Do not ignore competence, let alone genius, because the person who demonstrates it is black (or Asian, or Hispanic, or "Indian" for that matter). One of Napoléon's greatest errors was his failing to recognize Toussaint Louverture's caliber. In writing his memoirs while in exile on the island of St. Helena, he called it one of his biggest mistakes[3].

Four: People who make white skin the criteria for distinction have done so as a matter of choice. Thinking that white is superior to everything else, under all circumstances, is something that arises from a crooked mind. This is judging a book by its cover, while being illiterate.

Five: Upon meeting intelligent and articulate men and women of color, stop thinking (and saying) that they are different from other

---

[3] According to the *Four Gospels* of Las Cases, Gourgaud, Montholon and Bertrand as edited by Robert Lafond.

blacks or Hispanics or Asians or "Indians" you think you have known. When your children pair with our sons and daughters, do not give your hearts and voices over to the fear that your children are signing up for a lifetime of battling well-established, "common sense-driven" traditions. Don't patronize your children and their beloveds. Think instead that you may be witnessing a miracle from God and that your family is about to witness firsthand that God doesn't make junk; that He creates geniuses of all colors and shades.

Six: Love justice. Ensure that your government officials and law enforcement personnel get the message that every person's life is a miracle of God. Desire that the representatives of your governments realize that when they stop a black man or woman on the road, he or she is to be served and protected. It is not enough that some law enforcement officers are of color. That is not the key to justice: it is the training that makes the real difference. In the exercise of his duty as a law enforcement officer, even a person of color may believe that, "All black persons are criminals unless they too are law enforcers or of the elite." Personal relationship with individual or even a select group of blacks is no indication of being a just person. For example, Justin Volpe, the New York City officer who brutalized Abner Louima in 1997, sodomizing him with a broomstick and holding the filthy stick to Louima's face, was engaged to a black woman (McWhorter, 2000).

Jacobus Elisa Joannes Capiteijn, the minister who wrote a doctoral thesis that was used as a justification for the slave trade, was born a black African. His thesis was based on his interpretation of a passage in Paul of Tarsus's second letter to the church of Corinthians where it is written, "Where the Spirit of the Lord is, there is liberty (Nederveen-Pieterse, 1992)." Capiteijn argued that the freedom written of in that epistle was a spiritual freedom rather than a physical one. A person who was a slave or was in chains could be considered a free person provided that he or she was a Christian. On the strength of this argument, Capiteijn graduated from Leiden University in 1742. He became a minister at Fort Elmina, the capital of the Dutch possessions on the Gold Coast of West Africa. The French, the Dutch, and the English, as well as the Catholic Church, used Capiteijn's thesis to defend slavery for more than another hundred years following its publication.

These six guidelines, if taken to heart, mind, and spirit, can help individuals handicapped by racism and ethnic or color prejudice become decent people. By fixing these attitudes in their minds and hearts, they might gain something for themselves and their children.

The legacy of slavery is sticky. It blinds all people that it touches: African, European, Indigenous and Asian; man, woman, and child; Caribbean and North American; Christian and non-Christian.

Now, Back to the Enormous Task of Explaining Haiti

Why were the people who became slaves on the middle passage sold? Maybe the Africans sold on the Middle Passage were social misfits, unfortunate brats in the habit of asking unwelcome questions. Maybe they were too much like the biblical Joseph, sold by their brothers because nobody likes a know-it-all - especially one who is gifted. Anyway, there the kidnapped Africans were, chained and shackled, given over to strangers who neither looked like them nor spoke their languages, packaged like cheap goods, auctioned like cattle, and given over to the wickedness of people who excused their greed and cold-heartedness as pleasing in the eyes of God. In the process, the force of Law and the law of Force dominated these people. They were handled, raped, starved, and covered in filth. The slave trade was a mind-killing, soul-warping vortex, a descent into an earthly hell that was destructive to both the victimized and the victimizers.

The culture of violence in Haiti is an example of the saying that violence begets violence. Perhaps it began in Africa, where a quadruple violence was committed against the African ancestors of the Haitian people. First, there was kidnapping and bondage by other Africans, strangers as well as neighbors, but all enemies. Then, there was eviction from their homeland. Third, was forced emigration through the demoralizing and brutal transport on reeking slave ships. Fourth was their sale (and branding) like cattle upon arrival in the Americas. Inside the human garbage pit of American slavery, the mothers and fathers of Haiti were continuously and creatively violated. They were not permitted to live together, build together, or love. In the man-created Hell that was Haiti, the vicious and pragmatic French slave owners had calculated that it made more economic sense to work slaves to death and buy new ones, rather than provide for their basic needs.

Survival dictated that the slaves refrain from trusting. The only weapons they had were those that could not be taken away from them physically: instincts. For a long time, the instinct of conservation made for enslaved people who were staunch individualists. These were people who could not build together. The bundling together that made the

Haitian revolt successful was a unity forged on charcoal. It was temporary.

There was little love or intellectual chemistry among the Africans who rebelled against the French. In general, their only commitment was to immediate, personal freedom. Freedom was defined in extreme, limited terms: getting away from hell. The habits and tactics that facilitated the beating of the French colonials from the island, the dismantling of slavery, and the establishment of freedom from the French were not conducive to nation building or to the maintenance of a community of equals.

How did Haitian slavery and the Haitian revolution account for the fractiousness of Haitian society and politics? By drawing upon Jung and Freud's theories of the subconscious, as Milburn and Conrad have, it can be argued that anyone who survives physical violence is likely to subconsciously accept it, even if they hate it. From accepting the hypothetical necessity of violence, even subconsciously, a person may go on to embody it.

The pain a person has endured is not the only determining factor of his or her future behavior: the message and attitude of the person or people inflicting the violence act like subliminal invaders (Milburn & Conrad). Subliminal invaders are the attitudes toward violence embodied in the words, expressions, and emotions of the abusers. During a violent episode, the person being abused absorbs these invaders, consciously and unconsciously. In his or her agony, the recipient of that violence might not consciously notice what's being said, but their subconscious will. In the subconscious, the effects of the violence and aggression are warped and amplified. The subliminal invaders sink into the subconscious like bad seeds. The effects will spring up like choking weeds. They are translated from physical events into psychic events. As psychic events, they become equivalent to the strings of a puppet master.

Commonly, victims of abuse and oppression are coerced to deny the injustice of the encounter and the accompanying pain by the people committing the violence against them. The victims are encouraged to deny the evil motives and to accept the consequences of the violent encounter. The abusers make the abused complicit in the abuse. The abused comply and believe as a means to surviving the horrible experience. When the abusive person holds a socially recognized position of authority over the person who has experienced violence, what lingers in the mind of the violated is that the pain is not that bad - that the pain may even be necessary. Sooner or later victims will use pain as a way of solving problems and resolving conflicts, especially against people they consider weaker than themselves or against those whom they fear. In simplest terms, problem solving will involve either accepting blame, or inflicting it on others. Milburn and Conrad proposed this theory to explain the reactionary, rigid, and punitive bent of American politics, relating corporal punishment as an acceptable child-rearing practice to brutality and incivility in politics and societal conflict.

For the most part, Haiti's founders were fresh off the slave ships. They had survived, more or less, the horrors of the Middle Passage. They were the absolute possessions of people determined to work them to death. Paradoxically, Haitians won freedom from their oppressors and exploiters by using violence and brutality to put an end to being brutalized and violated by the slave owners and their representatives, but as a people, Haitians made violence and brutality a way of life for themselves and their descendants.

Building upon Jung's theory of subliminal invaders, Michael Milburn and Sheree Conrad illustrate how a people can perpetuate a culture of violence through the child-rearing practices employed by parents and other authority figures. In *The Politics of Denial*, Milburn and Conrad provide a theory that offers insight into the paradox of Haitian cultural violence. Conrad and Milburn wanted to know how people who had suffered violence and injustice - like Americans who had been subjected to harsh corporal punishment and emotional/mental abuse as children - could be indifferent to it, and worse, embrace it as a way of life. The parallel with Haitians and Haitian society is both compelling and appalling. As slaves, Haitians were subject to horrendous violence. As adults, as descendants of those people, some modern Haitians, are at best indifferent to it, and at worst, seem to have embraced it as a way of life.

The descendants of people who were valued less than four-legged beasts of burden, the enslaved of colonial Haiti, are quick to inflict violence upon the land, people and animals. In the name of building the country, violent acts have become acceptable and admirable. For two hundred years, Haitians as a people have condoned zombification, murderous witchcraft, and black magic by government officials in the name of cultural identity. Haitian society has accepted and blessed trigger-happy neurotics in the Haitian police and military. Haitians of all levels of society have watched with approval as impeccably uniformed brutes - many of them wife-beaters - have paraded with their daughters, sisters, and cousins on the finest dance floors. Members of a just society should have shunned these monstrous men long ago, thus clearing the way for men of excellence to succeed in the military. Perhaps today Haiti would field military and police forces worthy of admiration.

In Haitian churches, people have retreated behind dogma and false doctrines as they inflict verbal violence upon the relatively less powerful. Virtuous men and women have been scolded and demonized, and children's spirits have been broken. Breaking a child's spirit is akin to killing the drive that enables one to build a country of equals.

In *The Politics of Denial*, Conrad and Milburn argue that punitive and violent politics are a consequence of violent upbringing. Three observations supported their claim:

1. People use denial to avoid recalling painful experiences and memories.
2. Aggression in child-rearing is counterproductive
3. Over time, unexpressed anger transforms into semi-conscious hatred directed against either the self or against substitute persons.

Conrad and Milburn observe that the denial of wrong, consciously or subconsciously, is often a psychological defense mechanism. People deny that something wrong has occurred in order to cope with harsh realities. As Conrad and Milburn put it, "Denial is a psychological defense mechanism, an unconscious maneuver that cancels or obscures painful reality." People use denial so they can hear no evil, see no evil, and hence feel no pain; they run the risk of cutting themselves off from vital portions of their conscience, consciousness, and ethical sensibilities. They stunt their understanding of themselves and their place in the world. When people are in denial, they avoid confronting or changing things that have power over them. They do not have to examine their motives, intentions, and actions, or those of other people, other interests, or governments.

When a person suffers torture at the hands of people with whom they are condemned to spend their lives, some denial of reality is inevitable; it's a psychological defense mechanism for survival. In that denial of harsh reality, the individual retreats into a mental comfort zone where pain, wrong, and suffering are rationalized or minimized. While the violence is occurring and the violated are being told - by words, attitudes, and actions - that they are bad and that the punishment is earned, necessary, unavoidable, and for their own good, they begin believing it. Hitting someone who is dependent or subordinate to you, and then telling that person that your treatment will help him or her become a better or more civilized person, is like giving someone's conscience the *coup de grace* after the firing squad. In that process, the victim learns to laugh at pain, toy with misery, and accept suffering as an unavoidable and necessary part of life. Even when away from the aggressor or the immediate ordeal, the victim holds onto the companions of misery, those influential subliminal invaders mentioned earlier. Later, when opportunity presents itself, the victim may use violence, or the threat of it, against others. Haitians may use the threat of violence every day, even in words;

When an educated Haitian, smiling a grin of satisfaction, curses another Haitian with the phrase, "Colon get manman-ou" don't they really mean may the colonist get your mother? What is he or she really wishing? That a white man catches and rapes that woman? What satisfaction is derived from using the threat or specter or memory of violence? Who does the speaker identify with at that moment? Is this good soil for women's rights to freedom? Ki lwa sa'a ki dansé nan têt Ayitien pou fe'l blié malè maman-l?[4]

Milburn and Conrad's second relevant observation is that inflicting physical pain on children in order to discipline them is destructive. Conrad and Milburn skillfully describe the ill effects of the mindset that favors child beating. Child beating is counterproductive. Whipping is wrong. After convincingly establishing that corporal punishment predisposes a child to become hard-hearted and indifferent to other people's suffering, Conrad and Milburn further demonstrate that corporal punishment in childhood has wide-ranging adult consequences. It shapes the child's views of the world, life, society, God, and government well into adulthood.

Milburn and Conrad, drawing upon the work of Alice Miller, outlined the underlying motives of that practice of that pedagogy:

1. The unconscious need to pass on to others the humiliation one has undergone in one's past.
2. The need to provide "repressed feelings" an outlet.
3. The need to possess and have at one's disposal a vital object to manipulate.

---

[4] What's possessed you that you forget your mother's misery and nightmares?

4. Self-defense: that is, the need to idealize one's childhood and one's parents by dogmatically applying the parents' pedagogical principles to one's own children.
5. Fear of freedom.
6. Fear of reappearance of what one has repressed, which one reencounters in one's child and must try to stamp out, having killed it in oneself earlier.
7. Revenge for the pain one has suffered.

Milburn and Conrad's third observation was that over time, unexpressed anger transforms into hatred directed against the self or substitute persons. That hatred will seek to discharge itself in various ways permissible and suitable for an adult (Miller, 1997).

To summarize these observations into one four-step conclusion:

1. During a violent encounter, subliminal invasion of the subconscious occurs. Along with the need to survive the encounter, other subliminal invaders (that is, words that claim the encounter is for the victim's own good) force victims to deny their pain and suffering.
2. The worst part of being forced to withstand physical violence isn't so much the pain inflicted, but the insistence on the part of the aggressor that the pain and punishment are for the benefit of the victim. It's a double violation that reinforces an abuse survivor's need for denial. Denial is a psychological defense mechanism that minimizes or hides painful realities of abuse in the mind - not in reality.
3. Information processed through denial, or other forms of repression during torture or mistreatment, program the subconscious for insensitivity. It makes a person insensitive and inclined to accept violence as a way of life.
4. Since violence against children has the same negative impact as violence against adults, to break the cycle of violence requires sparing children from it as children have more years ahead of them during which to act out their learned aggressions.

When the four observations are considered alongside Haitian child-rearing practices, the Haitian problem becomes all the more complicated. On top of misery, they have co-opted a religious fundamentalism that makes it hopeless. The religious fundamentalism of Haitian Protestantism is riddled with the shortcomings of an imported doctrine.

Right or wrong, historical Christianity appears to maintain a love affair with violence. It is a religion that too many times has failed the narrator of the story of the Good Samaritan because it judges the wounded man collapsed on the side of the road as deserving of his fate rather than showing compassion for him. It is a religion of intellectual divides that foments a culture of drift and discrimination, not of peace, love, and harmony as it stood yesterday and as it stands today, a culture of just retribution and fair condemnation.

Christians have learned to accept violence as compatible with the will of God. Consider the following statement made by a preacher who appeared in 2006 on the Trinity Broadcasting Network: "Christians should not be against capital punishment because God is not against it. If He was, while Jesus was on the cross, that was the time to speak against it and He didn't." How hard is it to relate to that preacher? Through the Bible Christians become acquainted with blood sacrifice of animal and humans; a king's daughter's dowry of two hundred foreskins; the slaughter of hundreds of infants for the sake of one baby; an angry god's demand for the death of all firstborn Egyptian children, probably innocent of the sins of one wicked Pharaoh; and David, a man often described as a person after God's own heart, killing the sons of one woman and leaving her in such grief that she lay under their corpses until their bones dried out.

Even in the New Testament, violence is graphically depicted. There are the tortures preceding Jesus' crucifixion and the actual crucifixion; the story of Ananias and Sapphira being struck dead by a merciless Peter who is described as being filled with the Holy Spirit; and the claim in Paul's letter to the Roman believers, "Without the shedding of blood there is no remission for sin." Somehow, what's written as necessary for salvation and atonement for sin translates into child-rearing practices.

In the Old Testament it is written, "Spare the rod, spoil the child." Right or wrong, whether it is for personal salvation or because it's the only way God knows how to do it, the Bible is used to support violence in a family context. Physical brutality toward children and others who depend on someone for guidance may also draw from the biblical example of the Father who evicted his children from the only home they ever knew to the Father who oversaw and approved the ugly death of

His only sinless Son on the bloody cross, even though that son had cried out, "My God, my God why has thou forsaken me?"

This is not to say that the Bible is all about violence, nor is it to deny the ultimate message of God's redeeming love in the Bible. This is about pointing to the packaging of the message likely to affect the subconscious in a way contrary to God's plan. And if this is true, it is the responsibility of those who are enlightened to break the ugly shell, throw it away, and present the pearl - not the other way around.

In *The Politics of Denial*, Conrad and Milburn cite American heavyweights of the cloth as being the products and the advocates of the Christian culture of the whip. They mentioned Oral Robert's experience with corporal punishment. They viewed Roberts's statement, "My father believed in the stars and stripes. He gave the stripes, we saw the stars" as an indication of his getting whipped religiously in more than one sense. Milburn and Conrad pointed out the attitudes of Christian psychologists toward parenting styles and parental discipline by quoting James Dobson. Dobson teaches that after being spanked, a child should only be allowed to cry for a short time, "Two minutes or less...after which I would require him to stop the protest crying, usually by offering him a little more of whatever caused the original tears."

Considering the popularity of Roberts and Dobson, it would be incorrect to consider them and their views as exceptions. According to Milburn and Conrad's investigation, corporal punishment is a practice condoned by 92% of the American public, most of them Christian. They found that the culture in question gave rise to the polarization of the American electorate while leaning toward the extreme right, to conservative views in favor of capital punishment, to intolerance for liberal laws on abortion and homosexuality and the high threshold of sensitivity toward repressive regimes, or mass murder.

There is enough in the letter of the Bible to explain why people under the authority of historical Christianity appear to have had no problem repressing people and their rights (that is, burning them at the stake, carrying the sword into the temple in Jerusalem or elsewhere); that fascism, Nazism, and white supremacists have billed themselves as traditional Christians' homegrown products. An example of a biblical story that appears to put a gloss on cruelty and violence involves Gehazi being stricken with leprosy for an all-too-human mistake. Another is about Achan being mortally singled out over petty theft. A third story depicts children being eaten alive by bears because they made fun of the prophet Elisha. This culture, in which people who should know better prefer to sit in judgment of others rather than work for peace through love and forgiveness, favors fear of God over the love of God. After the tragedy of September 11, 2001, one preacher said, "Oh, how I love it when something that bad happens because it is then that people remember the Lord and rush back to Church." On CNN, with Larry King as moderator, a cross-section of the religious establishment debated what should be done in response to the September 11th attacks. The members were a Catholic priest, a Jewish rabbi, a Muslim religious leader, a Protestant pastor, and Deepak Chopra. It was comforting to see and hear the priest make constructive comments; the rabbi was right to the point; the Muslim was measured and helpful; and Deepak Chopra was very wise. All participants, except one, stressed people's responsibility to work for world peace, love, and harmony. One of them even said that what was most pleasant in the sight of God was taking place right then around the table of discussion: children of God sitting together to explore ways for them to get along with one another.

The pastor was the lone dissident. He claimed what had happened were events predicted by Jesus Christ. He said that we had to pray that these events happen fast so that prophecies could be fulfilled. In the meantime, all we needed to do was accept Jesus Christ as our Savior and pray that His kingdom come soon.

How convenient! Not only was the violence acceptable and divinely sanctioned, but the Reverend Pastor and other believers in God need not do anything nor question anything. The Reverend Pastor failed to entertain the possibility that something should be done on behalf of those who had died and those who had survived.

Where is love in all of this? What would Jesus have said? What happens to people's God-given talents? Likewise, one can feel the inner satisfaction in the voice of preachers describing the atrocities of hell for those who unlike them can't make it to Paradise. Their exultant, intense satisfaction is palpable, but where is their compassion? What happens to the prayer of Abraham: "God, will you spare them, if twenty, ten, are good?" Similar to some American Christian beliefs, Haitian-co-opted Christianity has combined with a history of oppression and injustice and has allowed for violence and indifference - pervasive, physical, spiritual, and emotional. (In Haiti's case, the violence is a legacy of French colonial slavery.) This sort of deliberate cruelty and contradictory "love" makes for people who are sensitive to other people's vulnerability but lacking in both sympathy and empathy for the underdog.

Haiti ought to break away from the cycle of violence, and Haitian parents must, while embracing God with all their might and with all their souls and with all their thoughts, move away from those violent preachers and listen exclusively to Jesus Christ, the preacher of unconditional love. There are no simple solutions for complex problems. Redressing the errors of a culture of violence is not easy, but beginning in childrearing it is important to differentiate between discipline and punishment, malice aforethought, and confusion.

People must stop beating their children. They must discard their understanding of the Old Testament tenet, "Spare the rod and spoil the child" and reconsider its meaning, thus following the actual prescription, laid out by Jesus Christ when he said, "Suffer that the little children come to me, and do not hinder them, for the kingdom of God belongs to such as these (Matthew 19:14)." The Old Testament's prescription, Jesus might say, was there because of hardness of hearts. His could be, "Try love and more patience, or remember, you parents, how well God treats you, how much He's been patient with you."

Jesus did not advocate whipping children. If He believed in corporal punishment when the little children were brought to Him that was the time to say so: but He didn't. Paul didn't encourage corporal punishment of children either. Rather, he charged parents to guard their behavior toward their children. He petitioned fathers to go gently with their children. He wrote, "Fathers, do not provoke your children to anger, but bring them up in the discipline and instruction of the Lord (Ephesians 6:4)."

Even though Haitians love their Bible, verses like Ephesians 6:4 are not popular. But they do lean on their Bible. Tap-taps, the colorfully painted van-like taxis, have Bible verses written on their hoods and doors. In the most remote corners of the country, over the mountains and in the valleys, people read the Bible or listen to it being read. The learned and the illiterate name their children after biblical heroes and saints. In the 1960s and 1970s, it was not uncommon for the most brutal paramilitary chiefs and law enforcement officers to be Bible-thumpers and that inside their Bibles there were more ear-marked verses and psalms than in a Sunday school teacher's. And here, we are talking about unconditional hatchet men in the service of a repressive government, killers who did their job with a smile. A literal, primitive interpretation of the Sacred Book allows a comfort zone to these warped souls. There is much better than that in the Bible, but it takes a special grace from God and decent reading comprehension to perceive it. So another question is warranted: in searching for the pearl, must the hard-to-digest, ugly shell be swallowed?

In the Bible, so much of God's message is crusted over by a shell of confusing negatives. A Bible reader may easily mistake what he or she has read and embrace negatives. For biblical literalism to be disastrous, readers only need to have been coached to accept everything they have read, even things read half-attentively. Yet, God's message of love is disclosed when critical, humble analysis is aligned with the Holy Spirit. Being Christian doesn't mean kissing your God-given brain goodbye. Haitian laity and clergy must find a different way to read their Bible with their hearts.

Here is a short list of sayings taken from the Bible that, when taken literally or out of context, have inspired Haiti's and historical Christianity's affinity for violence.

First: "Come out of her [Babylon], my people." This expression is often used to exhort believers, especially the young, to avoid anything or anyone deemed sinful or unholy. In Protestant circles, Babylon has too often been used to refer to the Catholic Church, namely the Vatican. On the basis of this verse and others like it, people are warned against having certain playmates (Catholics or Protestants), attending certain gatherings (like dance parties), or joining particular professions (that is, the military). Many gifted and talented young Christians have been dissuaded from pursuing professions that they could have entered with honor because of their church leaders' perception of the will of God.

Other verses that could contradict this point of view such as "You are the salt of the earth" or "You are the light of the world...let your light shine before men (Matthew 5:30-14)" have not always been included in considerations regarding the injunctions against fraternizing with so-called enemies of the true faith.

Second: "Do not love the world or anything in the world. If anyone loves the world, the love of the Father is not in him (1st John 2:15)." Often used like the "come out of Babylon" verse, it has been given as a command to "true" believers to separate themselves completely from the world. This encourages a sort of "heavenly-mindedness" that discourages believers from the practical considerations of living at relative peace with people who don't think exactly like they or their leaders say they should. It makes those who obey that command unfit for respectful diversity. In this use, it flies in the face of the phrase "For God so loves the world, He gave it His son (John 3:16)" ignoring it as evidence of God's love for the world or specifically, the people in it. Haitian Christians who are more concerned with avoiding the world and things worldly because they fear contamination from the world fail to ask why God would go to the trouble of creating a beautiful world and encourage the people living in it to despise it. This chain of thought does not make sense. Unfortunately, there are Bible verses that can be taken out of context to make this isolationism palatable to believers who are at odds with the world and choose "worldly" people as suitable targets for their inner anger.

Christians should not shun the world. They should work, pray, and listen to improve it. They should spend their time and talents in the effort of making it more lovable. Jesus set that example while here on earth. His willingness to mingle with people and earn the right to speak into their lives, to meet them where they were, and to accept them as they were enabled him to change them for the better. Supposedly, this was also the recommendation of Lord Krishna to civic and moral-minded people ("Seek the company of the wicked in order to reform him.") Maybe Psalm 1:1-2 is not a demand for believers to ostracize nonbelievers or God's wonderful world but to be mindful of God in everything done by those who claim to love and honor God.

Third: "Spare the rod spoil the child" is drawn from the Book of Proverbs (13:24). It is at the center of Christian exhortations to use corporal punishment in raising children. Consider the words attributed to Christ, such as:

> "Suffer that the little children come to me. For, the kingdom of God belongs to such as these (Mark 10:14)."

> "Do not exasperate your children (Ephesians 6:4)."

> "When you do this to the least of these, you do it to me (Matthew 25:40)."

> "He called a little child and had him stand among them. And he said: 'I tell you the truth, unless you change and become like little children, you will never enter the kingdom of heaven. And whoever welcomes a little child like this in my name welcomes me. But if anyone causes one

of these little ones who believe in me to sin, - (if, for instance, an adult or person in position of authority over that child manages to poison his subconscious, perhaps?) - it would be better for him to have a large millstone hung around his neck and to be drowned in the depths of the sea' (Matthew 18:2-6)."

These instructions are written as if coming straight from the Master's mouth. The Lord had a profound respect for children. His attitude toward them was tender and patient. Where is the tenderness or patience in beating a child? Where is the tenderness in using one's physical force against them to inflict pain? If Jesus is indeed the Lord as so many believers claim, and as the Lord he is the ultimate authority, and as the ultimate authority he did not advocate the use of physical force against children, what are his people doing when they purport to physically discipline their own children or the children of other people?

Fourth: The expression "Let his blood fall on us and on our children" was twisted when it entered the subconscious of Martin Luther the Reformer. Is it wrong to surmise that this was the basis of his anti-Jewish rationale? Could it be that as someone who was at odds with the Catholic Church and Catholic secular authorities that he had been twisted by physical, emotional, and spiritual violence and in despising Jews, he found an outlet? In his hatred, Luther recommended that the Jewish ghettos be burned and that the surviving Jews be prohibited from living amongst Christians or from buying land and property. How did Luther not see that this opposed Jesus' cry from the heart in regard to the Jews who had called out for his blood so many hundreds of years before Luther: "Father, forgive them for they know not what they do"?

Fifth: "A woman must not wear men's clothing, nor a man wear women's clothing, for the Lord your God detests anyone who does this (Deuteronomy 22:5)." Yet it is also written, "Therefore, there is now no condemnation for those who are in Christ Jesus, because through Christ Jesus the law of the Spirit of life set me free from the law of sin and death (Romans 8:1)."

Sixth: "If a man has a stubborn and rebellious son who does not obey his father and mother and will not listen to them when they discipline him, his father and mother shall take hold of him and bring him to the elders at the gate of his town. They shall say to the elders,

'This son of ours is stubborn and rebellious. He will not obey us. He is profligate and a drunkard.' Then all the men of his town shall stone him to death. You must purge the evil from among you. All Israel will hear of it and will be afraid (Deuteronomy 21:20)."

How does the harsh executive order to stone a disobedient son contrast with Jesus' parable of the prodigal son? Jesus recommended that the father forgive his rebellious son seventy times seven. And what of the parable of the rebellious son who was named the better son after he changed his mind and did what his father had asked him to do, in contrast to his brother who said he'd do what his father wanted but ultimately did not?

4

Perceptions of God and Religion

Haiti's religious leadership has failed the Church by misperceiving God, religion, the Bible, spirituality, and holiness. A Haitian citizen of the United States made a family trip to Haiti for the funeral of a beloved aunt. The night they arrived, they listened to a radio talk show. At first, one of the political leaders being interviewed struggled to voice his opinion on the role of members of the Haitian Diaspora in Haitian politics. Unexpectedly, the topic changed when a caller brought up religion. The anchorman answered the caller in frenzy, "I am tired, fed up by you people, singing and chanting that you are children of God, sons of a king, and yet you're poor, miserable, hungry, and unable to even afford a shower. You're crazy! It's about time you face reality. You are kidding yourselves. You're nothing! Give me a break!" The listeners, a religious group of individuals, took those words like a punch to their collective gut.

They discussed the anchor's comments. What if the anchor was right? Wasn't praising God in the midst of such squalor and stench an exercise in futility? What did being the sons and daughters of God inside such a hell as Haiti's slums mean? Where was God?

As they meditated, it dawned upon them that perhaps Haitians do not mean what they say when speaking Christianese. That those believers are reciting verses and the lyrics of religious songs like parrots: without being in it with the words and the truths behind them or in real conversation with God. Rather than judging and faulting God, they reevaluated the Haitian journey as they'd known it with God and religion.

As they meditated on what had happened on the radio, a sad truth came to them, like a warning written on a giant screen: "If it's true that a nation has the government it deserves, for change to happen, it will have to come from the base." They questioned themselves and their experiences, like students of elementary mathematics struggling to solve a difficult problem. Unexpectedly but forcefully, the solution unfolded, "Change is only possible when the religious leadership assumes its true responsibility. And for that to happen, religious leadership must be open-minded, exhaustively informed, and with all personal and sectarian prejudices in check."

Christians ought to be more focused on the redemptive force of the love of God, the true message and mission of Jesus Christ. They should abandon intellectually hostile biblical literalism that has contributed so much to general confusion. If this is going to be a first in this world, then like the first black revolt that made Haiti independent against the odds, let Haiti do it again to show the world that when God's children turn to Him and worship Him in spirit and in truth, all things work for their good and the miracle called success becomes inevitable.

If it is true that people have the government they deserve, then change is necessary. In 1982, one Haitian political leader said, "For what we want to accomplish in Haiti, Haitians need to be changed from that raw material we have now into a finer product." (*Il faut changer l'Haïtien, ce produit brut, en un produit fini.*) One high-ranking French official, supportive of the Haitian cause, said the same thing with more emphasis to a Haitian who hoped to change his country. "You have much work to do, young man, for your people are not ready." At the time, the Haitian in question did not fully grasp what the Frenchman meant, perhaps because he was in denial or had taken those words as irrationalities uttered in anger. Or because he was still angry at the robbery the French had done the Haitian people by forcing the Haitians to pay reparation after France lost to them in the war of 1803.

Perhaps there has never been any great political achievement without a spiritual or religious primer *(Un mordançage spiritual)*. Was it coincidence that Haiti's Dutty Boukman, India's Gandhi, and America's Martin Luther King were religious people? Or that by the side of Nelson Mandela was Bishop Desmond Tutu? The founding of the

United States of America coincided with a spiritual awakening. George Washington, Thomas Jefferson, Ben Franklin, and John Adams, among others, were determined, educated individuals of deep religious conviction. Yet America was not founded on biblical literalism or Christian dogmas. They may not have held beliefs like those of more traditional, anti-intellectual Christians of the sort currently active in Haiti and in the United States of America, but their perceptions of God, and the examples of Indigenous modes of governance (the Iroquois Federation), inspired them to shape an amazing, almost-representative government. Their perceptions of the Great Divinity and their duty as believers were far ahead of their time and, perhaps, ahead of these times.

John Adams took issue with a variety of dogmas, the idea that the Bible was the inspired Word, and the sincerity of preachers. He wrote the following in one of his many letters:

> What do you mean by the ideas, the thoughts, the reason, the intelligence or the speech of God? His intelligence is a subject too vast, too incomprehensible for Plato, Philo, Paul, or Peter, Jews, Gentiles, or Christians. Let us adore, not presume, nor dogmatize. Even the great Teacher may not reveal this subject. There never was, is not, and never will be more than one Being in the universe capable of comprehending it. At least this is the humble and adoring opinion of the writer of this note...was there ever a popular religion that did not pretend to divine instruction? ...Was there ever a country, in which philosophers, politicians, and theologians believed what they taught to the vulgar? (Bernstein, 2002)

To Benjamin Rush, John Adams once wrote:
> Bigotry, superstition, and enthusiasm on religious subjects I have long since set at defiance. I have attended public worship in all countries and with all sects and believe them all much better than no religion, though I have not thought myself obliged to believe all I heard. Religion I hold to be essential to morals; I never read of any irreligious character in Greek or Roman history, nor have I known one in life, who was not a rascal. Name one if you can, living or dead (Bernstein, 2002).

To Thomas Jefferson, John Adams sent:
> ...For the last year or two I have devoted myself to this kind of study [i.e. the history of religion]...Romances all! I have learned nothing of importance to me, for they have made no change in my moral or religious creed, which has for 50 or 60 years been contained in four short words "be just and good." In this result they all agree with me (Bernstein, 2002).

On the Christian Bible and American laws designed to punish those who did not believe in biblical inerrancy, Adams wrote this to Jefferson:
> There exists I believe throughout the whole Christian world a law which makes it a blasphemy to deny the divine inspiration of all the books of the old and new Testaments from Genesis to Revelation...I think such laws a great embarrassment, great obstructions to the improvement of the human mind. Books that cannot bear examination ought not to be established as divine inspiration by penal laws (Bernstein, 2002).

These are the words of a man who was respectful of other people's beliefs and religions. John Adams supported the right to not only think freely but to question, in good faith, everything said about God and everything written in the Bible. Some founding fathers, while embracing God, did not seek to impose their choices on their countrymen or the world. They also embraced reason and laid the groundwork for much good to be done in America and the world. Unlike the reformer Martin Luther, a biblical literalist whose reading of the scripture may have done as much damage as help, the founding fathers respected the classical scholars. Luther spoke of Aristotle with hatred and loathed Erasmus. Luther was convinced that reason could lead to atheism (Armstrong, 2001).

Through his "faith", Luther convinced himself that God had retreated from the physical world. Little wonder that Luther tried to deny women relief from labor pains or that he wanted to burn Jews (Ellerbe, 1995). Luther used the Bible like an axe, discouraging peasants and other humble people from viewing the Reformation as a movement that could improve their miserable lives. Author Karen Armstrong (2001) put it well, "Like the conservative Muslim reformers, the Protestant reformers were both revolutionary and reactionary."

The founding fathers of America availed themselves of a great deal of wisdom and self-restraint in their dealings with the nineteenth century's so-called prophets. Many of those prophets were anti-intellectual demagogues, the nineteenth century equivalent of fundamentalists-televangelists bent on hijacking America's moral conscience. John Adams viewed the European settlements of the Americas as part of God's plan for the enlightenment of all humanity. Thomas Payne was convinced that Americans could start the world anew (Armstrong, 2001). What a far cry those sentiments are from political creeds that the only relevant guide for American foreign policy is American interest. Or the stupidity in the speech that held, "America should not go elsewhere and engage in nation building." Were the authors of that statement unaware that America's founders had long been in the business of nation building (if not always in the right way, nor always for the right reasons)? Long after America's founding fathers had completed their work, their successors also left their mark on Haiti. President Franklin Delano Roosevelt boasted of having single-handedly written a Haitian constitution in one afternoon (Dorestant, 1998). As president, Woodrow Wilson inflicted southern marines on Haiti in 1915.

Judging by what America's founding fathers tried to realize in the world, based upon the ideas of prophets and spiritual leaders the world over, America's true calling and mission may be to prime the world for the coming kingdom of God (Spaulding, 1996), not to trample it in a destructive exercise of self righteousness wed to ham-handed imperialism. President John F. Kennedy may have understood this calling when he shared the following vision in his 1961 inaugural address:

> The world is very different now for man holds in his mortal hands the power to abolish all forms of human poverty and all forms of human life...To those people in the huts and villages across the globe, struggling to break the bounds of mass misery, we pledge our best efforts to help them help themselves, for whatever period is required - not because the communists may be doing it, not because we seek their votes, but because it is right. If a free society cannot help the many who are poor, it cannot save the few who are rich.

What a difference from the stingy, vulgar rhetoric, "It's all about America's interests"! The Americas need real leaders, people with an expansive vision of the world, of freedom, and of America. Participation in politics, for Christians, should be more like a sacrament than a rat-race. Political leadership should be reserved for a certain level of achievement. Undercover, power-driven preachers' pets on a mission to hijack the country's religious consciousness for political gain should not be permitted to work out their dimly understood salvation on the basis of other people's fear and trembling - or add to their personal wealth while manipulating national and public resources.

In post-colonial Virginia, Thomas Jefferson disestablished the Anglican Church. That was his church (Armstrong, 2001). The deciding bill declared that coercion in matters of faith was sinful as well as tyrannical; truth would prevail if people were allowed their own opinions; and there should be a wall of separation between religion and politics. If Jefferson and Adams had stayed in Europe, where the Church (across sects) was so powerful, they might have been politically neutralized, ostracized, or, like François Marie Arouet (Voltaire), slandered and made out to be what they were not - atheists.

Yet if this book is about Haiti, why focus on Napoléon, Jefferson, Adams, America, politics, religion, culture, and theology? Haiti's problem is at the intersection of everything that has happened and is happening in the world. For those who believe there is a God Who created the world and Who has a vested interest in the affairs of men and this world, there is no getting away from the premise that everything in reality is interconnected. Saving Haiti requires framing of the problems of Haiti. Framing the problems of Haiti requires placing the country in a historical and geopolitical context.

Theologically speaking, every major unsolved problem, and every social or political disaster, is a result of people straying from God's design specifications. Some of them, Christian leaders, have been mistaken in their stewardship of believers - individually and collectively. Haitians, like Americans, have strayed from the light that guided men and women of the eighteenth century to the principles that began transforming the world for the better. People have taken to playing down, as if ashamed, the greatness of Thomas Jefferson, George Washington, Ben Franklin, and John Adams. Over time, these great souls have received the same treatment from the religious establishment that the genius of Toussaint Louverture received in the era of revolutions. While the brilliance of these men is obscured, fundamental - if attractive - flaws of people like Napoléon are down-played. Napoléon failed (America's founding fathers only went short of breath) to ensure that the rights of man extended to all those under their authority. It appears that efforts to airbrush this so egregious of Napoléon's flaws has been transposed to American's sense of history - which, admittedly, is not strong.

How often do Americans discuss the French revolutionary motto, "All men are created equal before the law"? Or even the great American proclamation, "All men are created equal and endowed by their Creator of the unalienable rights to Life, Liberty, and the pursuit of Happiness"? These fine thoughts have been superseded by a gospel of American interests, which translates into power and control - the limitation of the lives and happiness of others. That falls short of Thomas Jefferson's critique of Napoléon: "We believe no more in Napoléon fighting for the liberty of the seas nor in Great Britain fighting for the liberty of mankind. The object is the same: to draw to themselves the power, the wealth and the resources of other nations."

The duty of the first republics of the Americas was to highlight that France failed in the post-Revolutionary confusion of Danton and the intransigence of Robespierre. Like the Americans who destroyed the highest aims of the Declaration of Independence, Danton, Robespierre, and their ideological contemporaries strayed from the Light of what was best. God's will was not the focus of their dream and struggle. That failure turned a revolution into a reign of terror. The French revolutionary motto was "All men are created equal before the law." In the Declaration of Independence, America's founding fathers proclaimed that God endowed all men with those important rights. They appealed to more than the Law - they drew upon their reasoned and inspired understanding of God.

It is tragic that America's founding fathers would not reject slavery while midwiving the United States, even though they wrote its condemnations in its defining documents. Embracing the belief that God has endowed all men and women with certain rights may be one example of the obedience that God prefers to sacrifices. It is better to have a commander-in-chief who has given his or her heart to the belief that God has endowed all people with important rights. It is better for all people when leaders obey the golden rule. When obedience is chosen, we get peace. When leaders choose sacrifice, we get war.

Yes, children in America should have long been told that in all probability, China still stands and probably will continue to stand, while the Soviet Union failed miserably, because in China there is an *esprit de corps* characteristic of the People - an *"e pluribus unum"* which is godly, while the Soviet Union prized ungodliness. Consider the statement colloquially credited to cosmonaut Yuri Gagarin, "I have searched in space, but I did not find God." It resembles an arrogant surgeon's boast, "I have not found the soul at the tip of my scalpel."

Wake up, America! You may have long strayed from the faith. You may have long reaped the rewards given to your nation's founding fathers for their willingness to live in light of what they had given their hearts to, while erroneously crediting current prosperity to yourself in self-righteousness. If men and women return to the faith that inspired the founding fathers at their best, America's best is yet to come.

America was not made to trample on the rest of the world with surgical strikes, autonomous corporations, and special interests. America's military might was to be like the reward of money to the hardworking person - an insurance policy, so to speak. American's calling was, and is, to carry good news: to prime the world for God's kingdom by upholding the best ideals. Those men craved God and glimpsed who God really was: not a bigot, not a devotee of any particular religion, but the Lord of the Universe who made the sun shine and the rain fall for all children, providing for their welfare.

The founding fathers saw the Light and tried to walk in its path. They got a glimpse of that Supreme God who so loves the world and manifests many times in all shapes and forms to Moses, to Jacob, to Abraham, to the nations of pre-colonial "Mexico" and the Mayan peninsula, the Muslims, the Hindus, the Buddhists, and certainly Christians. The God Who, once in a while, picked a man or woman and elevated them to be repairers of the breaches. Political power should be a tool used in the course of stewardship. It should be respected as a God-granted privilege to participate in the on-going work of creation, the continuously expanding universe (Hawking, 1998). A believer's politics should mirror their love for and faith in God. One Muslim living in America put it beautifully this way: "There must be an intelligently placed wall between religion and politics, but they should not be so separated as to cancel each other out. In that regard, participation in politics should be like a sacrament (Hossain, 2006)."

It's a lovely idea, a fine and lofty one. If, however, a person were to go to Washington and speak with members of Congress, the Secretary of State, and other high-ranking officials, would that idea be considered a fit topic for discussion? Consider that in 2006 and 2007, formal polls indicated that the American electorate's faith in Congress had plummeted.

"Real politick," as opposed to ideals that might effectively work for widespread benefit, appears to be the only variable deemed fit for consideration. Dreamers and idealists seem to be out of fashion. But who were John Adams or Benjamin Franklin? Down-to-earth dreamers who managed to align reason with their enthusiasm for God. A God-loving liberal may be more in tune with what is good than a Bible-throwing selective literalist. Leaders such as these apparent literalists are quick to inflict punishment and consider compassion unrealistic. Leaders who profess Christ, but consistently interact with the world in "realistic" terms cherish power, control, and money more than God's people and that's sinful. Is it outrageous to claim that among the great men who founded this country there were those who would have wanted corporate America not to be so unmerciful, so ungodly?

America's technology, the creation of jobs and opportunities, and the pursuit of happiness, while keeping Americans at the top, could be kindly made available to the rest of the world in a more generous manner. According to President Jimmy Carter, while a country like Norway gives almost 3% of its national income to humanitarian causes, the United States gives only one sixth of 1% (2002). Carter went on to share that a 1995 public opinion poll showed that almost two-thirds of Americans agreed that the United States should use part of its wealth to assist less fortunate people abroad. Despite the American government's financial support record, Americans always have been a generous people (Carter, 2005). Instead of being a nation represented and led by those who seem to know only how to sell, cherishing profit rather than the value of the merchandise sold to the buyer, the people of this country could be even more generous children of God through whom the whole world would be blessed. The believers of the United States would then be a true beacon of light in the world for the sake of God.

Unfortunately, it is easier to distribute Bibles, to send preachers and MTV to Russia, and to otherwise keep wallets and hearts shut than it is to provide practical help. Though practical help may be needed, it may not always be wanted. The lessons taught by other believers, in times past still muddy the waters. The Kikuyu, the Zulu and the Xhosa know something about that. Among them it is said, "When the settlers first arrived they had the Bible, we had the land; they said: let's close our eyes and pray. Thereafter, when we opened ours eyes, we had the Bible and they had the land."

Some Americans would rather undermine China's efforts to raise their people's standard of living, giving them unfair competition instead of intelligently assisting them as asked because they've deemed the Chinese "non-Christians." When the Chinese sense that attitude, why should their reaction be kind? Why do Christian countries wish to ignore the sacred Newton's law that to every action there is an equal reaction? A people of God should not behave so selfishly, should not run so scared, or be so insecure. It is a faithless child, forgetful or simply greedy, who resents the help his or her father is willing to give their neighbors-in-need and who tries to rationalize their inner poverty by pointing out the things their neighbor has done that may have contributed to their current difficulties. Never mind that they've been told, "Stop judging. Don't be greedy. I'm not going to let you starve."

Haiti's religiosity feeds on American Protestantism. Its distortions and vices mirror the shortcomings of American theologies. America too misunderstands religion, God, spirituality, and holiness. Its people probably also have a thwarted concept of sin, and for that, repentance is in order. In order to make amends, the momentum set in motion by the founding fathers must be seized. The torch must be picked up and carried further and higher. People should hesitate before crucifying political leaders while blinding themselves to well-packaged ungodliness.

America's founding fathers may have meant well to all in everything they did. At their best, they had the right vision for America and the world. They were men of good will who obviously digested the French translation of the Christmas message, "Peace on earth to all men of good will." What doubt is there that had their enlightenment prevailed in America there would be peace on earth or at least there would be active pursuit of it with good chance to secure it today?

Is it unreasonable to suppose that neither John nor Abigail Adams, nor Thomas Jefferson nor Benjamin Franklin would have been guests on the Trinity Broadcasting Network (TBN) bragging about the Bible being the inerrant inspired word of God? Would they insist on displaying the Ten Commandments on court properties? Or would they, instead, busy themselves with priming the world for the advancement of God's kingdom and preach by example? Instead of the gospel of Machiavelli ("Better to be feared than loved") or the preachers of Armageddon ("Let the bloody prophecies be fulfilled") they would promote the Gospel of Salvation ("Let your light be shining, be the city upon a hill"). Participation in America's politics would promote her people to higher ground in the Sacred. The whole world would follow America, wanting to emulate in the sense of good versus evil, instead of trying to outdo Americans in cunning and self-righteousness. Sadly, the current style of leadership is telling the world that might is right - and perhaps the only right. No wonder friends and foes want to stockpile lethal weapons. With such world leadership, the other countries too can and will avail themselves of those weapons which, now, seem to be the only assets that matter. As the existentialist maxim says, "Morality and politics are not the same but how much good politics can be without morality?" Too many believers lack the faith of that "mustard seed" to move their mountains; therefore, in military might they trust.

God has not prevented this. Nevertheless, that should not be the primary face worn when publicly or covertly interacting with the rest of the world. The believers' reputation should be what America was created for: to be part of God's plan to save the world. Today, because we have fallen into temptation, the temptation of Old Great Britain or Spain to dominate the world *per fas et nefas*, we have dropped the ball (spiritually speaking) and almost exclusively retreated behind our military might, somewhat suspicious that God could call us any time into judgment. Then we rationalize our poor spiritual stamina by saying, "Anyway, we live in a dangerous world," almost oblivious to the sad reality that we too have contributed to make it dangerous. Yet, we still have the ability and the opportunity to right the wrong.

America should not be intent on doing what Haiti did, dropping the ball and embarking on a selfish struggle for survival or to impress the world. Others have been where America is now: at the top. They are history today - bywords for failure and shortsightedness. America, so far, has prevailed. Why? In two key respects, the country has been faithful in the eyes of God:

1. Many of the founding fathers were respectful of God's might and authority, while at the same time expecting much of themselves and their intellect.
2. Unlike in Ancient Rome, many American citizens have shown wisdom and compassion, dedicating their lives to supporting weaker and less powerful people of their nation.

There are wise and compassionate people in America, even among the social Christians, dominionists, and self-styled atheists. In that regard, the difference between atheists and believers may be that some believers may trick you, beat you, rob you, and expect to get away with it given God's grace (if it is not God's will for them to do so). And whatever they take from others they can rationalize as blessings from God. And if they give a percentage of the loot to charity, what need is there for remorse? Atheists know they don't have that option. Even if by their own definition they are ungodly, some may be better neighbors for they have less familiarity with rationalizing their behavior on the basis of their ideas about God. Many hold themselves as accountable to people as they do to their ideals.

Compassionate wisdom is probably worth much more than sacrifices. Some American authorities allowed Martin Luther King to have part of his say when they could have resorted to do what Rochambeau, Leclerc, and Napoléon tried to do to Haitians - total annihilation of free blacks and mulâtres.

America had the weapons and the political clout to crush the demonstrators. That black people succeeded in gaining civil rights on paper without having to kill all their enemies indicates that the pressure on the wicked was not solely from the victims but also from well-minded, wise, and compassionate whites who saw the injustice and worked to end it. By contributing to the victory, they helped save the day without stealing the show. That's godly humility and decency. Isn't it telling that the greatest evangelist in America, Billy Graham, met and talked with Martin Luther King in secret? Graham may not have publicly endorsed Martin Luther King, but he told King to take to the streets while he'd take to the stadiums where he would only preach the truth?

America must recoup, grab the torch, and carry it further and higher. America is not supposed to be only breadbasket. That would be plain, dry, barren idealism. America needs to be *good*. The foreign policy ought to stop being amoral. The world doesn't crave charity. Instead, the world needs America to help it make bread and fish; not to donate bread and fish. On that note: Churn more butter. Sell fewer guns.

The same moral obligation that was given as a gift to the Haitian elite (a group that Americans have called the most repugnant elite) and the Haitians could apply to the United States with regard to the rest of the struggling world. Refusing to carry that ball down the field and through the goal will produce the same miserable effects - a country rich in history and human spirit but impoverished by social Darwinism, greed, and false-piety. If the great experiment of America fails, Americans may find themselves asking how God let it happen. God may answer, "How could you?" They must not repeat the Haitians' mistakes then blame the coach for the defeat when they were the ones who lost the game. Americans would do well to look at Haiti and see a warning. Even when you are created for greatness, you may, like Haiti, fail and your culture may become a byword for injustice, creative brutality, and social Darwinism.

Guidance only goes so far. It is time to stop telling church people, "Before you do anything ask, 'What would Jesus do?'" when as a body, the members of the church have confused Jesus with marketing. What does the What Would Jesus Do (WWJD) movement signify when "born-again" political leaders who can't stand the sight of a partially nude Lady Justice statue allow one question to guide their policies: What's in it for me politically? What is in it for America? Where is the oil, beef, land, coal, uranium and water?

The question believers should ask is "What is God's good?" For its own sake, America must fight poverty, illiteracy, hunger, joblessness and suffering throughout the world, especially in settings where Americans have contributed to poverty, illiteracy, hunger, and joblessness. It is the surest way to secure America's wealth and happiness. America was not created to be selfish. That is why one of the worst things that can happen is that penurious souls hold significant control in America. We need the perspectives of people like Ben Franklin, John and Abigail Adams, Thomas Jefferson, Alexander Hamilton, Charles Summer, and Wendell Phillips. Americans need to reclaim the moral authority embodied in those leaders who opened the door to God for their blessings and to inspire the world. Take, for instance, peace in the Middle East. It's only a moral authority that demonstrates unconditional love to all who could tell the Palestinians, "Forget about it. Don't dream about the Jews getting out of Israel, for who having endured so much pain and suffering at the hands of so many nations is going to risk being kicked out of the motherland? That is a dream that will never come true. It's either living with them or perishing with them (Moore, 2002)." The voice of authority must practice what it preaches, and if that authority is Christian, it must fall back on Jesus' recommendation that those who would presume to lead first try leading His way. This is not to encourage imposing Jesus on the Jews but to encourage those who have given their hearts to the Lord to find a way to include His precepts in their agendas. Tell the Zionist Jews, "We don't want you to disarm. We want you to stay focused, but try love. It's a wise investment. Put yourselves mentally in the place of the adversary and listen to one who says, 'Love even your enemy'." For the Zionists to listen to such advice, they must view the advice giver as a moral authority that preaches primarily by example. If the advice-givers have demonstrated a blood-soaked inconsistency of speech, story, and actual behavior, the advice will fall on deaf ears.

5

Of Religions and Spiritual Consciousness

If religion is to make a difference in Haiti, its many faith-ways must present a united front against the divisive rhetoric of overzealous preachers. This "ours is better than yours" attitude and demeanor must go away. God is bigger than anybody's perception of God. Enticing people to view themselves as better than others in matters of "faith" feeds into bigotry.

Perhaps the best analogy for the interrelatedness of religions is that of the enormous elephant being examined by blindfolded examiners. Suppose those examiners could neither smell, nor hear, nor taste; their ability to move around the animal was limited; and they were only allowed to touch the animal with their hands and fingers. Each person will define the animal according to what he or she feels, depending on what he or she touches. Thus it may be like this and all of earth's religions. God is immense. There may be clashes and wars over differing experiences of God; nevertheless, almost all definitions of Him apply. In the Bible, in the gospel of John (1:18), it is written that no one has ever seen God, but God the One and only (the Christ), who is at the Father's side has made him known. Take that to mean that until one is like Christ or the Christ in them is real, the believer is only guessing. Christ being real in him or her, or being like Christ, won't come from self-promotion or their own conceited proclamations. Someday, by a miracle of Christ's own, "We shall see God face to face."

Until then, believers must stop fighting over their definitions of God. Clashes over which religion or religious sect understands God best must end. Individual believers must not permit their small perception of God to be a source of problems for the rest of humanity. God is so immense and so powerful that God owns the right to reveal His or Herself on His or Her own terms. Perceptions of God, even from Christians, may not be the full picture but only a glimpse. And certainly, God is too big to be locked up inside a book.

In Psalms 19:1 it is written:

> The Heavens declare the glory of God; the skies proclaim the work of His hands. Day after day they put forth speech; night after night they display knowledge. There is no speech or language where his voice is not heard. Their voice goes out into all the earth, their words to the ends of the world.

Equating God with a book, calling every word of it His own, making it sound like a correspondence by fax from His throne, is idolatry, a concerted effort to minimize the greatness of God.

Religion derives from the Latin word *religere* ("religare," meaning "to tie back"). Religions represent people's efforts to be tied back to God, to return to the Source. The pagan's velleities or actual volition for spirituality ought not to be discounted. These are steps in the right direction. However, by their human methods, no religion is the epitome of perfection. All have their risks and pitfalls, but it cannot be stated strongly enough: even the pagan's effort toward spirituality has merit.

One thing that plagues humanity is the pretense of some religions to exclusivity. This sickening pretense supports attempts for devout politicos to impose their creed on others by any and all means. And worse, a certain intellectual laziness keeps overzealous preachers from leaving their comfort zones, causing them to act as if they are scared of finding the truth, preventing them from analyzing more than well-packaged lies. In stereotyping non-Christians, the words *pagan* and *heathen* have become conflated with wicked, savage, and primitive. Smart terminologies have obscured the truth to the point where concerned, responsible children of God, arguably the real Christians, are labeled "bleeding-heart liberals." And yet, guess who would get the whipping in the Temple? Who are most similar to the Temple's vendors?

As to the pagans, what if they are not nearly as ungodly as they are made to appear in Christian books and sermons? For instance, it's not as if Voltaire was a practicing atheist. Perhaps pagans' reputations were subject to similar treatment. There is historical evidence to the effect that believers' sacraments, rituals, and beliefs are familiar to the pagan world, having been talked of, written about, and etched in sculpture. Some evidence indicates that historical Christianity, not satisfied with keeping silent about inconvenient truths, hid them. Rather than admitting that there is possible kinship between Christianity and Paganism (the Old Religion), some prefer to claim that the Adversary had knowledge of God's plan and sought to circumvent it by creating decoys long before the advent of Christ. Likewise, the theory that Prophet Samuel's ghost, as it appeared to Saul through the powers of the witch of Endor, was actually a demonic entity impersonating Samuel.

When convenience dictates, these same preachers will not hesitate to say that Satan cannot read minds or drive a car or operate a computer. In fact, this second position is probably closer to the truth, because wherever evil is on the rise, man is a necessary agent. It took Hitler and his wicked hatchet men to create the Holocaust, and it took actual men and women to institute slavery and its atrocities. Whenever man pays lip service to God while detaching himself from the Great Divinity, he stops focusing on good, he freelances for the devil, and he unleashes his inner demons on earth.

In the light of this lack of integrity, a simple question is whether historical Christianity was afraid or ashamed of publicly sharing beliefs and traditions with pagans? A much better question is whether believers plagiarized the pagans or whether God equally inspired Christians and pagans? How impossible is it that God visited the pagans, became one of them, and lived among them to show them the Way, the Resurrection, and the Life? Even preachers claim that God is no respecter of anybody's religion.

What is the true value of Christianity if not to reconfirm previous teachings of virtue, love and selflessness, through Jesus, so that God's children can live and work *e pluribus unum,* like the cells of a healthy human body? And in the same vein, could it be that many so-called atheists are not atheists at all, but are instead smart people under indictment for asking inconvenient questions? The most vocal atheist is probably a thoughtful person asking questions that are not yet answered or for which he cannot yet find answers. Certainly, there are atheists who want to be viewed as impenitent. Indeed many of them are philosophical busybodies, restless, and sometimes iconoclastic questioners. But as evangelical minister Pastor Fresnel Charlot once said, even bickering about the existence of God is testimony of people's efforts to answer the ultimate question. "Man's thirst for God is natural. People crave the Higher-Up with the same ardor the leaping flames of a bonfire seek the sky." Self-appointed defenders of the faith, who were quicker to kill messengers than seek answers to the questioning messages, branded many intellectuals and scholars as atheists. In that regard, hearing out atheists might be worthwhile. They may be in the position of not being able to accept what is offered to them on what they believe to be insufficient grounds.

Why do Christians favor this belief in atonement for sins, a concept that permits believers to become chronic repeat offenders (that is, holy on Sundays but wicked and forgetful as of the following Monday)?

Jesus may have accepted his crucifixion because he knew that Good Friday was an exercise in futility. Jesus had the foresight, or might have, quite responsibly, concluded that in the inevitable confrontation of good and evil, good would achieve a crushing victory. This had to be done to save the world. Surely His divinity overcame any foolishness of people. However, saying God planned it, whatever "it" may be, is perhaps a way to duck personal responsibility: something more in tune with being fascinated by violence and the desire to be exonerated for crimes already committed and about to be committed rather than an expression of faith and joy.

It's been observed that many religions are in the habit of pinning people's mistakes and sins on innocent (or at least wordless) beings. First, it was a scarlet cloth; later, a white cloth dipped in blood attached to an animal's back, head, or horns (bull, sheep, lamb, goat as in "scapegoat"). The animal was then released into the wilderness where it would run wild. While the animal ran wild, the cloth or fabric would be exposed to the weather. Eventually, the red became white, signifying that the fault, the sin, or the crime had been bleached out and therefore forgiven. From that concept, people moved from using animals to performing human sacrifices. Eventually, a doctrine developed that somebody, something, or some Holy One must pay a blood penalty for moral blunders. Without the shedding of blood there is no remission for sin (Hebrews 9:22).

Moral blunders range from mistakes that erring people make during the pilgrimage of life, to horrendous, planned crimes. The least of these came to necessitate dragging God from his throne in heaven and murdering him? Nothing less would quench divine wrath? Could these be in tune with Pope Gregory the VII's "Cursed be the man who holds back his sword from shedding blood"? Or doesn't St. Augustine's justification for the Church's violent suppression of heretics in his *Cognite Intrare* carry the day?

"The wounds of a friend are better than the kisses of an enemy." Does this ring a bell? And consider Bishop Arnaud's instruction to the Crusaders: "Kill them all, for God knows His own," when asked how the Church's soldiers could tell Catholics apart from Cathars. Incidentally, not a single child was spared.

Could the Church followers' fascination with blood explain Pope Innocent III's assertion that anyone who attempted to construe a personal view of God which conflicted with Church dogma must be burned without pity? Christians, think hard, for in the light of this new era of accurate information, the survival of Christian religions may depend on integrity and respect for truth.

Christians, wake up! Preachers must leave their hermetic comfort zone and work harder. Read more. The Bible is a great book, but should it be the only good book a good Christian reads? The Bible represents a conscious effort to relate everything to God; it is a great book in which the name God is so often mentioned with sincerity. That may be where its power resides. Rather than arguing that every single word of the Bible is God-inspired, it is more truthful to affirm that there is a humble and intelligent way to read the Bible that always makes the book inspiring.

Ask the Holy Spirit to be the driving energy in searches for truth. Love the Bible, but go beyond it for the love of God. Today is the moment of truth. The time has come when anyone who reads only the Bible and locks himself and God in their understanding of the Bible is no better than a music composer who, having discovered the beauty of the pentatonic scale, chooses to go no further. The same applies to someone who looks at their religion or its doctrines and declares that those arguments and thoughts are the only way to God. There are more than five keys on the piano keyboard. It's doubtful that it be the will of God that believers restrict themselves to only one scale.

The Bible is a book. Who would trust a doctor whose knowledge is confined to only one book? The Bible was codified by people of diverse opinions: some of whom believed the earth was flat; some who believed that women were inferior creatures; others who trusted that slavery was fair, and some who held that leprosy was an incurable disease. The narrators and writers would have scoffed at the idea of in-vitro fertilization and sent its proponents to the scaffold or burned them at the stake. Imagine what they would do to Stephen Hawking! Finally, some of the New Testament's highly-praised heroes thought the return of Christ so imminent that they almost gave up "living" and urged believers to focus only on "things above." St. Paul thought marriage, therefore, unnecessary and only relented when it became obvious that ill-advised celibacy was creating too many problems, more problems than the early Church could handle (Deloria, 1994). In retrospect, even their understanding of the message of Christ appears to have been quite limited. They could only envision God as a rigid, intolerant, punitive supreme Commander-in-Chief of a big army against Satan's rather than an all-loving, comforting, and redeeming Presence dedicated to working wonders through us.

We ought to know God better by now, thanks to the extreme patience demonstrated by God to humankind. Where is the patient today who would want treatment for tuberculosis based upon Hippocrates' prescription? A person's understanding of God is proportionate with his or her humility and clarity of mind. People are not perfect, and their understanding is not perfect, but there is such a thing as common sense and wisdom. We are just children in the process of growing up, and God is patient with us. It is not God who changes - it is perceptions of God that must change. They have caused too much misery for our fellow humans.

It's time for truth to prevail over prejudices, cultural biases, personal preferences, and mistaken personal convictions of scriptural correctness. Truth, when allowed to illuminate, exposes and redeems hidden agendas for power and control.

Christians must have a godly approach to the religions they so wickedly denigrate out of their sinful fear and pride. In 2005, a preacher on a Haitian radio station in Miami said, "I am arrogant and rightfully so about my Christian religion." But believers' words and deeds must breathe humility. They must, like Jesus, show love to everybody and reject arrogance and wickedness everywhere (including arrogance and wickedness within their ranks).

Christians must stop being conceited, and they must stop calling their sect-ridden religion the only way to peace with God. Christians don't have an exclusive on the doctrines or the sacraments. Take baptism for instance. Not only Christians use it as a symbol for renunciation of bad behavior and pride. It existed for thousands of years before John the Baptist called the people of Israel to repentance. Even baptisms where the faithful roll in mud or clay are plunges into humility.

In the same vein, holding Vodou responsible for a country's ills, be the focus New Orleans or Gonaïves, may be unfair. Christians in Haiti and abroad blame Vodou for the poverty, violence, and hopelessness. What if it's not Vodou that is the problem? What if it is the Haitian refusal to give up slavery whether in the guise of restavek or zombie? Maybe what has preserved America despite its similarities to Haiti is that America, as a nation, has turned away from slavery and has laws that forbid and protect against exploitation of the weakest and the most vulnerable. Perhaps what condemns a nation to ignominy and contempt, what makes them cursed by God, is the willingness to tolerate slavery of any type (like sharecropping). Human origin is divine. Even the restavek and the zombie. Even the migrant worker. Even the sweatshop worker. We're all children of God.

Who doesn't crave the infinite? Not one person is immune to that thirst, whether he or she is modern or primitive, pagan or Christian, scholarly or illiterate. Christians, Buddhists, Hindus, Zoroastrians, Jews, and Animists all have this in common. If believers focus on that common ground and fight evil together, God is honored and the world is readied for the big redemption to come. God will finish what believers start. If this is the case, then it's reasonable to ask: "So what is evil?" What identifies evil as such? Some inescapable inner flame that's vocal in all of us?

God's task becomes more pleasant when families play their part with humility and love for God's creations. God is honored and pours out blessing untold when people, like some of the founding fathers of America, submit to God's will, defer to God's plan, and when they stop letting one tree obscure their view of the forest.

Religions represent humanity's efforts to deal with the unknown and with uncontrollable events and phenomena. The unknown upsets people, especially when the unknown, the not-yet-understood hurts them. When they consider the future, fearing it or hoping for a better situation than their present one, they are apprehensive and restless in body, soul, and spirit. Caught between wanting information and reassurance, their curiosity and apprehension combine to lead them to think in ruts. In seeking comfort and reassurance, people ask questions, create and lean on symbols, hypothesize, theorize, philosophize, extrapolate from the environment and their experiences, they imagine, and they question. Could this be how the history of humanity and the chronology of creation in the book of Genesis came to be?

Oh, yes, we may already hear the objectors: How could primitive people come with such a profound and time-tested dissertation unless God personally uploaded the information into their brains? The truth is, a peasant great-grandson turned physician or physicist is no smarter than his great-great grandfather or great-great-grandmother; he simply has access to more knowledge by virtue of the era into which he was born. Being smart is an equal opportunity blessing across generations, and progress is in the knowledge. Dear reader, you are not smarter than your oldest ancestor. You are simply more knowledgeable. Your knowledge today is a drop in the cup, as compared with your child's knowledge of tomorrow. Our perception of God yesterday is not - and should not be - the same as we move forward. But God does not change.

Humans have always asked: Where are we going? From where did we come? What are we made of? Why are we here? Where is the better tomorrow? What must be done to make the not-too-distant future safe? What happens after death?

When a person finds hope, he or she romanticizes it, making it dramatically colorful, and giving it what the existentialists call *la fumée métaphysique* (a metaphysical smokescreen). Hope becomes myth, but reality cannot be ignored. Being hungry, stubbing one's toe against a rock, and being burned by the fire are all real. There's no guessing or dreaming. A person must face reality and discern patterns and create a formula. Reason (*logos*) is needed. Life goes on between the two extremes of reason and hope (Armstrong, 2001). Like the crutches of a person with a broken leg, such life companions provide balance.

The satisfaction of knowledge is short-lived. People always long for more. There is always something new that matters, and even if reason (*logos*) is so wonderful, even if there is gratitude for having been pulled out of the dark ages by reason, there is a desire to build temples and places of worship because reason doesn't satisfy. It stops short of filling us up completely. There is unsatisfied thirst and worry. Mythos is needed; the trauma of uncertainty does not disappear. Indeed, reason and her child, science, do not assuage all longings. Science asks more questions than it provides answers. When answers are provided, they bring a heavy price and are slow in coming. It's been said, "Science's trajectory is a vast graveyard." Reason has other children besides science that have left their stamp on world events. Based on rational acts, these attitudes and movements have been destructive rather than beneficial. Some of these terrible, illegitimate children (as defined by John Ralston Saul) include the murderous Inquisition; Hitler's Nazism; Mussolini's Fascism; corporate America's crushing greed; and the logic of McNamara's politics of world armament.

For sure, reason does not provide comfort from pain and sorrow. When there is grief and scarcity and when there is despair, hope in the form of mythos enables people to open themselves and the situation to compassionate energy. Pure reason gives rise to Darwinism, the survival of the "meanest," but hope for a better solution allows compassion for the despised. Hope delivers people from the rational urge to ignore or destroy others for the sake of narrow self-interest. Leaning 100% on reason is bad, and so is depending too much on mythos. Serenity breathes in the middle ground.

Most religions make a mockery of reason and common sense. Imposing myths has been their besetting sin. Most people admit that truth lives somewhere between science and faith, and that God is greater than both *Logos* and *Mythos,* but why do some make a God out of reason? Why chain God up in myths? In part, some people are more concerned with having servants than with being free.

The time has come to pursue a multiplicity of perspectives and to allow reason to sift the truth. Jesus said, "The truth shall set you free." When will that prophecy be fulfilled? The sincerely devout, and the cynically observant, should guard against hijacking God and dressing God up to their liking, in accordance with their prejudices, cultural biases, and personal preferences. The search for power and control over others is a deceptive and persistent vice that too many believers are unwilling to relinquish. Christians' sacred opportunity is to open the door to God's influence and let God work amongst people. Believers do not have a mandate to impose our creeds on others. It is not our task to judge, nor to kill, coerce, or alienate in His name. And, for God's sake, let us not tell lies, conceal, destroy documents, demonize people, or fabricate evidence. To do that is evil. That cannot be God's agenda.

Supporters of historical Christianity have been too eager to overwhelm people's minds and trust in themselves. The struggle for control of people's behavior has caused too much coercion, double-speech, and manipulation. The truths about America's founding fathers' beliefs regarding religion have been glossed over by people seeking control over other people's lives. When the founding fathers created America, they had a particular vision of the world. Reality has fallen short of that vision. Not only do we need to do more but like Reverend W. Lamont Hardison says, we need to guarantee that our government, instead of having America take its moral cue from the world, give its cue to the world.

Christians stop short of denying that the founding fathers were Christians, but call them Deists (as if that's a dirty word). Now that believers are divided into theists, animists, spiritists, what is next? How did it happen that one word translated into different languages created a lexicon for different religions? This serves as evidence of the visceral craving for people to consider their thoughts as greater than the thoughts of others. The adherents of historical Christianity have had that disease for too long. It's led to Christians having lied, killed, and resorted to merciless repression to impose their creeds across sects and cultures. Is it arrogant to think that God knows more than the greatest theologians and apologists? Perhaps God is too big to be encapsulated by any book, no matter its inspiration.

Christians should know that they represent a minority. God created humanity. Believers must stop acting like the youngest child, who in his conceit proclaims himself his father's only heir and tries to disown those born before him, or from other mothers, unless they pray, eat, talk, and dress like him. It should not be doubted that God treasures people who love mercy and justice; enlightened Christians, Buddhists, Muslims, and Hindus. Nor should it be taken lightly that believers have killed so many human beings. This has happened because of self-righteousness, lust for power, and pride. Probably the same wickedness, the same power that wanted to separate blacks and natives from whites is still at work building walls between God-worshiping people. Beware!

It matters that believers get along so that false religious excuses for injustice cease. Too many children of God have died at the feet of cruel parents. Though it is true that the purpose of religions is to reconnect people to God, violence is not an acceptable way to enforce God-honoring behavior. When violent acts are committed in the name of God, the victims and perpetrators of violence adopt violence as a convenient way to solve problems and resolve conflicts.

In casting doubt upon another's merit and importance, religions entertain bigotry, mutual mistrust, and tension. On the other hand, the fascination of all religions is spiritual. If people focus on that instead of their differences, common ground will be unearthed and religions may claim their rightful place in the world: building bridges instead erecting of walls. Ultimately, when all the lies and legends have been set aside, religion will emerge as a force for unification. It may be that religion's true role is to resolve conflicts and prevent wars.

As a nation, Haiti illustrates what may happen when a country marked out as the staging area for religion's true role, a nation of extraordinary destiny, can be manipulated by outside interests and betrayed by its trustees. In Haiti's case, embracing racial prejudice and classism, and abandoning the highest aims of the revolutionary spirit was equal to embracing the devil, not in finding strength in traditional African religions. In becoming materialistic, the people of Haiti dropped the ball and mimicked the mistakes of America's founding fathers.

Considering the personal writings of America's founding fathers, the idea that God's plan for the world allowed for the birth of the United States of America may not be farfetched, nor is the idea that God wanted Haiti for a special purpose! It is plainly obvious that this approach to understanding religions and spiritual matters has been the endeavor of many God-loving souls among the founding fathers and founding mothers of this great country. Among John Adams' writings is a frantic plea for people to give religions credit where credit is due ("Religion I hold to be essential to Morals") but to also be objective ("I have not thought myself obliged to believe all I heard") as to their realities and limitations. For example, Adams advocated a more responsible reading of the Bible. America's founding fathers who strove, with their eyes and minds fixed on the Great Divinity, to establish a society where politics and religion interacted in mutually beneficial ways, intended religion and politics to enjoy a peaceful and informed coexistence. This is a far cry from how religion and politics now attempt to hold each other hostage - especially at election time. In the 2004 presidential elections, some preachers consented to use of their churches for canvassing votes. Some who presumed to "seize the country for God" believed, perhaps in good faith, that voting for Democratic candidates meant voting for the Anti-Christ. Consider the frequency, and to what effect, the phrase "separation of church and state" is used. Any society stands to benefit from a functional interaction of the three consciences: social, religious, and political. Religious leaders require a political conscience, and their political conscience should enrich their understanding that governments fail their mission when they favor one religion over another.

The government and the state exist for all citizens. The sacred duty of government is to protect everyone who obeys the law of the land. When solving problems, political leadership will and must use methods independent from those used by churches or temples. Consider the pressing issue of teenage sexual activity. It makes sense that churches preach abstinence, yet abstinence is only one approach to solving the multifaceted problem of sexually transmitted diseases and of teenage pregnancy. Realistically, some teens will not abstain; even those who attend church. What about the social and economic problems that accompany unplanned and unwanted pregnancies? What about the health of adolescents and the population at large when ignorance and sexual activities spread disease? The solutions must begin with good will toward all.

The Church's preaching is only one contribution to the general solution. The political leadership owes society a more comprehensive strategy. The social and political consciences of religious leaders should lead them to consider the costs of choices made by them on behalf of their people and how much before imposing unwise burdens on the rest of the nation. A religious conscience in political leadership should make political leaders more respectful of the deep religious of their colleagues and the electorate in a framework of intelligent mutual understanding rather than political exploitation or abuse of power.

We need social and political conscience in religion; social and religious conscience in politics; and political and religious conscience for social concerns. In short, there should be respect for everyone's rights. Given respect for everyone's rights, love for everybody is just a few steps away - which is what God demands. God's grace and our intelligence should do the rest. That's the powerful Christmas message (according to a translation from the French) - "Peace on earth to all men of goodwill." When people act with good will, they open the door for God to work, they act out the second sentence of the Lord's Prayer, and they invite "Thy will be done on earth as it is in Heaven."

When religious leadership rises above sectarianism and takes its rightful place as moderator, it inspires concord and harmony. It acts as the voice of reason in the midst of turmoil, a lighthouse in the turbulent seas of a troubled moment. Several examples of this are detailed in Johnston's and Sampson's *Religion the Missing Dimension in Statecraft* (1994). Contributor Edward Luttwak argued that the post-World War II reconciliation of France and Germany was made possible by the leadership of different religious denominations working together. Bruce Nichols described how a similar approach salvaged a fragile political alliance in Nicaragua. Cynthia Sampson detailed how Quakers helped stop the civil war in Nigeria. Most inspiring was Wooster's account of how the Catholic Church led ecumenical initiative to aid the people of the Philippines during and after the regime of Ferdinand Marcos.

Under Marcos, the Catholic Church chose the path least traveled by authority. The Catholic Bishops Conference of the Philippines had enough practical morality to realize that the regime had lost "its moral legitimacy to govern." Siding with the people rather than catering to the representatives of the status quo, the Church saved the country from chaos. Guided by the principles of clearly articulated common ground, Cardinal Jaime Sin - backed up by a strong cohort of enlightened nuns and priests - offered an ecumenical olive branch to other religious groups. The leaders of this diverse religious group resisted seduction attempts, ignored official and unofficial intimidation, and overcame patronization from the totalitarian, selfish, pretentious power.

Until Philippino religious leaders unearthed their common ground as believers and non-political leaders, the United States had backed Marcos, but when persuaded by the display of unflinching resolve, the U.S. government loaned its weight to the Church-led Philippinos. That development of U.S. involvement thwarted the plans of the Marxists to steal the show. In the end, evil was overcome. The graceful and gracious intervention of the Catholic Church made that miracle possible. It involved the principled engagement of the religious leadership, a spiritual interpretation of Biblical texts - rather than a semantic one - and an open humility with regard to the focus on the will of God. Father Moraleda of Manila believed that the Church must be an instrument of liberation and, in keeping with humanist impulses of Marxism, must bring the society of the future kingdom of God into being (Wooster, 1994).

In that contest between institutionalized injustice and revolutionary violence, the Church traveled the Way of Wisdom. Catholic Bishops suggested that the love proclaimed in the Gospel had the power to transform people and society, that social transformation required authentic reconciliation with God and one another, and that the chief means to bring about social transformation is a conversion of hearts among the powerful (Wooster, 1994).

To President Marcos, who had sent threats, they offered the following unequivocal message:

> The increasing use of force to dominate people is a frightening reality that we as pastors cannot ignore (Wooster, 1994).

Then, as is often the case when a political power tries and fails to beat the Church, a voice representing the establishment told them, in effect, to shut up. On behalf of the interested religious leaders, Cardinal Sin responded with:

> I am reminded...of the wise man who said that war was too important a business to be left exclusively in the hands of generals. Might not the same be said of government, that government is much too important a business to be left in the sole hands of politicians and political scientists? (Wooster, 1994)

Haiti needs this kind of religious leadership. The whole world needs stewards who understand the necessity of keeping politics and religion separate but not to the point that they cancel each other out. Spiritually minded people need courage to stand up to powers that have lost the moral legitimacy to govern. Wisdom is needed to distinguish between the decency of abstaining from partisan politics and the cowardice of condoning politics that threaten faith and morals. That's only one lesson from the Philippines miracle.

There Are No Sinless Religions

All religions have their problems. But how often in their spiritual and religious observances, or secular education, do Christians get an opportunity to look at other religions other than through the lens of bigotry?

According to John Snelling (1998), Buddhism is the only major world religion that has not served as a platform for mass killings, pogroms, and burnings. He credits Buddhism with respecting humans' basic instinct to reach for highest spirituality and understanding that there are many approaches to the mysteries of ultimate reality. This differs from the idea expressed in 1st Timothy 2:5 that there is one God and one Mediator between God and men, the man Christ Jesus.

In thinking of that Mediator in the third person, some believers may want to control how other people think of the historical Jesus. Perhaps it would be better for all believers if Christians did not consider the above verse as grounds for the exclusive righteousness of their religion. They may take this belief to the point of resenting people who do not agree with them, going so far to consign them to hell. Why? If there is only one Mediator between God and individuals, why do Christians try to involve themselves so much in this process? Why do some Christians set themselves up as mediators in religious and spiritual matters? Another way of viewing the aforementioned verse is that perhaps the concept would be more unifying if it could be thought of as referring to the Christ in Jesus that He wants in all people who would be one with God. Maybe Christ in Jesus, and Christ in all believers, is what makes all believers one in the Father. Is it not written that Christ is in those who believe in Him and those who believe in Him are in Him? Why then is there such a multiplicity of Christian sects? Why, instead of imitating Jesus do we choose instead to dress Him up to our liking and shove Him down the throats of reluctant listeners?

As for other religions, what is the purpose of the insistence that Christianity is the one true religion? A multiplicity of spiritual narratives suggest that the practice of Christianity repeats precepts that had been taught by Lord Krishna, Buddha, and other sages prior to the time of Jesus. Maybe one of the reasons Jesus lived and taught as he did was to confirm those teachings as being "the right stuff." Here are some teachings attributed to Lord Krishna that appear to be along the same lines of those taught by Jesus and the prophets before him:

1. When the poor man knocks at your door, take him and administer to his wants, for the poor are the chosen of God.
2. Above all things, cultivate love for your neighbor.
3. Do good for its own sake and expect not your reward for it on earth.
4. It is better to forgive an injury than to avenge it.
5. What you blame in others do not practice yourself.

Purportedly, a man born some 1,200 years before the time of Christ spoke these maxims. Are these devil-inspired precepts or a preview of Jesus Christ's moral code, a precursor of the sermon of the Mount? Let the critical reader be the judge.

What about these precepts from the Vedas?

1. God curses him who is cursed by woman.
2. God will punish him who laughs at a woman's suffering.
3. When a woman is honored God is honored.
4. The virtuous woman will have one husband and the right-minded man one wife.
5. It is the highest crime to take advantage of the weakness of a woman.
6. Women should be loved, respected, and protected by husbands, fathers and brothers, etc.

What about the following from the moral code of the Buddhists?

1. Thou shall not kill.
2. Thou shall not steal.
3. Thou shall not commit adultery.
4. Thou shall not lie.
5. Thou shall not intoxicate yourself.

Some of the founding fathers had made their own comparative study of religions. John Adams said, "Religions I hold to be essential to morals." For the followers of one religion to claim superiority over all others, however, is a vile exercise in self-righteousness. For when religions are used to teach distrust and fear they create civil war in the minds of believers and convert them into soldiers of hate. Protestant children growing up in Haiti of the 1950's and 1960's, remember the tension, mutual contempt, and mistrust between Catholics and Protestants; harassment on the schoolyard and inside the classrooms; the condescending attitudes of the teachers; and the aura of darkness they were brainwashed to see or feel around Vodou people. It didn't get better when Catholic priests, as professors of religion, would appear in the classrooms to hammer on individual Protestant children - "cursed sons of heretics" - from the lecterns. Those were painful experiences, and certainly not conducive to mutual respect, to love, or to nation building. They were fertile ground for self-hate.

Considering the moral principles listed above, particularly the Hindu Vedas, it is ironic that Christians are so often at odds with the adherents of a religion such as Hinduism. Perhaps it has something to do with the difference between the Vedas and the scriptures regarding attitudes toward women. To decide that the statements drawn from the Vedas are of the devil, however, would be dishonest. Christians, wake up! Christianity must be rescued from its traditions of exclusivity, which are based, at least in part, upon ignorance, fear, and lies.

God, Spirituality and Vodou

Persecuted by the Church, denounced by the Haitian elite, discredited by most foreigners, and often disowned by those that practice it nevertheless, Vodou in Haiti has stood the test of time.

Vodou has impregnated Haitian culture. Haitian music - secular or sacred - Haitian art, and day-to-day Haitian-to-Haitian interaction are permeated by that powerful way of life. One must then ask the question: how can so many get it so wrong? Haitians are not alone in holding on to what some describe as a false, primitive, or backward religion, a practice that some denounce as not being a religion at all.

Elsewhere it is named Santeria, Candomble, Obeah, Shango, and Macumba, among other terms.

In considering God, spirituality and Vodou, some pertinent questions persist: Is Vodou so evil as to demonize its entire people? Is it that any evil in a Vodou worshipper ruins what is an otherwise normal religion? Could it be that critics of Vodou have been criticizing a dirtied dress (the religion) rather than the habits of the people choosing to wear that dress (the worshippers)?

An approach that combines critical analysis along with thoughtful spirituality may provide a better frame for suitable questions and in some cases, answers. There are many ways to make a literal reading of the Bible. If one is willing to consider a variety of angles of a particular situation, one may deepen their understanding of who the people of the Bible were and what they were about.

It is written that Father Abraham was willing to offer God a human sacrifice. Abraham believed that God told him to sacrifice his son. How did Abraham know that God wanted this of him? Did God tell Abraham this in a vision while he was awake or in a dream while he was asleep? Did God tell Abraham this directly, speaking from Divine consciousness into Abraham's consciousness? Maybe Abraham consulted with an oracle (not unlike the way advice is sought in some Vodou circles) and believed that sacrificing his son Isaac was what God wanted from him (not unlike some Vodou believers believe that sacrificing their children is what is required of them by God).

In any case, Abraham's willingness (reluctant or otherwise) to sacrifice Isaac suggests that Abraham lived in a culture in which human sacrifice was neither unheard of nor unacceptable. When Jacob took his wives and ran away from his father-in-law Laban, one of Jacob's wives took Laban's *theraphim* (called a "god" in some translations; in Vodou parlance one would say *ouanga*) with her. Saul, the King of Israel, asked the Witch of Endor to summon the ghost of the prophet Samuel for him. The religious law forbade consulting with witches, but Saul did it anyway. These three examples illustrate acts that Vodou worshippers and Christians familiar with Vodou call Vodou. Even with these practices as a part of their lives (and households) God built upon what they had and did not forsake them.

Vodou is an ancient religion, older than Judaism. It employs ways of seeking out God's opinion that are different from strict Judeo-Christian practices. Vodou is another approach to spirituality, commensurate with evolution of the mind. That many Haitians favor this religion over Christianity has less to do with being primitive or sinful than with the fact that white European colonials used Christianity to dehumanize, enslave, and exploit them and their immediate predecessors.

During the days of the slave trade and slavery, European slave traffickers and French slave owners hid behind the cross of Christ. They preached at the enslaved, demanding that the slaves be obedient to merciless and brutal (but Bible-toting) white men. As far as the enslaved were concerned, Satan, no matter how negatively described by the Church, was a more gracious figure than the white Christians they knew. For Haitians, Hell was already on earth. It was the white Christians' debased spirituality that justified and excused the evils of colonialism and the African slave trade. Living with the fruits of this debased Christianity made that kind of thinking reasonable.

Now consider the spirituality of Vodou. If the aspects of Vodou spirituality that are most easily warped by the wickedness inherent to humankind are corrected, the "dress" of Vodou can be cleaned. One of the ways Vodou can be brought out of malignance is if a strong civil - but respectful - society demands that murderous witchcraft be removed from the Vodou religion. For example, "zombification" could be outlawed in pretty much the same way the United States federal government forced Mormons to repudiate polygamy - and hopefully, by steering clear of more martial methods, with more success.

If trusted and moral government says to the Vodou worshipper, "Listen, if you want to be protected by the law of the land, you cannot go on with unacceptable practices." If it is said to Vodou adherents, "You no longer have to take the law into your own hands: you have a government that is going to see to it that justice be served," Vodou will become and stay clean. If love is demonstrated to the people, Vodou will be a dress that remains clean on its wearer. If Haitians do this, they won't be making the mistake of throwing the baby out with the bath water. For this is what Haitians have done in dismissing customs connected to the Vodou religion as backward, primitive, and savage.

Take, for instance, the ceremony at Bwa Kayiman, where the successful Haitian slave revolt exploded into life. The events there electrified Haiti's forebears, inspiring them to fight the French slave masters and win. It was a collective spiritual experience for those slaves who did not have to know about the real Jesus Christ and His sacrifice on Calvary.

The following is the prayer of Boukman[5] (the Haitian founding father who had come from Jamaica), the master of ceremonies and chief priest officiating at Bwa Kayiman:

God who made the Sun,
God who sends us light from above,
God who moves the tidal waves,
God who made the thunder roar,
The god of the other people heard of our misery.
He went hiding behind the clouds.
There he takes a look at us
And sees all the wrong the white man has done
And like an idiot does nothing.
The white man's God is only good to the white man.
White man's God wants nothing to do with blacks.
The white man's God is Satan.
He craves blood.
He delights in the white man's sucking our blood.
The white man's God demands crime.
Our God wants what is good.
He gives us strength,
He grants us courage,
He gives us endurance.
Our God wants all to live.
He means well for all of us.
He wants everybody to live like people.

How was this prayer ungodly prayer? Boukman's perception of God may not have been right on the mark, but if this was a test, surely he made more than a passing grade. Boukman's prayer energized the enslaved men and women. They fought against enormous odds and triumphed because they believed, and because they had faith in a God who was greater than the cruelty and might of their earthly masters.

The *Slave Prayer*, another artifact of the Haitian Vodou experience, is reserved only for certain Vodou initiates. The late Dr. Beauvoir Edmond, great-great-grandson of Jean-Jacques Dessalines told a group of Haitians that he managed to get hold of the original *Slave Prayer*. According to Dr. Edmond, the original prayer is so well crafted, so deep and powerful, that after reading it, he remained convinced that it

---

[5] The original Creole text was provided courtesy of Librari Mapou in Miami, Florida.

was the Holy Spirit that had lifted up the rebelling blacks and led them to victory over Napoléon's forces.

The Spirit at Bwa Kayiman was of God. It would have remained so, to this day, if ignorance had not credited other forces with the French defeat. That is the root of the problem: not the events of Bwa Kayiman but the forces most often given credit for that miracle. Vodou worshippers make this error when crediting someone or something else for something God has done for them. Sometimes, people even credit themselves for miraculous accomplishments because they want to be God.

The same may be said about the spirituality at work in the Vodou circle. People are essentially spiritual. According to the Book of John, we are divine (John 10:34). By renouncing ego to reconnect with the Source, people can resonate with the divine and permit God's presence, motives, and aims to saturate their being; thus immersed, they may do astonishing things. Nothing is really diabolic until handed over to the devil - the devil being real or imaginary - or when the actor willingly disconnects his or herself from God or otherwise willingly does evil.

How is this possible? Because, believe it or not, God made human beings better than the devil. It is written in the Hebrews 2:7, "God made us a little bit under the angels," probably in connecting our divine nature to this sophisticated, wonderful but perishable flesh. Believers, however, are mistaken when they take this to mean *they are just like God.* Having the option of blending with Jesus, of having the Christ within them, they are promoted to a higher level where flesh or everything else is transcended.

In *What If Vodou Was Better Than We Think?* Joseph Augustin of Montreal, a former Catholic Priest, argued in favor of the idea that the crisis of possession in Vodou worship is not necessarily from the devil. The crisis of possession refers to the phenomena that exemplify what people can accomplish when they access their spiritual dimension, let go of their ego, and set faith free. Examples of this include walking on incandescent coals, spending hours under water, or dancing atop the very tip of a fragile antenna.

Perhaps it is a specially blessed people who can put on such a show of spirituality. Another, more homely example, is the situation of a mother who is in a car accident with her child and regains consciousness only to discover that her child is trapped under the capsized car. In a sudden frenzy, the mother finds the strength to heave up the car and free her child. It could be said that in that moment, the mother experienced a crisis of possession that made the miraculous possible. That's God or spirituality at work!

Of course, the person who experiences such an amazing event has the option of crediting the wrong power for what happened. People always have that choice, and it seems that many choose the wrong one. As a people, Haitians did it by returning to Bwa Kayiman and indiscriminately dedicating the country to the Spirits of Africa. That is a sad example of ignorance overpowering common sense. Indeed, many people take issue with this definition of God's blessing, but attributing God's blessing to malefic forces constitutes true blasphemy. It would be better to critically and scientifically credit the wickedness of the white slave owner for the slave's crisis of possession than any other evil forces. And here is why: inescapable physical and mental misery forces the survivor to escape from sad reality by extraordinary means. Call this escape *denial* or *rationalizing of the mind,* but nevertheless, it is the power of the mind's ability to escape into a world of its own creation. In that world, the spiritual dimension of the victim momentarily dissociates itself from the body. The spiritual dimension can look at it, laugh at it, and can even mock the stupidity in the aggressor. Inescapable torture, when it stops short of physically killing the victim, opens a window for the spiritual and metaphysical. That is what vanquished Haiti's slave owners and slave drivers. That is what defeated Napoléon in Haiti. That was God's way of saying to institutionalized evil, "Enough is enough." The wickedness of the white masters forced the black Africans to access their spiritual dimension in an extraordinary way. To describe it in a spiritual way, God avenged the mayhem unleashed on the world by giving his enslaved black children the upper hand.

Someday, the descendants of former slaves will acknowledge God in all that they do and see. They will know to give credit to whom credit is due. Then they'll triumph. They'll be the wonder of the world. Little Mariella, dancing on her perch atop a seventy-five foot tall television antenna, will cry, "Then sings my soul, my Savior God to Thee, How great thou art!" Rather than, "Agwé Tarroyo sa sa yé" and that will not be the greatest of the wonders known.

People who disagree with this vision of hope are likely one of three types:

1. The trembling racists upset by the idea of God-loving black people having access to power.

2. The miscreants among the Vodou faithful who are incapable or unwilling to let go of murderous witchcraft and zombification - in short, the social misfit-sadists.
3. The victims of secular, sin-riddled Vodou practices. People who have suffered so much because of Vodou problem-solving tactics that they are flooded with unbearable, horrible memories when they hear the faintest whisper of the most innocent Vodou melodies.

The people of the third category must receive as much respect and compassion as great Haitian hearts can offer. The first two are in need of grace - but their works cannot be tolerated. Compassion for them is necessary; tolerance for their tactics and habits is not.

Vodou, the complex philosophy-religion derived from many nations of Africa, was the crutch slaves and maroons leaned on because that is all that was left to them after kidnapping, torture, forcible transport, and more torture. But God had eyes on the African. Instead of forsaking the enslaved people, he built upon what they had. The crisis of possession came from the window of opportunity that was supposedly the slave's destruction. The torturers were taken by surprise because it was the merciless violence - the soul-crushing torture - that gave the enslaved an escape into their raw spirituality.

7

Timeliness, Truths, and Thinking

Marie Curie, co-discoverer of radioactivity, said, "Nothing in life is to be feared, it is only to be understood." Too many lies have been told for too long. There have been too many misunderstandings and too much alienation and hatred in the name of God! Today is the time for repentance. The truth can no longer be hidden or twisted as it has been for nearly 2000 years. God's people must think rather than rearrange their prejudices. That is how they will allow truth into their lives.

"You shall know the truth and the truth shall set you free." Those are Jesus' words, according to the Bible. Jesus knew a time would come when little could bar access to information. Indeed, with nearly unfettered access to the Internet in the industrialized nations, satellite communication, television with its documentaries and biographies, movies, radio, reader-friendly bookstores, and public libraries, researchers, scholars, entertainers, and regular folks eagerly search and share their truths. Books that were condemned in the past are emerging from their hiding places and into the public eye.

Was Voltaire really an atheist? He took the local Catholic Church at Ferney under his protection, going so far as to have *Deo erexit Voltaire* inscribed on it (Parton, 1881). According to James Boswell, Voltaire's venerated the "Supreme Being" and expressed desire to resemble the "Authour of Goodness" by being good himself (Redman, 1949). When Boswell questioned Voltaire's sincerity Voltaire replied, "Before God I am." Perhaps it was not that Voltaire didn't believe in God, but rather that he rejected the version of God presented to him by the Catholic Church. According to Parton, Voltaire could not swallow the Catholic Church's claims of supernatural authority and enforcement of those claims by punishment using the resources and power of government. The Church presented those claims as sound theology. Voltaire viewed them as self-serving half-truths and outright lies. This truth being out about Voltaire, suggests that the problem is not in having churches built in the village but in deifying the Church hierarchy. While Protestants may be guilty of enshrining the Bible at the expense of God Almighty, Catholics, in enshrining the Church hierarchy and power may have sinned no less.

Translations and Literalism

The Bible certainly is a great book to love, to treasure like a gem, but not one to worship and use for political control. Scriptural correctness and selective literalism are double-edged swords that may maim. Whatever the translation, the Bible is an extraordinary book. Consisting of a collection of writings created by many people over thousands of years, it contains the entire message of redemption. God's majesty and will transcend all perfectibility suspected or evident in the book. That the voice of God, God's message, is so substantially part of the Bible is a miracle. The Bible, however, is not God. God is too big and too deep, too independent and too alive, to be parsed by a book.

Dear reader, if you grew up being told that every single word in the Bible was to be accepted at face value, you - like the authors - were misled. Here is why: some self-appointed powers decided that in order to protect our faith, we should only be fed "food appropriate for children." Too many believers have not been taught about the secular origins of the Bible; the circumstances surrounding the compilation and selection of its texts; or the actual criterion for rejection or inclusion of the various testimonies, letters, chapters, and gospels. That kind of discussion and instruction was far above the concerns of ordinary people.

The collection of documents known as *The New Testament* was compiled, at the behest of a powerful non-Christian. The writings selected for inclusion were chosen to serve a particular political purpose. Fortunately, enough is now known about the contributions of Emperor Constantine to the Bible. Though known as the Christian Roman Emperor, Constantine was not a Christian (Ellerbe, 1995). He was a murderer and a dictator until the day he took his last breath (Ellerbe).

He had his own son killed on the basis of his third wife's accusation. Later, when he realized the wife had lied, he had her boiled alive. It was only on his deathbed, when he had nearly taken his last breath, did he accept Christian baptism. According to some, it was because he was too weak to protest (Ellerbe).

Nevertheless, Constantine was the driving political force behind the Council of Nicea. Whether or not Jesus was the Son of God, the idea of Jesus as God was used to consolidate power while excusing the abuses of the Powers-that-be. Insisting that Jesus is God without doing what Jesus asked his followers to do is a shell game (*piké kolé*). It has served many times the malignant purpose of those running the game and deceiving the believers. Before the Council of Nicea, Christians did not unanimously preach that Jesus was the Son of God. That was not their priority; perhaps they did not have to preach it, let alone believe it, to be called followers of Christ. It is said that imitation is the highest form of flattery, so the most dignified way to acknowledge Jesus may be to imitate Him in what He is, what He stands for, and to obey His rule.

Additionally, as the driving force behind the formation of this council, Constantine probably approved the final selection of the texts of the New Testament. Texts that did not support the doctrines that Constantine favored may have been excluded for political, not theological, reasons. Fortunately there is enough information available to explain the absence of a gospel according to Mary or Mary of Magdalene. The absence of any Gospel of Mary may have less to do with lack of inspiration or authenticity and more to do with misogynist propensities of the leaders of the ancient Church. The simple fact that those discarded books may have been written or unearthed much later than the approved ones is no valid reason for rejection. One may ask, "Were those people ever invited to share or write their testimonies in time? Did the powers-that-be ever value them?"

In his fictional thriller *The Da Vinci Code*, Dan Brown writes, "Jesus was declared God by a vote." Perhaps the church fathers desired to present Jesus Christ to Christians in a way that supported an ungodly dream of world domination. Some scholars see the hand of Constantine in the church father's declaration that God was completely and utterly removed from humanity. Constantine may have needed a promoted Jesus to weaken the power of the idea of Him. Maybe it served some political purpose to elevate a historical person, a rebel and a teacher, someone far removed from the "things of this earth," thus leaving room for a Messiah necessary for a dream of a World Government, and whose sandals he, the emperor, could easily fill. Hence the fitness of the expression *Constantinian imperial Christianity* as used by Cornel West (2004) to describe our history, actual performance and accomplishment, thus far. To borrow from Paul of Tarsus, Jesus wished to humanize himself, and he did so by submitting to the humility of death on the cross. Even before the crucifixion, He was humble enough to weep with His friends and reduce himself to the status of a lowly servant when He washed his apostles' feet at the Last Supper.

These thoughts on the political usefulness of the declared divinity of Jesus, as sponsored by a political opportunist and the aims of Jesus himself, raise many questions. Here are some pertinent ones:

Is the Bible really a linear textbook? Is the message of salvation as easily deciphered as some pretend, or does it hide within the pages like pearls in oysters, or diamonds in ore? That is, only retrievable through loving intelligence, genuine thirst for the truth, and ceaseless prayer (what some Buddhists call being in the constant mindfulness of God)? What to make of the enormous difference between versions of the Holy Bible? Perhaps what makes the Sacred Book so powerful is far from what people's limited sight may comprehend. Isn't it through a miracle that the Bible, despite its imperfections, leads to Christ whose way is the truth, life, and the only way?

The following sums up what is known about the Old Testament: The first books of the Bible were written in Hebrew and Aramaic. By 250 BC, those languages passed from common usage. The sacred texts were translated into Greek, and thus the Hebrew "Bible" became the Greek Septuagint. Around that time, a legendary tale was circulated. According to that story, 72 old men working independently over the course of 72 days produced 72 identical Greek translations of the Old Testament. In later retellings, the number shrank to 70 (hence the title Septuagint). Nonetheless, despite this glorious beginning, the Jewish cannon would later disown some of the texts of the Greek Septuagint as inadmissible.

Revisions opened the era of a plurality of bibles. They differed from one another by the number of texts added or removed. Some were the Catholic Bible, the Protestant Bible, and the Eastern Orthodox Christian Bible. Later, while Hellenic civilization was losing its direct influence and Roman civilization was gaining ascendance, Latin became the language of the Bible. Jerome, Church father from 327 to

420 CE, abandoned the Greek text and arranged for a direct translation from Hebrew and Aramaic. Jerome's recommended switch supports the idea that someone important had questions about the accuracy or inerrancy of the Greek Septuagint.

Parallel to the Christian effort to create a more faithful translation of the original sacred Hebrew texts was the move by Jewish scholars to return to the Hebrew original. The so-called *Masoretic Bible* was written with added vowels and accents to words (Davis, 2001). Until then, written Hebrew used no vowels, a situation that could have made writing and translating a chore in any language.

How possible is it that these many translations and retranslations suggest a lack of consensus among the translators? The translations and retranslations dismantle the claim that every word in the Bible is to be obeyed to the last letter, which in turn challenges the claim that every word in the Bible was inspired by God and is to be obeyed as if coming directly from God. Should we believe that Saint Jerome's Bible, the so-called Vulgate, is better or more authentic than the others on the basis of its popularity?

The act of translation also allows for errors. It has already been said that "translation is treason." Taken a step further, translation is sometimes murder. Every language has its own inexorable genius, and every translator has his or her own weakness and prejudices that can nullify and curtail that genius. There are word choices that have more to do with the psychology of the moment or the translator's social context - in other words, "The actual or current content of the mind." (*Le contenu actuel de la pensée*). Ancient words lose their meaning, and the current connotations differ, sometimes violently, from the etymologic history. For example, the author of Song of Songs may not have been astonished that his darling was both beautiful and dark-skinned. According to some scholars, "Thou art black but beautiful" could easily have been translated as, "Thou art black and beautiful." The word "but" rather than the word "and" may have been chosen because in the mind of the translators, or the princes who funded them, blackness and beauty cannot exist in the same person without comment.

The Bible is read in many different languages. Simple word order may give rise to a host of meanings. Across languages and versions, translations vary. For example, in the case of the Angel's heraldic Christmas message, the French translation of that verse is closer to, "Peace on earth to men of good will." The English version of Luke 2:14 reads, "Peace on earth and goodwill to men." These two translations make for at least two different teachings about world peace. Another example of the inconsistencies of translation involves the description of Solomon's temple. What would happen if someone attempted to rebuild the Temple of Solomon according to the scripture? If they should try to build the Temple of Solomon according to the design specifications as translated in different languages, could architects and contractors come up with the same blueprint and build identical temples? Check how differently Matthew 11:12 sounds in the *New International Version (NIV)* from the *New American Standard Bible (NASB)*. The NIV reads, "...The kingdom of heaven has been forcefully advancing and forceful men lay hold of it." What does the NASB read? "...The kingdom of heaven suffers violence and violent men take it by force." While neither statement disowns coercion or aggressiveness, the second translation sounds emphatic about unqualified violence, its desirability, or absolute necessity. Who can tell how much this apology of violence inspired the likes of anti-Native Reverend John Chivington or the crusaders, the Inquisition's executioners, the killers of Joan of Arc, or how it drove the thoughts of Jew-hating Martin Luther or Hitler? Who can tell how much suffering was visited upon God's children because of these two probably equally inaccurate translations or out-of-context interpretations?

The problem arises not only with translations. Bart D. Ehrman (2003) points out the prevailing illiteracy, adding that the very art of writing was in its infancy (no punctuations, no capitals, no spaces between words - as in Dr Ehrman's "*godisnowhere*" versus "God is no where" versus "God is now here"). It may be impossible to know which manuscripts faithfully represented unaltered statements from the presumed authors, and which are copies of translations of the original texts. Using one example, St. Paul's epistle to the Galatians, Ehrman, proved that no one can guarantee that a translation has made it through unaltered from the lips (or pen) of the revered Apostle to the many churches of his concern in Galatia. Therefore, assuming that there exists an original Bible that is exactly the inspired Word of God, a pertinent question remains: Where is that original Word of God? Where do we find it in the midst of all those willfully or accidentally altered versions? With Professor Ehrman, the question is much better phrased: "How does it help us to say that the Bible is the inerrant word of God if in fact we don't have the words that God inerrantly inspired, but only the words copied by the scribes?"

In addition, there are at least eight essential points to consider when reading any version of the Bible:

1. The original language of the books that made up the Bible lacked vowels.
2. The original texts were in poor physical condition when discovered.
3. Sections of the Bible appear to have been inspired by earlier writings from other cultures. Why do the laws of Moses resemble the code of Hammurabi (which predates the Bible)? Why do Solomon's proverbs resemble those of his contemporary, Egyptian sage Amen-em-ope (Davis)? Why does the story of Moses being smuggled into the Pharaoh's palace, including the basket, mirror the legend of King Sargon of Mesopotamia (Davis, 1999)? If Moses authored the first five books of the Old Testament, how could he have written the true history of his death? Does the argument of the selective literalists carry so much weight? Did Moses, being a prophet, foresee his own death and write of it beforehand? If so, why wasn't the account of his death described as a prophecy in the actual text?
4. Careful readings of the sacred texts have revealed differences in style and in the chronology of narration, thus establishing the existence of several authors for single texts (including the book of Genesis).
5. Arguments used to justify dogmas can be simplistic and irrational. Iraeneus de Lyons gave the following as the reason for four gospels: "There are four winds, four corners of the Universe, four pillars that support Heaven; therefore, there could not be more than four gospels. The number four (4) is supported by the notion of a flat earth, center of the universe, supported by four posts (Ellerbe)."
6. Current knowledge regarding the unreliability of memory and the myth of historic truth cast doubt upon the accuracy of narratives written decades after the events they aim to describe.
7. The political machine behind the creation or revision of the set of documents that became the Bible was finalized by the tyrant Emperor Constantine. Considering his history and aims, it is reasonable to question the purity of intention, the intellectual probity, the integrity, and the sincerity of all the

    participants of that council and the accuracy of certain testimonies.
 8. Texts and documents that had been suppressed have become available for review and analysis. It appears that the criterion for selection or exclusion from the Bible was dependent upon doctrines previously taught as absolute truth.

Ideas of the inaccuracies of misleading translations aside, what is to be made of the apparent contradictions in sordid biblical tales? When reading the Bible, contradictions, inconsistencies, and errors of translation or departures from the original texts leap off the page. Some passages reek of the prejudices, cultural biases, and personal tastes of the translators. Words that reek of bias and prejudice sometimes result from the difficulty of translating ideas from one language to another - or vice versa.

The Bible is full of stories that refer to events and personalities that appear inconsistent with decency and mercy. In 1st Kings 13, one prophet's lie has horrible consequences for the prophet he deceives. What's to be made of the blessings heaped upon Jacob? He was described as a notorious liar, so deceitful that as a child he was given a nickname that identified him as a sneak. And what of David? He lied to the priest Ahimeleck, a man of God. He schemed against Saul, God's anointed. He colluded with Jonathan, Saul's own son. Or what of Moses' shady inclusion in the house of Pharaoh? God allowed Moses to be smuggled into Pharaoh's palace. In some respects, his rescue resembles illegal immigration. Then there's Abraham's cowardly spin on his relationship with his wife, Sarah. While he was traveling through a foreign country where he had no natural allies, Abraham pretended that Sarah was only his sister. Abraham feared the attention Sarah might attract from the men of that country as she was a beautiful woman. When the king took interest in Sarah, and claimed her for himself, Abraham raised no protest. If one can be sympathetic to a rapist, it may be worth nothing that it was the King who was punished for the incident.

In the New Testament, other problematic narratives exist. Consider the fate of Ananias and Sapphira, the believers who correctly thought Jesus Christ was not returning right away. They tried to play it smart, not willing to make the mistake everybody else made, but Peter had no mercy. Using the Holy Spirit as a weapon of husband-and-wife destruction, Peter had them struck dead. Upon their collapse, Peter ordered that they be buried. Normal people try to revive collapsed individuals. Today we call it CPR. Did Ananias and Saphira really die right-a-way? They weren't simply buried alive? From the scriptures it appears better to deal with the Lord than with one of his representatives.

Consider some sayings that are considered synonymous with Christianity. "Do not love the world, nor the things in the world. If any one loves the world, there is no love in his heart for the Father (1st John 2:15)." Yet, in John 3:16 it is emphatically stated, "For God so loved the world, that He gave His only begotten Son." What is to be made of these two statements in relation to one another?

The Bible contains God's message, but it does not contain the entire word of God. God's message is coded in the sacred collection of books. It takes critical thinking and creative analysis, allied with the Holy Spirit, to decipher that message. Some believers argue that if you have the Holy Spirit you don't need to make sense of contradictory biblical passages." That is a form of sacrilege. God wants his people to be humble, but humility does not equate with stupidity. God's people are to be obedient, not blind. Human intelligence is a spark of God's wisdom. Allied with the Holy Spirit, intelligence takes people to the Source. As far as Christians are concerned, it will take them to God through Jesus Christ.

Distorted biblical literalism has created a loss of knowledge over time. Spotlighting problems caused by biblical literalism is important because solutions cannot be found when problems go unacknowledged. This has always been a daring venture. Indeed, many people have been burned in fires, put on the rack, or ostracized because they dared to address the excesses of selective biblical literalism.

For example: "Thou art black but beautiful (Song of Songs)" could easily have been translated as, "Thou art black and beautiful." The Christmas message as translated in the French means, "Peace on earth to men of good will" not "Peace on earth and good will to men." The biblical saying, "God hates liars," contrasts with the love God lavished on some of the biggest liars in the Old Testament. It appears God may worry less about the telling of some lies. For example, consider the prophet who tricked another man of God into involuntary disobedience and claimed the right to bury the man he tricked when that man died because of it (1st Kings 13). Or consider the accountant in the Gospel of Luke, who rightly believed that his boss was about to fire him and resolved to cushion himself by ingratiating himself with the people who owed his employer money. He contacted his employer's biggest debtors and wrote off their debts. Could it be that God's ethics are yet to be fathomed by humanity? Or is it, as suggested by Bruce Chilton (2002) that in comparison to the people of this age Jesus was a primitive, illiterate man, belonging to an alien culture whose ideas of doing business contrasted with modern and post-modern ideas? Nevertheless, the right question here is what does the average Christian preacher seek to convey to the neophyte about this story? Or is this one of those tragic, unprocessed subliminal invaders of the subconscious that subverts thoughts and warps behaviors?

Those who insist on using the Bible like a cookbook or a surgeon's operative manual when ministering to people or passing judgments on others ought to consider the long trail of dead bodies left by professing Christians around the world (the genocide of the First Nations, the middle passage, the Third Reich, the Crusades, the Inquisition, the American and European witch trials), the continuing bickering among sects, and the subtle but unrelenting race and color discrimination anywhere Christian Europeans settled. Those who see themselves as completely dependant on the Bible for guidance and inspiration should ask themselves whether this cookbook is safe in all hands. To understand the Bible, to synthesize the gems hidden in it, we need humility, God's grace, and God's Holy Spirit. We need wisdom and we need unconditional love for our fellow people and for ourselves. Then, emulating Jesus the Christ, we will thrill at being on the right track. No cookbook, and no operative manual, that inspired people to destroy so many, would be declared safe as is. Even if the disasters could be blamed on failure to understand the actual recipes or the true meaning of the texts.

Religion, Selective Literalism, and Brutality

In addition to translations and prejudices of believers who fail to correspond to God's love and delight in creations, there is a penchant for hate and animosity toward God's creations that is expressed through religious vehicles. The murders, the deceptions, and the strategic killings - in short, the merciless and cheap brutality so often depicted in the Old Testament - are ripe for discussion in the interest of ensuring that Christians do not repeat old failures.

David married a princess he did not care for, Saul's daughter, because it helped secure his political power. David cynically cloistered her so she couldn't marry somebody else who could then challenge his claim to the throne. And yet, it was for her that David offered two hundred foreskins (perhaps two hundred severed penises) as dowry (1st Samuel 18:26-27). And last but not least, there is the story of the seven sons of the deceased King Saul, released by David to the Gabaonites so that they could be killed in expiation for an alleged curse. The grief of one of the mothers, who lay beneath their corpses until the corpses became dried bones, elicited no compassion according to the scriptures (1st Samuel 21).

The rationale for daring to venture into these biblical dark alleys is to make this point: When the clear conscience reads the Bible with the preconception that all the letters, stories, and pronouncements were God-inspired, and that every prescription handed down from Moses to

Saint Paul are the immutable words of God, the mind struggles to make the message of God's unconditional love compatible with all the violent stories. A psychological compromise takes place: the message of love and grace is acknowledged by the conscious, but that which is inconsistent with God's love and grace - the deep cruelties, the casual brutalities, and the cruel behaviors and visions - are relegated to the subconscious. They resurface later, haunting the mind and warping behavior.

Christians who cause the world so much harm by endorsing slavery, organizations like the KKK, ideologies like Nazism, have joyfully sacrificed lives for the sake of their ideas of law and order. To make these shortfalls of grace, mercy, and love acceptable, people's right to free choice have dressed God to suit ungodly purposes.

The prolongation of slavery in the Western world was due, in part, to selective biblical literalism. Nowhere in the Bible is there an injunction against the practice of slavery. The French prelate Bossuet, a seventeenth century orator, stated, "To abolish slavery would be to rebel against the Holy Spirit, which through the lips of St. Peter ordered that the slave accept his condition and made no demand on the master to set him free. England rejected the advice of William Wilberforce to abolish slavery on biblical grounds. According to the Anglican Church of that time, Christianity's duty was to free people from eternal damnation, not from the chains of slavery. Christianity provided a freedom from sin, Satan, lust, passions, and inordinate desires. Neither baptism nor becoming a Christian changed the fact of physical slavery (Ellerbe, 1995).

The violence characteristic of the racist militias, Nazism, and colonialism is a sad consequence of biblical literalism and the religion of white supremacy. Perhaps in his subconscious, the racist terrorist thinks of himself as justified in destroying a person of color, believing that he is rightfully prosecuting the cursed son of Ham. Deep inside himself, he may believe that he is doing it for the salvation of the world; thus, his crime is not really a crime because he is taking it upon himself to do the work of God. He (or she) is exacting justice for the sake of God. He is obeying a biblical ordinance. In this dark alley, Protestants and Catholics have much in common. For whether it was Calvin ordering heretics nailed by their earlobes, Puritan-supported witch-hunts in Salem, Massachusetts, or Catholic priests forcibly baptizing captured American aboriginals and Africans as part of turning them into slaves, it's all the same display of intolerance, greed, and perversion.

Martin Luther's movement may just have been an accident of the ascending curve. Luther, the most outspoken and perhaps the most brutal biblical literalist ever, took exception with the Catholic Church's departure from the written words agreed upon by the authorities of his time. He wanted Catholic words and actions to conform to the letter and spirit of his understanding of the sentiments expressed in the Bible. He wanted to hold the Church accountable to the words as written, as if honoring a signed contract.

This may seem logical, but it is not good enough. There is a higher calling than legality, and not just because the words in the Bible are far from consistent. This imperfect contract is open to a variety of interpretations. Understandings change, and readings of the Bible are amended and reassessed. Does this mean that God changes? Is the King of the Universe as vague and inconsistent as those who serve Him? More likely, it means that man's understanding is fallible and subject to man's prejudices, failings, and blind spots.

For instance, Constantine, the driving force behind the final choice of the documents included in the New Testament, and perhaps the Old Testament, did not have the same agenda as the church's holy fathers. Constantine wanted to gain control of a political power that had been eluding him. The church fathers found themselves in the position of being a politically important group. In the beginning they were weak and obligated to be careful, lest they be thrown into the arenas to be devoured and raped by lions and tigers. Martyrdom was the alternative to sharing real power, honor, glory, and wealth. What were they supposed to do? In effect, they yielded to temptation. Sometimes, the message of Jesus Christ's suffering was thrown to the back burner. Constantine called upon the Christians as advised by his magicians. It was his dream of a cross in the sky with the inscription, "In this sign Thou shall conquer" that prompted him to go to his magicians for help. Constantine's magicians advised him to invite the Christians to join him in consolidating his power. To that end, the Council of Nicea was called. The Nicean Creed was created, and thus the Christian religion became the official religion of the Roman Empire.

Surely the idea of basing the principles of behavior, common sense, social mores, and societal foundations in a written document has long been the obsession of men and women of power. Examples of books written by people who wanted to explain and change the world include

Mao's *Little Red Book;* Marx's *Manifest of the Communist Party:* François Duvalier's *The Elements of a Doctrine;* and Hitler's *Mein Kampf.* Constantine may not have written the Bible, but in calling for the creation of a universal point of reference for the Christian community he attempted to control that community. The universal point of reference Constantine sponsored was intended to serve purposes similar to the political aims of Mao, Marx, Duvalier, and Hitler - in short, domination and control.

A testament to God's glory is that even when sacred words and ideas are twisted to suit the purpose of those who would enslave people, matters pertaining to God cannot be mocked for long. That is why God's message of redemptive, enduring love made it through the Scripture intact despite politicking, intrigue, slander, misogyny, classicism, ethnocentrism, mistranslations, errors of omission, and good faith embellishments. God's message, however, may not be for the fearful, lazy, or vanquished.

The message of God is in the Bible by a sheer miracle from God who is all-wise. It is present despite the selfishness, duplicity, and brutality of people, their instinct of conservation, and their desire to control others. God cannot be mocked. God will always have the last word.

God's dearly beloved Christians should no longer hide from truths. The survival of this beautiful religion is at stake. Christians craving for power and control risk their credibility. For too long, salesmanship has triumphed over moral integrity and intellectual probity. Dogmas, doctrines and self-righteousness have removed compassion from religious observance. It's time for repentance. Let us acknowledge the truth: Hitler and his devoted butchers believed themselves to be true Christians who were justified by the Bible in massacring wicked people who killed Jesus on a cross (Ellerbe, 1995).

The concentration camp gas chambers were the invention of Eastern Europe's Christians Inquisition (Ellerbe, 1995). When Hitler wanted to make the Jews pay for what the Bible reported them saying about Jesus' execution - that His blood should fall on them and their children - those mass murder devices came in handy (Saul, 1992). Adolph Hitler is said to have written that the agenda for the ultimate triumph of Nazism was to follow the blueprint of the Catholic Church with its "traditional adherence to dogma" and its "fanatical intolerance" (Kaltreider, 1998). Hitler admired the "efficiency" of the genocide of the native people of North America (Kaltreider). The words of Martin Luther, the first Protestant, gave the Nazis a Christian "go" signal when they were robbing and killing the Jews of Europe. Luther, the great reformer, had written that the Jews should be expelled from Christian lands and their ghettos and their synagogues be burnt (Ellerbe, 1995).

When the members of the certain terrorist organizations assault a citizen, they may gather behind a burning cross, a bitter reminder of the Inquisition, when a crucifix would be held to the face of one of the Inquisition's victims about to be burned at the stake. The last message the judges and accusers want the condemned to carry into eternity was that of the flaming cross.

When Christian members of groups like the KKK hold up a burning cross, they are vindicating the theory that abusers are trying to rationalize their crimes for the sake of their precarious mental balance. The burning cross represents the effort of violent, hate-filled Christians to justify their behavior. In a sense, they are saying, "I'm no criminal. It's not me who condemns you to death. It's the cross of Jesus Christ Himself. I'm carrying out my sacred duty."

The mental acrobatics of the perpetrators of these crimes absolve them, in their minds, of breaking the commandments against killing, stealing, and bearing false witness against their neighbor. The breaker of both God and humanity's laws will be in Church on Sunday, or another religious gathering of his or her choice, with neither pain nor remorse thanks to a subconscious poisoned long ago and an unwillingness to challenge themselves as they would challenge others. If it is true that what comes around goes around, they've opened the door to destruction of themselves and their children. They've done the equivalent of sowing salt in the fields of their lives and their children's lives.

The violence that accompanied false doctrines did not quite pass away with the advent of the twentieth century. Interpretations of heartbreaking stories such as the summary eviction of Adam and Eve from the Garden of Eden, the lonely injustice of the scenes at Calvary, and the infamous saying "Spare the rod spoil the child" prepare one to either endure violence or to inflict it. No wonder Christians have repressed and killed so many. Some Christian hardliners so adore being different from the rest of the world that unconsciously or in full awareness, they sit in constant judgment of others. Relishing the role of Saint James the Major, they kill snakes, which they imagine they see nearly everywhere. Sadly enough, even giving one's heart to the idea that he or she is righteous does not mean that children and pregnant women are always spared the wrath of those in pursuit of satisfaction. That quality of mercy is lacking.

Haitian Selective Literalists

Many Haitian men and women have done much to inspire younger generations and promote the love of Christ. Unfortunately, some of us fall short of the call to heal. God's children need reminders, whether they are rich or poor, influential or anonymous, admirable or bland. Don't view mentions of child abuse and the abuse of pregnant women as trivial muckraking. Looking upon the negatives is part of attempting to comply with the aims of the One who said, "Whenever you do this to the least of these, you do it unto Me." It's one way of revisiting the recipe for God's blessings on the nations of the Americas, like Haiti and the United States, by helping the needy. When healing a wound or illness, the treatment doesn't always consist of sugarcoated pills. Even when the injury is located under a nail, the entire body receives the remedy through the mouth and absorbs the cure. Pain, sometimes, is part of getting better. Even dressing a wound causes real pain.

The following stories involve real people. Their names have been changed to respect their privacy.

Case 1: Little Nicholas

Ten year-old Nicholas is about to learn that a little boy has no business answering back to the reverend-in-chief, especially if there is bad blood between that pastor and his father. Nicholas's father, who holds the subordinate position in the church as an evangelist, thinks to augment his meager salary by buying coffee from the peasants and re-selling it for export. The reverend-in-chief does not approve of this. One day, Nicholas and three other kids are playing with the wheel of a disassembled bicycle out on the schoolyard. The schoolyard is the personal fiefdom of the reverend-in-chief.

That pastor comes upon the children and says, "What gives you the right to be playing with my property?" In a fury, he signals to Nicholas and says, "Bring in the wheel and then kneel down with it for the rest of the day."

Nicholas replies, "But, Pastor, there are four of us playing with that wheel. Why am I the only one to b e punished? Is it because you're still angry with my father about that coffee thing?"

Immediately, it is like being in a vortex, a volcanic eruption; it is hell. God, thank you for the numbness! The ordained minister of God orders four big men to drag the kid to him. The reverend-in-chief savagely beats that child with a thick wooden rule, aiming blows to the child's head and shoulders. The child is bleeding from the mouth, nose, and ears as that reverend swings his wooden ruler with precision. Nicholas breaks free for a second but big hands catch him, yanking him back to that pastor where he is repeatedly cursed at and hit. When Nicholas is close to passing out, he is forced on his knees. Those assisting the pastor are told to make sure Nicholas knelt until nightfall.

Exhausted from administering the savage beating and wanting some fresh air, the pastor jumps into his car for a drive, but before taking off he has one last thing to say: "Nicholas is expelled without appeal. I no longer want to see him in my school."

That man of God kept his position and was never reprimanded, let alone taken to justice. This man enjoyed the support and advantages of being a Christian authority.

Case 2: The Pig and Sister Inez

In this story, human and "divine" justice combine. A church stands on a vast property where the pastor and his family also maintain a home. Members of the church congregation, a small group of maids and gardeners, live on that property in their own little huts courtesy of the pastor's generosity. The size of the holding allows for small-scale farming (pigs, chickens, and goats). One of the pastor's pigs mysteriously vanishes. A quick investigation discloses that one of the pastor's adoptive sons sold the pig and loaned the proceeds to Sister Inez, a foot soldier in the small army of domestics. It is understood that Sister Inez used the money but had every intention of repaying the seller. The pastoral decision is to have both culprits arrested, taken to court, and then jailed.

Soon afterward, a heartbreaking scene unfolds. The poor lady, Sister Inez, is humiliated for borrowing money that had been stolen from her pastor. She can be seen in the very neighborhood where she lives, wearing a prison uniform, sweeping the streets, and picking up trash. How difficult would it have been for her pastor to find another way to deal with the problem? The pastor pronounces that Sister Inez is excommunicated for a set period of time for the purposes of expiation.

Sister Inez' story worsens. When she is eventually released from jail, she gets down on her knees before the pastor to apologize. She also thanks him for allowing her back into the church. What Sister Inez has suffered affects her family as well as her. Her daughter grows into a distraught, rebellious adult with no self-esteem. Is it so difficult to recognize the connection between the harsh treatment Sister Inez received at the hands of the pastor and the misery of Inez's adult child?

Case 3: Church Ladies, Dress Codes, and the Absence of Grace

Just across the fence from the church property lives Sister Ti Nann. One of the lady deacons, she is the fearless leader of the sanctified bunch. She preaches faithfulness to God, patience in affliction, and perseverance in prayer. These are good things. Sister Ti Nan prays long prayers and visits every sick member of the church. There is more: she sometimes is rebuked by the ill, for she insists that they are ill because of hidden sins they must confess before being healed. Other than that, Sister Ti Nann is considered a paragon of virtue, a mother of the church whose house is a sanctuary (although women who do not respect Sister Ti Nann's dress code are unwelcome).

There is a disturbance in Sister Ti Nann's house. Two dollars that had been reserved to pay for a dress that was to be worn at a wedding disappear from the bedroom. Felicia is a new addition to the extended family. She is prostitute who has been impregnated by Sister Ti Nann's son. She is suspected of stealing the money. The police attaché, a member of the Church, is summoned. He is paid two gourdes (about $0.40) to extract a confession from Felicia. The children growing up in that Christian neighborhood were made to watch. Though Felicia is in the last week of her pregnancy, the police attaché orders her to lie down so he can beat her. She begs to be allowed to stand because her belly will not allow her to lie on the ground. She is allowed to take her whipping while standing but is not spared a single blow. Sister Ti Nann is heard to declare, "Spare the belly, because the child is ours." Eventually, the person who reported the money as missing finds it.

This is far from Christ's recommendation to his disciples to treat the person with the least status in the community as if they were Christ. None of these three incidents illustrates people who bothered to do what Jesus would have done. Did the Reverend Pastor, the pastor pig owner, or Sister Ti Nann believe themselves to be sinners? Of course not, nor were they aware that they had gone against Jesus' instructions. Instead, like the Inquisition's judges and enforcers, they may have felt in compliance with St. Paul's prescription in 1st Corinthians 5:5 "Deliver such one to Satan for the destruction of the flesh, that his spirit may be saved in the day of the Lord." Their behavior was the consequence of their subconscious having been warped by a simplistic interpretation of the words of the Bible. The children who witnessed the beatings sided with the self-appointed God-avengers rather than the victims, because they were told - and believed - that the victims were the likes of Acan, Gehazi, or Judas Iscariot.

When the Christian leaders of those congregations read the Bible, they preach and live as if some irresistible compulsion has directed them to swallow the worst aspects of biblical heroes rather than the best. Stories of the mercilessness of King David, Elisha, and Peter are twisted to teach the faithful that accepting or inflicting pain is a righteous manner of problem solving; that it is proper for someone to perish as long as their soul is being saved; and that the wounds of a fellow believer are better than the kisses of an enemy. In short, by threats of the wrath of God, the Father draws souls to the Son (Ellerbe, 1995).

What happens to the person bent on making sense of the world or to the children who have witnessed these events? How are they to be convinced that a hougan (witch doctor) who comforts and heals the sick is more wicked than a pastor who beats a 10-year-old child in the head or that a hounsi kanzo is worse than a gathering of church ladies who beat pregnant women? Whipping pregnant women differs from turning one's enemies into zombies? Beating children to death, or near enough to it, differs from siccing loup-garous on your enemies' children?

How did Christians and other believers who embrace brutality create their double-minded existence? Selective biblical literalism is dangerous in that it is limited by the readers' reading comprehension. Reading the Bible with unbalanced literalism allows people to think and feel justified in their wretched actions. Even though they meditated upon the word of God, studied it, and memorized it, they were guilty of great cruelty. How can the God of Love and Compassion be happy when children and pregnant women are beaten? Or when nursing infants are yanked from their mothers' breasts by one leg and have their heads smashed open or are thrown alive to hungry dogs (Kaltreider, 1998)? It makes sense to say that "bibliolatry" has in many instances taken Christians far away from godliness. The wickedness stamped upon the dark side of historical Christianity must not go unexorcized before a Truth and Reconciliation Body, like the commission established under Desmond Tutu in South Africa. Otherwise, the members of the body of Christ are in danger of missing God's blessings (among those being the miracle of progress and collective success for God's creation). Only then can we feel confident that the best is truly yet to come.

Biblical Literalism and Misogyny

Biblical literalism is also dangerous when fueling misogyny. It is written in the Bible, "Let women give birth in sorrows (Ellerbe, 1995)." Martin Luther said, "If women become tired or even die, that does not matter. Let them die in childbirth. That is why they are there" (Ellerbe). In reference to the introduction of chloroform in childbirth, a minister in New England claimed that chloroform was a decoy of Satan, offering itself to bless women but hardening society and robbing God of the deep earnest cries for help that arose in time of trouble (Ellerbe, 1995).

There again, one may ask, how does that concern Haiti? You see, many small Christian countries such as Haiti have yet to grab the message that in Christ there is no difference in importance between men and women. Jesus demonstrated that he would not deny women whatever pedestal His sacrifice affords men. Male chauvinism is not endangered in Christian countries. Christianity is not reputed for advocating equal rights for women. If anything, unconditional submissiveness to male authority is preached to women. So where culture permits, women may be battered, humiliated, ostracized in folk songs, mocked in theaters, and even killed with impunity. In 1970, a Haitian military sergeant shot his wife dead and went to jail for only a week. "Crime passionel," they said. It would be unfair to blame such cultural impropriety strictly on a remiss religious leadership. However, If Hegel is correct and that all human behavior, and thus human history, is rooted in a prior state of consciousness, such tragedies should have been challenged head-on by the general socio-religious consciousness. In a Christian country, one should hope the moral voices for that place would be in an uproar over such a display of indecency and take the powers-that-be to task, but it is not always the case.

Indeed, what organizations, or any other succession of authorities, have made pronouncements more abrasive or derogatory toward women than the Church? Bishop Odo de Clugny said, "To embrace a woman is to embrace a sack of manure (Ellerbe, 1995)." St. Thomas Aquinas said, "God perhaps made a mistake in creating women." The Lutherans of Wittenberg asked, "Are women really human beings (Ellerbe)?" The Orthodox Christian Church held that "women are responsible for all sins...of women came the biggest sin and thanks to her we must all die." The Inquisitor authors of the *Malleus Malefica-*

rum taught that women were only imperfect animals and crooked whereas man belongs to a privileged sex from whose midst Christ emerged."

Generally, it's all about testosterone in temples and sanctuaries, whereas feminine participation is discouraged. From where does this religious misogyny come? Even today, women are generally excluded from church leadership. The honor, respect, and admiration afforded to Mary, as the mother of Jesus, is real, but other women of virtue and extraordinary accomplishments have rarely been acknowledged for their actions and influence. Even in the Protestant Church, which in that regard could make the claim of being revolutionary, it is the men who receive the greater share of respect and regard. There are services women are not allowed to perform in some Christian sects (priest, pastors, deacons), and while they are permitted to fill rolls of leadership and guidance, they are subjected to special rules and regulations depending on the denomination.

The works of Kenneth C. Davis and Dan Brown, authors of *Don't Know Much about the Bible* and *The Da Vinci Code*, suggest that Christian misogyny did not spring from a vacuum. Brown's work is a novel, so it may not instruct with authority. There might be a possibility, however, that Jesus had an intimate relationship with Mary Magdalene and that they have physical descendants.

Brown whisks his readers to the sanctuary of a secret sect, whose members participate in a sacred ceremony. Forming a large circle that centers on the officiator, circling members pray, sing, and clap hands while the officiator engages in intimate relations with his wife. In another scene, the character professor Robert Landon explains to his students that sexual intercourse could be a spiritual experience. Disbelieving him, these students respond with sarcasm. Professor Landon challenges them with this statement: "The next time you find yourselves with a woman, look in your heart and see if you could not approach sexual intercourse as a mystic and spiritual act. Challenge yourselves to find that spark of divinity only attainable through the union with the Sacred Feminine." Later on, Brown writes:

> Early Jews believed that the Holy of Holies of Solomon's Temple housed not only God but also His powerful female equal Shekinah . . . The Jewish tetragrammation YHWH, the sacred name of God, is in fact derived from Jehovah, an androgynous physical union between the masculine JAH and the pre-Hebraic name for Eve, HAVAH...

Kenneth C. Davis (2001) offers a similar narrative that hints at the logic in the cultural clash between the Jews and The Canaanites:

> And among Baal's consorts were Astarte and Asherah, mythic female goddesses who must have been very alluring to the Children of Israel. The followers of Moses and their descendants kept getting into trouble with their Yahweh God because they continued to worship these fertility goddesses instead of Yahweh. Since worshipping Baal and his goddesses probably meant having sex or watching priests have sex, it was presumably more appealing to the masses than a religion that involved killing small animals and did not allow women in the temples.

In light of these perspectives, perhaps the cause for the Christian Church's resilient misogyny is as follows: in the beginning, people saw in sexual intercourse an occasion to praise and commune with the Divine. It is a practice sane by its purpose, yet fragile, and turned dangerous because man is somehow inclined to evil. Perhaps it was selfishness and abuse that caused such well-intentioned practices to degenerate, and in the end, to be rejected.

Picture the long list of possible abuses by those in positions of authority. Sex is often overemphasized and under-appreciated. Lack of respect for it sometimes leads to sexual addiction, sexual promiscuity (especially when alcohol and other drugs are involved), physical and moral traumas, and the psychological consequences of such traumas. Consider the difficulties attendant to unwanted pregnancies, the heartache of abortions (spontaneous, voluntary, or even criminal), and last but not least, the abandonment of so-called illegitimate children.

The picture is not beautiful at all.

Is it any wonder that the practice of ritual sex in the temple became so unappealing that sex in general became abhorrent? Nevertheless, one exaggeration yielded to another. This resulted in a blanket condemnation of sexual pleasure and of anything that might lead toward it: music, dance, cuisine, visual art, and even women themselves, whose beauty and grace could be deemed as tempting men to sin. When people of influence embraced these ideas, women ended up being demonized. They were denied access to the sanctuaries and were denied the right to participate in various religious activities, and obligated to hide their bodies and faces even outside the temple (that is, in public). Despite all of this, they remained subject to the unwanted sexual attention of men, no matter how modestly they dressed.

Human sexuality and religion interact in a puzzling love-hate relationship. Did ostracism of woman pre-date the Genesis narration? Probably yes. It is the first book in the Bible that presents woman as the catalyst for the first sin, the culprit responsible for the fall from Grace. All the faiths that draw relevance and strength from the first of Abraham's holy writ get the green light for their misogynistic ideas and principles. The emphatic anti-woman and anti-girl policies of the Church Fathers also draw support for their misogyny from holy writ.

Marriage and Children

> There is a tye more binding than Humanity and stronger than Friendship, which makes us anxious for the happiness and welfare of those to whom it binds us. It makes their misfortune, sorrows and afflictions our own...By this cord I am not ashamed to own myself bound, nor do I believe that you are wholly free from it.
> Abigail Smith to John Adams, 11 August 1763.

Considering the anti-sex, anti-women themes in the scriptural supports and inspiration for historical Christianity, is the pedestal that marriage is placed upon a godly prescription or a societal demand? By unconditionally exalting the institution of marriage, are believers wrongly stigmatizing people in the name of their understandings of God? Could traditional church wedding ceremonies be a vestige of the practice of temple ritual sex of time immemorial? Could sacred religious marriage be a reminder of the time when sexual initiation and the starting of a family began in a temple or a sanctuary?

Selective biblical literalists are often guilty of making the Bible say more than it means. Why? Are they so afraid of going against the letter that they swallow what they are told by others or what they absent-mindedly read? It is true that in the Sacred Book it is written, "What God has united let no man set apart" and "That is why man will leave his mother and father and will unite with a woman and both shall become one flesh." These verses do not necessarily mean marriage but rather that men and women, and people for that matter, united in love, are blessed. Nowhere in the Bible is it stated that God created marriage or celebrated in person a marriage ceremony, no matter what the literalists say.

That marriage, in general, is good for people, fantastic for children, most desirable in society, and a wonderful safety net for families is another story. To say marriage is a respectable institution is a truth. But perhaps, to say God created it is exaggeration.

It is known that Jesus honored a wedding in Cana with his presence. To some, like Laurence Gardner, author of *Bloodline of the Holy Grail*, the celebration at Cana was of Jesus' own wedding. He is said to have provided the best wine in performance of his first miracle. According to Genesis, in the Garden of Eden, God is described as saying, "Be fruitful and multiply." Taken together, how do these prove that God ordered or officiated at a wedding ceremony? God's command to be fruitful and multiply was directed to people *and* to animals. If these statements mandate marriage, why haven't animals been dragged to churches or town halls to get them married?

Marriage is a human construct, a social institution honored and blessed by God. Like computer networking, caesarian sections, and organ-transplants, marriage is another human construct that does not violate God's plan. To say these are tools people use for the good of others is the truth. To say God created these things and imposed the use of them upon all people - and to disparage people who don't care for these rituals - is deceitful. What is divine in marriage is the true love inhabiting the minds and spirits of those becoming married, not the pronouncement by the officiating religious leader or civil officer who declares the couple "man and wife." Surely, love is not an exclusive attribute of people married in a church or at city hall or by an Elvis Presley impersonator; true marriage is a union of the hearts.

This is important, for liberating Haiti means setting Haitians free from the nation's fears, guilt, and misperceptions of truth and of God - its demons. Haitians must pull each other out of the rubble of deceit and lies so they can feel the warm light of hope and grace upon their skin and in their souls. What Haiti needs is God - as God understands God - with no more embellishments in the narrations and no more mistranslated mysteries. The distance between Mythos and Logos must be shortened. Why can't now be the time for true worshippers to worship God in spirit and truth?

Too often, in Haiti, those in power are enemies of society, creators of hell-on-earth. Such leaders are rotten with self-contempt or a sad, double complex of inferiority and superiority in action. People whose subconsciouses are riddled with fear and self-hatred are too often freelancing for the devil. No Haitian - no person in the world, for that matter - should carry the stigma of "child of sin" or "illegitimate" because their parents were not formally married. No more should people be stigmatized as living in sin or living against God's will because they are not married or because their partnership did not begin with a wedding ceremony. This is important because historically in Haiti, laws regarding marriage, children, and inheritance were designed to push people around and control them. Even so, about 65% of the Haitian population was allegedly born out of wedlock. Dessalines may have understood this, which is why in 1805 he declared all Haitian children legitimate.

Once upon a time in Haiti, citizens could awake at 4 o'clock in the morning to the ringing of a church bell. This late-night ringing was the announcement that an anticipated wedding could not be celebrated in broad daylight because the bride was pregnant. What would the people who approve of that custom think of weddings in countries like Denmark or Sweden where it is customary for three to four children of the couple to lead the wedding procession?

God did not found the institute of marriage through a wedding ceremony, although it is obvious the Creator honors that celebration of love. It is even possible that the Divine Master, Jesus Himself was married.

Perhaps, the idea of a married Jesus is repugnant to many because by embracing marriage, Jesus would have given too much honor to women. Those who concealed the crimes of the Crusaders - fortune-hunters dripping with the blood of Muslims and Christians as they looted the temple of Jerusalem - judged Jesus as being too godly to be involved with a woman. These same champions took time in killing the legend that Jesus emerged from between the ribs of Mary instead of the usual route. Could it be that the persistence of the idea that Mary, the mother of Jesus, remained a virgin even after Jesus' birth comes from a similar anti-woman, anti-sex agenda?

One Miami pastor explains that the hypothesis of a married Jesus is plausible. "In the Jewish culture, for Jesus to be trusted and called 'Rabbi,' he very probably had to be married." Author Bruce Chilton (2002) writes, "Celebration of the divine kingdom was no abstract, puritanical affair. I would caution against the sanguine assumption that Jesus was celibate; the celebration was in Jesus' own analogy, a wedding feast. The inclusion of sexuality in the enjoyment of God's bounty is a classic feature of Judaism." If, historically speaking, it made more sense for Jesus to be married than unmarried, why is it so important to so many people of Christian faiths that Jesus was not married? A more logical Christian perspective could be that Jesus is God because of God's will. As such, He was born fully human and lived a full human life, so that we humans could relate to Him and let Him lead us to God. Jesus' birth and simplicity of his education are testimony that divinity is an equal opportunity blessing from God Almighty to all (Chilton, 2002; John 10:34). As equally logical should be that Jesus, as a full-fledged man, was free to embrace His divinity and His high calling or to run away from it. Perhaps that was the point about the temptation in the desert. Amongst human beings there are individuals who excel to remarkable levels. Among those who are thus respected and honored include Alexander the Great, Socrates, George Washington, Aristotle, and Albert Einstein. Yet, they were men who did everything men do. Would Jesus be denied his well-deserved glory, respect, and honor if it were common knowledge that He had been married? Despite His love and sacrifice? Despite his extraordinary ministry and accomplishments?

Why should His divinity suffer if He had allowed himself to be a woman's husband? Why are believers' thoughts still held hostage to the persistent dislike of women, girls, and the feminine? Why do warped minds deem women so inferior that Jesus could never have lived intimately with one without losing the qualities that made Him greatest in goodness and holiness? Christians who believe that Jesus is divine are correct, but now is the time to preach and practice true Christianity rather than trying to sell one that perpetuates lies and deceits and concentrates power in the hands of the self-aggrandizing, grasping, and hateful. One will please God by searching for and preaching the truth, not by retreating to the comfort zone of parrots. Similarly, is it right to stigmatize people who love and live together without having knelt before an altar to receive a supposed blessing (for a fee)? Is it godly to shame and despise children whose parents never married according to Church doctrine or state law?

Psychologically, externally imposed guilt and shame have a variety of horrible effects. They compel people to view misfortunes and failures as punishments from Above. They can diminish people's desires to fight for their own best interests and other healthy drives. Guilt and shame become subliminal invaders that rot a personality from within, producing bitter changes in people, thus creating individuals bent on vengeance against society and fellow individuals within their sphere of influence (such as Shaka Zulu, François Duvalier, Elie Lescot, etc).

These individuals, who may or may not be in deep denial regarding their feelings of guilt and shame, can also show contempt for others, mistreat, and destroy. As subordinates, they react to authority with distrust and are inclined to conspiracy, their hearts full of one thing, their mouths and actions indicative of another.

Sadly, so many of Haiti's children are unjustly chained in guilt, shame, and inferiority complexes. For Haiti to be saved, its children must be in full possession of their better faculties. For the sake of our country, let us set all Haitians free. Even in the Bible there are instances in which the legitimate child is not favored over the bastard. Example: Solomon of Bathsheba. The firstborn son of David and Bathsheba died. Their second son, Solomon, arrived after Bathsheba was brought into David's household. He became the wisest, the most common-people-oriented, and richest king in the history of Israel. Also, consider what happened with Isaac and Ishmael. Ishmael was sent into the desert with his mother to die by a contrite Abraham, eager to assuage his wife's resentment and jealousy: God rescued them and promised to make a great nation of Ishmael's descendants. This is where it is good to remember that indeed "God sometimes works in mysterious ways."

And why not say it loud? In Haiti there is more love in some *plaçages* (informal domestic partnerships) than in some official marriages. At least there is more love in some of these man-mistresses, man-concubine relationships than there was in biblical David's marriage to the Princess Mical, daughter of King Saul. Unfortunately, by placing marriage in the highest position of honor, contempt for extra-marital and out-of-wedlock unions is systematically invited.

Certainly there is a difference between sinning against social norms and sinning against God. It is true that a happy marriage may be considered God's blessing, especially when God is invited into it; however, being married should be assessed and praised for what it is: a social construct, a cultural universal, not criteria for holiness or godliness. Hitler was married, as was Stalin. Hitler saw fit to marry Eva Braun hours before he engaged her and their children into their spectacularly shameful suicide pact. Congruently, Stalin's wife chose death rather than stay married to a butcher.

People should avoid confusing the moral, the cultural, the ethical, and the spiritual. With cultural polygamy, for instance, it is important not to rush to label it as sinful. Indeed, in some countries where polygamy is the norm, attacking it without assessing and defining it opens the way for the sins of selfishness, deceit, and greed.

For example, the government in one of the African countries where polygamy was legal decided to abolish it. The result was chaos. The declaration that a man could only have one wife, and was only legally responsible for one wife and her children, disrupted that society. Prior to the legal change, a man who could support more than one woman and her children was considered a distinguished person. He executed his obligations with responsible pride. The abolishment of polygamy forced married men into an alien way of life. The new law suppressed some of the married men's responsibilities, not the possibility and privileges of procreation. Culture and tradition did not equip these men to adjust to the new legalities in a manner that did them or their wives honor: they cheated. It became more difficult to go public with a second relationship and yet at the same time more convenient for married men not to take full responsibility for children fathered out of legal wedlock. There were dire financial consequences for the families involved - legitimate and otherwise. Financial resources were spread so thin that the legal wives themselves petitioned the government to rescind the law.

Likewise, when the missionaries landed in Haiti, they found a thriving peasant economy in some places where many men owned vast properties. These vast properties were administered by mistresses and concubines. These women got along well, and many became good friends. Sometimes, the children born out of those relationships were raised together in the common courtyard (*lakou*) by the network-of-mothers. Church missionaries entered Haitian society like elephants in a china-shop and declared that everybody with more than one woman was living in sin. To avoid eternal damnation, the men and women had to do it the Christian way: one married man to one married wife. One woman would become a wife in the eyes of the law and of the Church, but the other women and children were effectively abandoned.

Unfortunately, nothing had been enacted to care for the women who did not become wives. They and their children were disenfranchised. As a result, the peasant social fabric was destroyed in various towns and villages. After abandonment, discarded women and children lost their social standing. Shoved to the fringes of society, they suffered shame and financial hardship. This exemplifies the need for the

Church to enact changes that provide for all people. Social conscience must be exercised in religious duty.

Reading the Bible in a simplistic, shallow manner sometimes encourages love to be trivialized or held in contempt. Some traditional Christians are so obsessed with regulating sexual expression that they forgive the crime of mass murder ten times before forgiving sexual transgression. Whether it was a pastor or a simple church member who committed the sin, the sentence was social death and public humiliation. Was the penalty inspired by admiration for the vow of celibacy so dear to the Vatican?

In some Protestant circles, the news that so-and-so has "fallen into sin" quite literally means that someone has engaged in unsanctioned sexual behavior. Are not theft, abuse, and arrogance, hypocrisy, and deception big sins before God? Yes, but some Protestants reserve their true hate for matters involving sex. That sin enjoys so much importance in some establishments that it has befallen many a great predicator of the gospel and their exemplary ministries, while giving the upper hand to other hypocrites and self-serving powerbrokers.

Once upon a time in the Protestant churches of Haiti of the late 1950s, a gospel of austerity for the sake of godliness enjoyed popularity. Good Christians were called upon to nail their worldly ideals, particularly the things of youth, to the sacred, old, rugged cross of Sanctification. Christians did not play, dance, or laugh, and they did not dress fashionably. Women, old or young, who hot-combed their hair were often berated and sometimes excommunicated. Many of life's pleasures were forbidden to the Christians. In the midst of all that piety there was not one collective program to help even the faithful with their earthly struggles. This was in keeping with Church thinking. Quite early in the primary school careers, children were taught: every one for his self, God for all[6].

When the time came for a young person to chose a profession and go out into the world, going to a pastor for guidance wasn't necessarily the smartest choice. One pastor, upon learning from a gifted and intelligent young lady (the eldest of a large family) that she had been accepted into the school of nursing, advised her to choose another profession. The pastor said, "That profession of nursing would put you too close to those nuns who only swear by the Virgin Mary." Interestingly enough, that pastor was in a position to know that a woman who became a registered nurse would be able to make sure that her many

---

[6] Chacun pour soit: Dieu pour tous.

little brothers and sisters would have enough to eat (instead of go hungry as they had been since becoming fatherless). That same pastor was preparing to send his children to medical school. This pastor was primarily concerned for her spiritual welfare: or was he?

At about that same time, there was a young man, a son of the Church, with quite a different perspective in regard to the earthly concerns of those whose basic needs went unfulfilled. Having allowed his behavior to be dictated by an extraordinary perception of the will of God, he went to work with and for the benefit of the poor, creating and managing a health center that benefited the needy.

Without preaching inflammatory sermons or advocating class conflict, he was an inspiration to the youth. He was merely a bighearted young man full of energy and easy practicality who had dedicated his life to making a difference in a specific, physical way.

This imitator of the Good Samaritan was married to a Christian who did not share his vision. His work, however, put him in close contact with an intelligent co-worker who was devoted to the same cause. They fell in love and acted on that love. The consequences were dire, as the lady was married to one of the big financial supporters of the mother church. There was scandal in the family and a fall in disgrace. The Church swung against those two "criminals" with no mercy, leveling collective shame and pressure against them. Their commendable work in the slums carried no weight with their judges. Their ministry disappeared like smoke in a strong wind.

The intransigence of a few biblical literalists made no room for the good those two had done. The biblical literalists who judged and condemned them would have sent King David into exile following his relationship with Bathsheba (but maybe not for his murder of Uriah) oblivious to the fact that to remove a man of God from his God-inspired assignment is to postpone God's agenda *sine die*. Making no room for grace, the intransigence of biblical literalists forces a long march in the desert back to square one.

Anti-Intellectualism

Anti-intellectualism is a consequence of lackadaisical, uncritical, fear-filled, imagination-handicapped biblical literalism. What marks the divide between "believing intellectuals" and biblical literalists is that the intellectuals are unwilling to swallow what they do not understand; the literalists insist that everything within the Bible be accepted as absolute truth. Jesus said, "He who has ears let him hear." This was not the directive of someone who wanted people to believe without comprehension or blindly obey him. Are all attitudes of blind obedience acts of faith and trust? When Jesus said to Thomas, "Blessed are those who have not seen and yet have believed," Jesus was probably alluding to the spirit of discernment, what Pascal called *l'esprit de géométrie*. Thomas did not demonstrate the spirit of geometry, the spirit of balanced perspective when, in the wake of Jesus' resurrection, he demanded that Jesus show the wounds on His hands and feet. It is hard to give in to the assumption that Thomas was a mystic who knew what Jesus was capable of (performing miracles) and chose to put Him on the spot. In all likelihood, he was a doubter. Thomas deserved the gentle scolding because seeing was not necessarily believing. Sometimes believing involves capturing concepts with the mind - turning over the concepts with one's thoughts so one can visualize, imagine, and comprehend (like working on geometry problems, playing Tetris, or solving a Rubik's Cube).

Thomas's curiosity got a free ride thanks to Jesus' magnanimity. He led Thomas in a "time travel" experience where he could see the wounds of a bleeding Messiah. Poor Thomas was far from understanding that someone who had been raised from the dead had necessarily healed from all his wounds. According to the simple arithmetic, "he who can climb a mountain can climb stairs" (*Qui peut plus peut moins*)." Countering this calls for questioning whether Jesus really miraculously rose from the dead. It could give credence to Laurence Gardner's endeavor (*Bloodline of the Holy Grail*) to prove that Christ's crucifixion and resurrection were a masterpiece magic trick of Simon the Zealot with the help of Jesus' inner circle and facilitated by an unsuspecting or ambivalent Pontius Pilate.

Jesus congratulated Peter for knowing exactly who He was (Matthew 16:13-17). Peter's mind grabbed the truth in a flash. He did not say what he said to appease critics or to be seen as a believer or to avoid the accusation of blasphemy. No, his answer was firm, like someone who has seen the light. He understood and he believed, not unlike Archimedes who perceived, trusted his perception, and cried "Eureka!"

Faith doesn't negate a believer's brain. Faith is a firm assurance, a clear and convincing revelation awaiting the test of time. Probably it is only religious leaders' intellectual infirmity and their own lack of faith that moves them to demand that believers swallow what they don't understand. When these leaders resort to intimidation and other fear tactics to make believers accept their dogmas, they are only hiding their own insecurities. In religious parlance, "faith" is a commonly abused word. People express their belief in something and call that "faith." Belief is not necessarily faith. On our way toward having faith we may believe in the wrong thing until we see the light. Though we conventionally talk about the Protestant faith, the Seventh Day Adventist faith, and the Muslim faith, these expressions are misnomers; they refer to collective sets of beliefs in an idea or in a doctrine. The best definition of faith comes from St. Paul: "Faith is a firm assurance of things hoped for, a firm demonstration of things not yet seen (Hebrews 11:1)." In the mind it is intuitive knowledge.

Believing in something does not make that thing exist. Not necessarily. Beliefs color our realities. Believing that it is 6:00 p.m. does not make it true even if it is 6 o'clock where you are. True belief is a personal conviction; it is purely subjective. Faith is knowledge with the speed of thought. Belief is a choice; faith is a gift. While one's belief may never be confirmed, faith is 100%, or just awaiting the test of time. Faith is Peter capturing with his mind, without the shadow of a doubt, that Jesus is the son of the living God. Faith is Edison visualizing the light bulb before he held it in his hand and before the light brightened his retinas. Faith is the squirrel running on a wire several feet above ground, the monkey jumping from tree to tree, never doubting that he can do it. Paradoxically, elementary knowledge may stand in the way of faith. Educate squirrels and monkeys about gravity, and out of fear, they might stop doing what they do best.

Having faith does not mean saying, "yes" or "amen" to whatever dogma, doctrine, or sermon is being preached in order to avoid being singled out as a disbeliever, being accused of blasphemy, or even being cursed. Faith is a humble willingness to sweat through difficult concepts with the same clarity of mind as the mathematician who, having struggled for days to find the solution to a construction problem, suddenly finds what she's looking for in a window of light, and drops whatever else she's doing to write it down. Faith means being able to absorb with a suddenly magnified intelligence. Spiritually speaking, it is a miracle of the Holy Spirit. The Holy Spirit has never been the enemy of intelligence. God's spirit on earth, the holy comforter, sharpens our intelligence like ordinary light is amplified into a laser beam; then the conviction is immediate, the discovery complete and final.

Yes, faith is not inimical to intelligence, nor is it antagonistic to science. Science should be looked at as faith in slow motion. Faith is science in glorious action, understanding, and trust dancing with understanding at the speed of light. The difference between the two is that science may take a person there very slowly - too slowly - so that science's trajectory is like traveling through a vast cemetery while faith travels like lightning - faster and more efficiently. Faith and science can lead to the same destinations.

When annoyed by someone slow to believe them, preachers would be wise to consider the possibility that God may not be finished with that person yet. Too many Christians seem to believe that it is unprincipled to allow other people the freedom of their own convictions. Is John Eldredge (2006) correct that Christianity's problem is its preoccupation with principles that impair real conversation with God?

Not only is God not finished with the skeptical believer; God is still working on the person who is teaching and lecturing in God's name. That is why no book, including this one, is perfect. The concerned faithful would be wise to remember that God is hard at work in everybody's life. It is not the believers calling to judge, to condemn, no matter how knowledgeable, discerning, empathic, clear-sighted they may be.

As it is written, as it was prophesied, "The time has come, the kingdom of God is near, repent and believe the good news." The preaching of altered truths should be challenged. There is good news that tells of love and compassion: it leads to the deep truths and great hopes of God and righteous people. It is greater than dogma, doctrine, and the root causes of factionalism and war. Now is the time to embrace God and godliness out of love - not fear. If this dynamic interpretation of the Gospel would seize the minds of all Haitians, and if this Christ-driven Christianity is favored by religious leadership, Haiti certainly will show its true, beautiful face to the world. For too long we have not been permitted to think freely and to have faith. Too many young, dynamic intellectuals have been kicked out of the Church because they've asked embarrassing questions.

Anti-intellectualism amongst believers is a cancer. God sometimes uses the illiterate and unread as messengers, but if that's what God has to work with, He will. Fishermen or tax collectors: all people come into the world with a brain that surpasses the flexibility and power of a computer. However, people condition themselves and those dependent upon them to be limited, to be programmed in such a way that they only use a fraction of that power. Thanks to lack of faith, laziness, and cowardice, people's minds have been colonized by something foul and their hearts' hopes remain hidden from them.

Anti-intellectualism explains the apparently static character of Islam. Though one of the most socially conscious religions and quite paradoxically, one that has most contributed to scientific development and education (the same cannot be said of Christianity), it has fallen short of its early purity. Many of its more violent adherents advocate change through demonizing people who choose to live life in a way outside of their narrow definition of righteousness. Perhaps God used Mohammad, a man who could neither read nor write until very late in his life, to improve the lives of people living in a time of licentiousness and perverse injustice. Mohammad, however, did the best he could: far better than the most lettered people of this age.

It behooves those sitting at Mohammed's feet to build upon his work and to pursue dynamic truth with passion and intelligence. Indeed, Mohammad went beyond expectation for people of *his* time when he declared, "All religions in their pure form have positive values, and it is through the passing of time that they have become corrupted." He demanded that his disciples pay respect to all religions for the sake of that noble beginning. His authoritative opinion contrasts with the latter-day deviations and aberrations that have promoted violence, terrorism, and acceptance of honor killings and bloody revenge as a means of attaining unification with God in paradise. The twenty-first century is already littered with the horrors scriptural literalism can cause when practiced by those full of disgust and self-righteousness.

With regard to Christianity, anti-intellectualism is not a new disease. In medieval times, simply owning a Bible was a capital crime and it was sacrilege to translate it into a vernacular. As far as the Church leaders were concerned, Martin Luther's worst offense was translating the Latin Bible into German.

It is not wrong to believe that anti-intellectual Christianity is paradoxical. Anti-intellectual believers, who revere Saint Paul by putting him and his letters to the early Church on a pedestal, make little sense, as Paul is the intellectual of the New Testament. Unlike Peter, Mary Magdalene, or Thomas, Paul did not know Jesus in the flesh (or at least the Bible does not tell). He never physically sat down with Him, ate with Him, chatted with Him, and passed the time with Him. Yet, by intellect and Spirit, Paul drew close to Jesus, eventually becoming an acceptable papal substitute for the fledgling Reformation Church communities.

In many ways, Paul is a superstar Christian. As the foremost apologist of the New Testament, he has authored ideas that Catholics, and to a greater extent, Protestants, have accepted as holy writ. His opinions on Christ, holiness, marriage, women, slavery, and qualification for religious leadership, the resurrection of the dead, the relevance of Christ to Judaism, and the conversion of Gentiles are revered by many as if they had been faxed directly from God's desk to Paul's brain.

Some believers have broken ranks with the credulous and accepting, and have begun asking pertinent questions that call into question the relevance of contemporary concepts of heroicness and holiness. In his *Rescuing the Bible from Fundamentalism*, Reverend John Shelby Spong wonders if the "thorn in the flesh" Paul struggled to suppress was some urge toward homoerotic expression - an urge that was all the more disturbing because it was anathema to Paul's Jewish upbringing and his stature as a Pharisee. Paul despaired of "the thorn in his flesh," but he did not describe it. The ailment or handicap Paul described invites all sorts of conjecture. Other scholars and theologians believe that what Paul referred to as "a thorn in his flesh" was that the thorn in Paul's side was his public-speaking. Given his unspectacular oratory skills, there are several instances in the New Testament where it would have been better for him to write or pray in silence if not sleep. The first is when he spoke before the Commander and then before the Sanhedrin and could have been "torn into pieces (Acts 21-23)." The second was his appeal before Festus and King Agrippa. It delayed his being set free from prison. Lastly, one of Paul's lengthy speeches put a young man to sleep, upon which the fellow fell and nearly broke his neck.

It is important that the reader not read speculation of Paul being a terrible public speaker as dismissal of this impassioned defender of the Christian "faith." Paul was a powerful thinker and many Christians have lost sight of this. Some believe Paul's brain was of the same caliber as Ignatius de Loyola, founder of the Society of the Jesuits. It is a horrible shame that many believers have no conception of what that might mean, never mind respecting it. Saint Paul's intellect was such that he could create a doctrine that drafted an inclusive, world-encompassing "faith" from an exclusive, ethnic-based, theistic socio-religious lifestyle. Before and after his conversion, his was a mind that could have informed and challenged that of the world's spiritual leaders.

In Martin Scorsese's film *The Last Temptation of Christ,* Paul converses with a Jesus who had been taken down from the cross and had been living the life of a normal man. According to the film, that moment was probably the second meeting since Paul had seen Jesus on the road to Damascus. Jesus told Paul that he was alive, flesh and bone, with a wife and child. Jesus instructed Paul to tell the world the truth about his life. Paul refused because on the basis of the resurrection Christianity had become a great religion. According to Scorsese's Paul, it would serve no purpose to change the story of Jesus.

The film and the referenced scene are intellectual exercises from Martin Scorsese's artistic mind, used here to make the point that Saint Paul is not to be taken at face value. He's just a person like us who more than once allowed God to use him. Not everything he says is of God. Similarly, neither is everything said by Peter or the other Apostles. Christ was yesterday - and is today - people's true reality.

As for Paul, God Almighty encapsulated in that good man's perorations great messages for the benefit of the Church body. Only intelligence allied with the Holy Spirit can decode their meaning. For instance, consider the scripture verse, "Husbands love your wives like Christ has loved the Church." Paul, however, also left dissertations on his views of Jewish culture and Pharisaical philosophy and dogma. For example, why did he write of the resurrection of the flesh? "At the trumpet sound, at the voice of and Archangel...etc"? Arguably, of the New Testament authors, Paul wrote of the resurrection most often and most vividly. These details suggest that he was reciting the catechism he'd learned as a Pharisee prior to his conversion, not that he was writing as a Sadducee or an Essene as neither groups believed in the resurrection of the dead.

These words are not meant to cast doubt that Jesus Christ was resurrected and went to prepare a special place for believers in eternity. God, and only He, possesses the details of that great plan of redemption; not the man from Tarsus. In that vein, it is important that believers not swallow everything that is written or said about those "inspired men," including their views on authority, slavery, and the duties and roles of women. Those opinions are static reflections of their time.

Nor must believers go by the letter of the book of Revelation, lest they make the mistakes of international and domestic terrorists. Imprudent readings and interpretations of the Book of Revelation are already responsible for dissension, drift, false accusation, and ungodly hostility. Christians look upon one another with suspicion, fear, and even hatred. Some literalists declare that the papacy represents "the Beast" mentioned in the New Testament.

Simplistic doctrinarians embark on Catholic-bashing with the zeal of iconoclasts. A work of genius performed a magic trick that has stuck the Number of the Beast to the pope's hat, extracting the number 666 from the Latin inscription *Vicarius Filii Dei* on his mitre.

How is this responsible? Anyone who searches for support of a foregone conclusion will eventually find "evidence" that supports that conclusion. This is what intellectual gymnasts do. Unfortunately, this also happens in scientific research, and sound premises are often defeated by fabricated evidence. The truth is, there have been bad popes and great ones. Popes, like pastors, are people who could say, just like any honest person, "I am a human and nothing pertaining to our humanity [or to our humanness] is alien to me[7]."

When Pope John Paul II went to the Wailing Wall with a prayer crafted to make symbolical amends for the crimes Christians had committed against the Jewish people, that represented an act of healing. If the Jews forgive Christians, that is divine; and God would have been pleased. God wants the sincere reconciliation of all His children and their repentance. Pope John Paul II, while showing his special fascination with Jesus the Christ, gave indications that he too heard the "Prophetic voices for justice of the Old Testament" (West, 2004). He made himself an obstinate advocate for social justice for the peoples. As far as Haitians are concerned, the Pope showed he cared as much for us as he did for his native Poland. He went to Haiti and challenged the Duvalier dictatorship, insisting that something ought to change. Bless his soul! Can that much be said about traditional American evangelicals, today's heavyweights of the pulpit? They, who call upon and dine with dignitaries and heads-of-state the world over, have - but for a pitiful few - not set foot in the hell of Haiti while this poor country, biblically speaking, sits near the shadow of their home (the USA) like a stricken Lazarus languishing at the doorstep of the rich man's mansion. There is an American preacher who found it more convenient to scold former President Jimmy Carter for favoring "secular humanism". Would it not be nice if this critic re-read the Bible and realized how much Jesus cared for and advocated this particular expression of love? To be correct, Jesus' recommendations were sound financial advice to those who obey his command especially when he ordered that we love and care for our enemies. For, if one takes a good look at these recommendations, one sure beneficiary is the investor of

---

[7] Homo sum humani nihil a me alienum puto.

good will. Haiti is a very small place, vibrant with dynamic and willing souls, crying for Christian compassion. It would take just a few Christian millionaires to lift up this country. Haitians are no lazy people. They are talented, loyal, and productive individuals. Once empowered by a true, Christ-reoriented Christianity, they will overcome the vice of collective narcissism, and inspire the world.

Already, Haitians may have much to be grateful for with regards to Haiti's vicinity to the United States. For example, former president Jimmy Carter, Senator Sam Nunn, and Colin Powell intervened in Haitian politics in 1992. Their contributions succeeded in making Haiti's inevitable - and ongoing - occupation occur without bloodshed. These good men belong in the same gallery with Charles Sumner, the senator from Massachusetts who saved Mole St. Nicolas from being converted into a repository for coal by the United States of America or Frederick C. Douglass, the American ambassador who defended and lifted Haiti up in a manner never surpassed by any Haitian in the Diaspora and more recently, the Reverend Jesse Jackson.

The same cannot be said of South Carolina's Congressman Preston Brooks. Brooks so cherished the institution of slavery, and so despised Haiti and its defenders, that on May 22 of 1856, he entered the Senate Chamber and beat Senator Charles Sumner into unconsciousness with a gold-headed cane in retaliation for an antislavery speech Sumner had given (Donald, 1970). It took Sumner four years from the attack to recover enough from his physical injuries to return to his lawmaking duties. The citizens of Columbia, South Carolina, lionized Congressman Brooks for the attack. They awarded Brooks two silver goblets in tribute.

What tribute is deserved by the Americans that found it legitimate that Navassa Island be snatched away from Haiti, that same year, by an act of Congress? Congress authorized the theft of guano and kept the land as a bonus. A wealthy Christian nation stole a piece of property from the poorest nation in the world because God said so? Because might is right? Because slavery, and other kinds of theft, added to America's glory? Which was it?

It was Reverend Jessie Jackson who told the world that it was guns bearing the imprint "Made in the USA" that were being used to kill Haitians. What American traditions in regards to Haiti are we willing to continue today?

Fatalism and the Sacred Book

It isn't that the return of Jesus Christ is problematic. It's what happens to the believers who get stuck in survival mode and focus only on the imminent return of Christ. Most Haitians of the Protestant Church insist on taking the book of Revelation as-is and in doing so abandon earthly efficiency. Why work for a good life now, when any moment might mean the return of a triumphant Jesus-Christ? Why lobby for health care? Why protest corruption? Why study in school? Why master a profession? Why honor the flag? Why build anything material when everything earthly is scheduled to go up in flames? Why do anything outside of church business well when the only treasure that counts lies beyond the pearly gates?

What if what is written in the book of Revelation is perhaps a dream: the vision of a person who believed in the imminent and glorious return of Jesus Christ? Supposedly, Jesus loved John - the probable author of the book of Revelation - above all the other apostles. John may have been one of the trusted three who fell asleep when Jesus was sweating in the Garden of Gethsemane. What if remorse and guilt for having stood by when his master - and friend - was arrested and executed still tormented John? What if on the island of Patmos, where the book of Revelation was written, the apocalyptic scriptures of Isaiah, Ezekiel, Zecharia, and Daniel - visions John had studied all of his life - were flooding his mind?

The book of Revelation is one of the more difficult scriptures to interpret. In the fifth century, Revelation made it into the canon over Saint John Chrysostom's reservations. Revered by Fourth and Fifth century Church heavyweights, Chrysostom's ideas and beliefs were respected by Christians of not only the Eastern Orthodox Church, but also members of the Church of England and the Roman Catholic Church. To this day, the Greek Orthodox Church refrains from reading it publicly. Therefore, shouldn't every preacher exercise humility and caution in preaching from it? Here we only very cautiously suggest that John hoped Christ's return so imminent that he could have closed his eyes in meditation and have visions of it or Christ himself may have taken John into another realm. Did Jesus not show doubting Thomas His bleeding hands that should have been completely healed after His spectacular Resurrection? What John saw or heard on the island of Patmos might have been colored by unfamiliarity, wonder, or inexperience.

Another way to look at Revelation is that the book may have been written by someone engaged in an very important and dangerous undertaking, someone privy to privileged information that he had to write down but that he did not wish to see fall into the wrong hands; he then had to write it in codes, using symbols, allegories, and metaphors. One suggestion from the Apocalypse is that Judgment Day may be about individual sinners as well as about collectivities. John started his remarkable piece of work as an exhortation to seven Asian churches. Nations, therefore, should take heed, for on Judgment Day they may be held accountable for their treatment of one another. Then may come to light, fulfilled, the intriguing biblical prophecy: "The first shall be last and the last shall be first."

Must Religion Overrule Science?

Judging by the questions asked on Haitian talk shows on health matters, angry interventions from annoyed callers who introduce themselves as Bible readers, and arguments from well-meant preachers during debates on topics such as school clinics, congenital anomalies, sexual variances, and birth control, much work lies ahead and we should expect significant resistance in the coming task of setting Haiti free. Most objectors think religious beliefs must have veto power over everything in government and in science. It does not matter that theirs is an uninformed opinion; they are most vocal, ubiquitous, and unflinching, and not necessarily the least affluent or educated. That was the case for this very opinionated lady who called during a talk show.

The presentation focused on pseudo-hermaphrodites and other variances in sexuality. The lady wanted to know why such unpalatable topics were being discussed. She claimed that when a genetic male is born with a vagina, if a male child is born who is genetically female and a child that appears female at birth is a male, that family should pray for God's forgiveness because such a calamity should be understood only as a consequence of their sins.

Against such beliefs and attitude, living in the United States of America, where religious beliefs at times hold science on a leash, does not help. As late as in 1965, thirty states had laws prohibiting or restricting the sale or use of contraceptives (Lockwood, 2005). Connecticut, one of the states where the influence of the Puritans remained strong for a long time, enacted prohibitions against distribution and possession of contraceptives, even when the intent was to save a woman's life (Lockwood). Married couples could be arrested for using birth control even in their own homes (Lockwood).

It is enough for anyone to ask: Where is humility? Where has the wisdom of the old folks gone? President Eisenhower, for instance, ruled that money given in assistance to poor countries must not be used for population control (perhaps because he disapproved of the aims of eugenicists). But upon realizing that overpopulation was a major world problem, honest Ike - known as the man who, like George Washington, "could not tell a lie" - reportedly said, that if he had known before what he came to know later, he would have decided differently (Jalsevac, 2004). Contrast that to President George W. Bush, who has overruled scientists - men and women of ethics - in the debate over stem-cell research, merely on the merit of his religious beliefs?

Anti-scientific militancy is a danger of biblical literalism. Science without conscience ruins souls. A morality check on all scientific undertakings is needed, because people have too often revealed themselves as the biggest threat to others. To trust a well-funded scientist exploring the boundaries of current research from behind locked doors in ivory towers is to trust that people left to their own devices will always do the right thing, which is far from the truth.

However, when that morality check is imposed and enacted by religion, it represents double jeopardy for humankind. This is true for cloning, stem-cell harvesting, the treatment of anencephalic babies, and the process of in vitro fertilization. In Haitian circles and on radio talk shows, the most vehement interventions against family planning come from unprincipled preachers, biblical literalists who want the biblical tenet "be fruitful and multiply" to simply mean: "Have as many children as you can; it is God who makes them." And yet one of Haiti's major problems is chaotic demographic explosion not matched by life-sustaining resources. Common sense should have it that true immorality is for a Haitian man - married or unmarried - to die and leave behind sixty-four sons and daughters in the care of a younger brother, a struggling middle-class worker himself and a father of nine. Immorality is not a valid term for a God-loving, liberal preacher and his wife, for instance, who advocate or practice voluntary, sound family planning.

When religious establishments take it upon themselves to steal the show and dictate what should be or should not be done in science or in medicine, they would be wise to remember their track record. Helen Ellerbe challenges us to name a single great scientific recovery (or discovery) that was not opposed by the Church. Attacking reason and scientific methodology - the spirit of geometry - is what gave medieval times their name, "The Dark Age."

In The *Dark Side of Christian History,* Ellen Ellerbe wrote, "The losses in science were monumental. In some cases the Christian Church burning of books and repression of intellectual pursuit set humanity back as much as two millennia in its scientific understanding." Consider St. Augustine's defense of the theory that the earth was flat:

> It is impossible there should be inhabitants on the opposite side of the earth, since no such race is recorded by the scripture among the descendants of Adam.

How about that as a great example of stupid biblical literalism? Or Galileo being forced to recant his theory that the earth revolved around the Sun? In those difficult times, even mapmakers were held under suspicion by the Church.

Under the foot of religious authority, medicine itself was diseased. Autopsies were forbidden because it was written in the Bible that the body was the temple of the Holy Spirit. The medical discipline of obstetrics and gynecology was in a chokehold. Women in labor could only be examined through their clothes. If it were up to Martin Luther, pregnant women would never receive anesthesia during labor.

Illnesses, even the black plague, were considered divine punishment and therefore people were not supposed to do anything to relieve the suffering of the infected. The plague was an "act of God" and disease was a punishment for the sin of not obeying Church authority. The Church claimed the privilege of prescribing or justifying therapy. Christian monks taught that bleeding a person would prevent sexual desire (Ellerbe, 1995). The Church also tried to legislate sex and sexuality with a heavy hand. Ellerbe, drawing from Elaine Pagels's book *Adam, Eve and the Serpent,* reported that Clement of Alexandria strictly limited the types of sexual activity permissible to married couples. Even at night, it was important to behave modestly, in the light of reason, because even legitimate sexual activity was dangerous (Ellerbe). How far is that from Pope John Paul II's prohibition of sexual intercourse that is not intended for procreation?

Does being Christian automatically overcome or protect against suffering and poverty?

Another danger of biblical literalism is an acceptance of suffering and poverty in favor of hope and joy. Seventeenth century monk Antoine Godeau wrote, "A true Christian takes joy in having some afflictions to suffer, because suffering is the badge of a true Christian (Ellerbe, 1995)." This statement strongly suggests literalist intent in Paul's letter to the church in Rome: "Be joyful in hope, patient in affliction, and faithful in prayer (Romans 12:12)." Only it misses joy, hope, and faithfulness. Many Haitians fall for that trap. They feel the pain of misery, they grumble about it, but eventually, they embrace it as a Christian destiny on this planet earth. Many live resigned and go to church only to cling to the "old rugged cross" for a foretaste of "Glory Divine in the After Life." And, of course there is again the whispering hope of "Rapture that may come any time," thereby dismissing the need to keep fighting for a better life in this world - the principality of Satan.

In the movie *Luther*, people climb the steps of St. Peter's square on their knees, imploring forgiveness for their sins, while at the top of the stairs await representatives of the Church. With one hand, those representatives give the certificate of indulgence and with the other, they drop the money into the collection plate. It is hard to separate believing in God - as taught by religious authorities - from a willingness to suffer at the hands of people. For some reason that is convenient to some, there is a pernicious idea that without suffering, a man, woman, or child cannot achieve oneness with the Lord. All manner of brutalities are excused and accepted as good and fitting because of the idea that if Christ, the son of God, can be so brutally mistreated as to have his skin and flesh torn from his ribs, a believer in Christ should be willing to endure the same because, after all, Christ suffered the consequences of our sins. Films such as Gibson's *The Passion of the Christ* and Scorsese's *The Last Temptation of Christ* may have been presented as tributes, but their graphic violence suggests a glorification of injustice, an attendant message that God the Father condones human suffering.

Did the Father intend for Jesus to be beaten, scourged, brutalized, mocked, tortured, and suffocated? Or did our wickedness and our demons seek to thwart the plan of God and kill His son? Certainly Christ, out of love and sure of His divinity, endured our wickedness and forgave. Nailing Him on the cross was our doing because we crave violence, because we are mean, treacherous, and crass. For what kind of father would design such agony, in all its gruesome details, for his innocent son? Or did some powerful brain or brains, convinced, for the sake of world domination, that violence is inevitable, seek to legitimize it in making believe that God authorized it? The message seems clear: if salvation was impossible without the shedding of innocent blood, why dismiss violence as a tool for good? If God condones violence against the sinless, why should people scruple at the shedding of blood if the end justifies the means? And at the same time, if the brutal murder of an innocent man was God's choice for Himself, why should we, the wicked, be remorseful and take responsibility for inflicting suffering on Christ or on our fellow men for that matter?

Regarding Haiti, it's possible to see what state of mind results from that brand of theology. Theologies that justify violence and brutality play into the hands of those who uphold slavery and unconditional submission to bad, Satan-worshipping authorities. Violent theologies can encourage acceptance of social inequities. Worse, such theologies kill the drive and energy to fight constructively and be successful.

This theology may also be responsible for the misinterpretation of Matthew 6:33 and Luke 12:31 ("Seek first the kingdom of God and His righteousness, and all these things will be given to you as well") as injunctions to be 100% heavenly minded and disregard physical concerns. The message in this verse is so powerful that it is the core of this text. If people rightfully believed that their lives, possessions, and work were in line with the kingdom of God; if people dedicated everything they did to God and focused on Him in making their choices, then they would not have to worry about anything. They would need only to make the effort and accept the required sacrifice, and God's grace would bring every work to fruition. Instead, what is believed is what is too often preached in Haiti. The understanding of many believers is to renounce earthly gains and to forget the material; and that God is good and that all good things will come to you if you deserve them (and you really don't). In short, just pray.

Many Haitians who believe in Christ spend so much time on their knees that there is almost none left for them to work with their hands. While the first interpretation is proactive and accurate, the second one - the passive one - is a recipe for failure. That mistake is fueled (or compounded) by an apparent exaltation of poverty based upon the following: 1) a poor reading of the Sermon on the Mount; 2) the parable of the rich young man; 3) the tale of Lazarus and the rich man; and 4) the birth of Jesus in a manger where he was first worshipped by shepherds.

It may not be fair to single out Christianity as the only religion that markets poverty as something wonderful. Several major religions, in cautioning their faithful against putting wealth, glory, and honor on too high a pedestal, fail to distinguish simplicity from poverty. Instead, they invite confusion. The truth is that in the midst of blessings untold and joy unspeakable, during trial and tribulation, the Christian has a duty for humility. The idea is that no glory, honor, or fame should be able to make a Christian conceited or contemptuous. Unfortunately, the idea that simplicity is just as Christian as humility - and that it could prevent the son of the richest person from looking down on the poorest, or that it could make the strong willing to serve the weak - has not gained currency in traditional Christian circles. Here is the difference: While there is virtue in simplicity, poverty jeopardizes virtue.

Those who preach resignation in poverty have a hidden agenda. Enticing people into that way of thinking encourages them to accept a powerless condition. People who have surrendered their power in this way are easily controlled by the sheer fact of the poor being dependent. It's been said that there is a lot of money to be made - or power to be gained - in doing charity work. Likewise, one often hears about people taking vows of poverty. Perhaps those people have merely taken a vow of simplicity, which is commendable. However, a person who has a roof over his or her head isn't really poor. A person who stays hungry because he wants to fast, who dresses modestly by choice, who doesn't have money because he despises it, and who doesn't think about tomorrow being well-sheltered in a community he does not have to worry about these things, is not actually poor. Accepting poverty, preaching resignation, and encouraging suffering and deprivation, all in the name of God, only serves to consolidate the self-centered, irresponsible, brutal political leadership in this world. Consider the first chapter of Hebrews 13:17:

> Obey your leaders and submit to their authority. They keep watch over you as men who must give an account. Obey them so that their work will be a joy, not a burden, for that would be of no advantage to you.

And Romans 13:1-6:

> Everyone must submit himself to the governing authority, for there is no authority except that which God has established. God has established the authorities that exist. Consequently, he who rebels against the authority is rebelling against what God has instituted, and those who do so will bring judgment on themselves. For rulers hold no terror for those who do right, but for those who do wrong. Do you want to be free from fear of the one in authority? Then do what is right and he will commend you. For he is God's servant to do you good. But if you do wrong, be afraid, for he does not bear the sword for nothing. He is God's servant, an agent of wrath to bring punishment on the wrongdoer. Therefore it is necessary to submit to the authorities, not only because of possible punishment but also because of conscience. This is also why you pay taxes, for the authorities are God's servants, who give their full time to governing. Give everyone what you owe him: If you owe taxes, pay taxes; if revenue, then pay revenue; if respect, then respect; if honor, then honor.

This political speech, which patronizes the authorities of that time, should have been an embarrassment to Paul. Supposedly it came from a man who had received the harshest treatment at the hands of authorities for the simple "crime" of preaching the Gospel. That is the big contradiction: rather than taking Paul at his word that he was inspired by God to make those statements, wouldn't it be better to think that whoever wrote those statements was being astutely political but mistakenly so?

Consider the following: "Everyone must submit himself to the governing authority, for there is no authority except that which God has established?" Must the reader of the Bible believe that God put Hitler in authority to kill six million Jews? Did God give European whites authority to enslave blacks, or South-African whites to impose apartheid? What kind of God would abdicate His own authority in favor of that of scoundrels? Regrettably, those who espouse this Pauline political view flirt with ungodliness. In 1971, at the age of 19, Jean-Claude Duvalier, by his father François's fierce will and iron hand, became President of Haiti. The opening statement of his first speech began, "*Béni soit le Très-Haut de qui vient tout pouvoir.*" (Blessed be the All-High from Whom all powers come.)

Insistence that all authorities are in God's favor, regardless of what they do with that "God-given" authority, made the medieval times so dark. Sandwiched between a perceived intransigent God who constantly demanded penance and an aggressive and a merciless devil scheming in his burning hell, the believer had no choice but to submit to the established authority of the Church and the allied secular governments. The prescribed codes of behavior guaranteed complete control. Later, when the stranglehold of a monopolistic church loosened, it would not matter that those in control were Hitler, Mussolini, or any other self-serving, ruthless dictators. Those in charge were too happy that the cross reminds Christians that they should accept suffering, misery, slavery, and injustice. In short, they should be content with the lot that God, in his infinite wisdom, had chosen for them.

That blind faith in the letters of the sacred book explains that there was no remorse in these Christian Europeans who sought to subjugate Africans and aboriginals. Biblical correctness offered a comfort zone to self-proclaimed Christians. They should have known better. They had read about Jesus and they had heard the voices of wisdom in the exhortations to love and kindness from the likes of Father Antonio de Montesinos in Santo Domingo and Roger Williams in New England: "Tell me by what right, by what law do you keep these Indians in such cruel, such horrible bondage...are you not bound to love them as yourselves?" said Father de Montesinos (Deloria, 1994). Roger Williams admonished those so-called Christians with these words:

> "Remember, you too were persecuted in England and God, in His mercy, sent you here among these good people; buy from them, don't steal from them, do not con them." The majority of the Church-goers branded Williams a heretic and sided with Reverend John Chivington, the Methodist minister, who stated his intentions to "kill and scalp all little and big." That same Chivington, as he prepared to attack a village of peaceful Cheyennes and Arapahos, said (in the name of the Lord), "I shall long to wade in gore (Kaltreider, 1998)."

In 2003, on Gorée Island in Senegal, President George W. Bush said in a speech, "Small men took on the powers and airs of tyrants and masters. Years of unpunished brutality and bullying and rape produced a dullness and hardness of conscience. Christian men and women became blind to the clearest commands of their faith and added hypocrisy to injustice...My nation's journey toward justice has not been easy and is not over...The racial bigotry fed by slavery did not end with slavery or with segregation."

Even an informal apology such as former President Bill Clinton's in Uganda in 1998 was too much for some North Americans to handle, perhaps because their minds are still chained to St. Peter's view on slavery. Will there ever be a Truth and Reconciliation Commission in America that will once for all exorcize this sad past and set this country free to at long last sign the Genocide Convention that has been stalled in Congress since its acceptance by the United Nations in 1948? Perhaps failure to ratify a moral document that even the ungodly Soviet Union felt morally attracted too stems from the poorly expressed guilt in America for having itself committed genocide against Africans and American aboriginals. And perhaps subconsciously, the rationalizing in biblical correctness continues. In *American Indian Prophecies* (1998), Kurt Kaltreider wrote about the Puritan settlers of New England's justification for their violence against the original inhabitants of the land:

> ...the settlers often justified what they did through Scripture. Two passages that readily come to mind are Psalms 2:8, which says, "Ask of me and I shall give thee the heathen for thy inheritance, and the uttermost parts of the earth for thy possession"; and Romans 13:12, "Whosoever therefore resisteth the Power, resisteth the Ordinance of God, and they that resist, receive to themselves damnation.

Captain John Mason, an eighteenth century professing Christian and genocide, stated, "God laughed his Enemies and the Enemies of the People to Scorn; making them as a fiery Oven...Thus did the Lord among the Heathen, filling the place with dead Bodies." Captain John Underhill, Mason's co-leader, justified the slaughter with scripture by claiming that there was sufficient light from the word of God for the proceedings (Kaltreider, 1998).

Bibliolatry has moved Christianity far away from Christ.

Christian leaders, knowingly or subconsciously, accept horrible, unsettling, ugly things and patterns as "the will of God" when their true vocation is to reconcile people to one another and to God. This sad truth was made evident in the unqualified private and governmental support from the United States to the blood-soaked Duvalier regime and other dictatorships in Central and South America. This was made evident in what could be called the dark side of Reaganism, when the U.S. oversaw - or stood by watching - the merciless killing of the youth in Latin America toward the end of the Cold War. Christians, when they think themselves right, or when they are annoyed, may kill and maim mercilessly. And quite indecently too! When Pat Robertson, a pulpit heavyweight, publicly called for the assassination of Hugo Chavez of Venezuela, he was following a shameful tradition. On CNN, two reputable men of the cloth failed in 2005 to make the case for Christ while talking about the war in Iraq. Sadly, one stated, "Those Iraqis are bad people; if to blow them up it must take two days, two weeks, months, or years, let's blow them up in the name of the Lord." The other one, struggling to offer a rebuke, replied, "That does not sound biblical to me." Of course, that sounds biblical, the letter of the Bible is not against violence, and it is full of it. The good reply by Reverend Jesse Jackson should have been; "Which Lord are you talking about? When did "What would Jesus do?" become interchangeable with "Who would Jesus blow up"?

Oh, Christians, how soon do we all forget! Remember that the metamorphosis of the Great Persecutor, Saul of Tarsus, into Saint Paul was in part the result of prayers and actions by the persecuted Christians. They truly believed in the One who has shown that He too knows the merit of a timely, measured, and violent response (the overthrowing of the money-changers' tables, the whipping of the vendors in the temple), and yet still says, "Love your enemies, pray for those who persecute you...He who lives by the sword shall perish by the sword."

Christians Could Surely Do Better One-on-One or Country-to-Country

Indeed, rare are preachers with a social conscience who understand that God makes it rain and shine on all of God's children to entice believers to care for everyone indiscriminately. We are also quicker to point to the dire consequences of disobedience than to open windows of opportunity for blessings to the faithful.

Few will unconditionally give material aid to those in need. And yet, even in Haiti, pastors commonly preach from Malachi 3:10 as the best advice for a Christian seeking to help himself financially. It should be clear, however, that tithing is a surtax levied on the faithful's earnings, which should warrant some kind of social assistance, at least once in a while. Indeed a two-way give and take relationship is more than desirable in that sense between Haitians churches and their members.

The current practice whereby churches extract money from the faithful in exchange for spiritual shepherding, prayers, and moral support could be advantageously replaced by a more down-to-earth covenant of mutual servanthood. In that setting, people would more generously donate to the Church out of love instead of reluctantly out of fear. They would then find in their hearts and means to give more than 10% for there would be more blessings. In Haiti there is the so-called Feast of the Harvest where the peasants were asked to bring in the best of their crops for blessing. Wouldn't it have been nice if that occasion was used to bring everybody together to exchange tips and techniques on agriculture? Or to share ideas regarding how to improve production and how to protect against plant diseases?

It was 1950, the Church did not even think of taking a leading role in literacy campaigns. And yet some illiterate Haitians were so eager for knowledge they managed to locate the pages and sing almost correctly from the hymnals without much tutoring. By investing in the welfare of the faithful, churches would have worked for the advancement of the kingdom of God. Certainly the returns would have been manifold and more generous than the 10% preachers have been demanding over the centuries. When one gives out of love rather than out of fear, the generosity is akin to that of the widow who gave God all she had.

A miracle is possible in Haiti, but for that to happen, the religious leadership must be willing to break away from tradition. Religious life must not be "business as usual." It ought to be about spiritual well-being, physical and mental health, economic welfare, and prosperity for all under God. Together, Haitians must work the answer to the Lord's Prayer: "Thy kingdom come, thy will be done on earth as it is in heaven." God is not the Lord of grime and scarcity; the Prince of filth and thirst; the Duke of deforestation; Baron of drowned topsoil; or Count of burning greenery.

If prophets, priests, and pastors were to listen to who was actually chief within them (what God-loving thinkers truly hope is chief within them), rather than retreating to their comfort zone of self-righteousness and intellectual laziness, they would see the heavens open the floodgates of blessing over their heads and those of their children - beloved and despised. It is hoped that by truly listening to the Lord of their hearts, they will heed the advice of Jesus, as shared in Matthew 20:27: "Whosoever will be chief among you, let him be your servant." If these religious leaders schooled themselves in the behavior of the best of all shepherds, there would be for them and their flocks more blessings than they could count. Prosperity would be a sure thing, and where the reward would not be money, it would be the happiness that goes with the feeling of being part of something great, honorable, and glorious. Mother Theresa is proof that this is possible.

Indeed, God is intent on lavishing blessing on those who embrace a career or accept an occupation for the sake of helping others. None else was the secret of King Solomon's success. Consider his prayer to God on behalf of his people (2nd Chronicles 6):

> O Lord, God of Israel, there is no God like you in heaven above or on earth - you who keep your covenant of love with your servants who continue wholeheartedly in your way...Hear the cry and the prayer that your servant is praying in your presence this day...Hear the supplication of your servant and of your people Israel when they pray toward this place. Hear from heaven, your dwelling place, and when you hear, forgive...

> Judge between your servants, repaying the guilty by bringing down on his own head what he has done. Declare the innocent not guilty, and so establish his innocence.

> When your people Israel have been defeated by an enemy because they have sinned against you and they turn back to you and confess your name, praying and making supplication before to you in this temple, then hear from heaven and forgive the sin of your people Israel and bring them back to the land you gave to them and their fathers.

> When the heavens are shut up and there is no rain because your people have sinned against you, and when they pray toward this place and confess your name and turn from their sin because you have afflicted them, then hear from heaven and forgive the sin of your servants, your people of Israel. Teach them the right way to live, and send rain on the land you gave your people for an inheritance.

> When famine or plague come to the land, or blight or mildew, locusts or grass-hoppers, or an enemy besieges them in any of their cities, whatever disaster or disease may come, and when a prayer or plea is made by any of your people Israel - each one aware of his afflictions and pains...then hear from heaven, your dwelling place. Forgive, and deal with each man according to all he does, since you know his heart...
>
> When they sin against you - for there is no one who does not sin - and you become angry with them...and if they have a change of heart in the land where they are held captive, and repent...then from heaven, your dwelling place, hear their prayer and their plea, and uphold their cause.

This is the kind of prayer that carries power in the eyes of God. The supplicant quite forgets about himself to present the people to God. There is a wealth of respect and love in interceding for the people in the presence of God. Haitian religious and political leaders would be wise to emulate that. How many claim to be meritorious leaders, and yet, like President Sténio Vincent, hold the people in contempt? Or, like President-for-life François Duvalier, who gained his power on the platform that he wished to redeem the black nation and avenge past injustices, had the capacity and the chance to do so but could not because he had no respect for the very black men and women he claimed to care for? Duvalier did not balk at shedding Haitian blood. He proved on April 26, 1963 that only he and his family mattered, not the nation, when he threatened in words and action to level the country after an attempt on his children's life. Or, consider Jean-Bertrand Aristide, who seemed to have heard Jesus Christ's admonition, "Whosoever will be chief among you, let him be your servant," yet embraces class-hatred, and succumbs to the temptation of becoming those he had been criticizing and fighting?

King Solomon's prayer was not an exercise of pure intellect but a sincere cry of the heart. Not dialectics, but genuine loving intercession before God. God loves and blesses compassion more than intellectual gymnastics. Doctrines, dogmas, and decisions made at council levels are glorious when crafted in pursuit of excellence, but they are nothing without practical, humble love. Like King Solomon discovered, God is a God of prosperity only waiting for believers' obedience and love to grant that prosperity for the benefit of all.

Like so many hymns tell it, believers are sons and daughters of a King. The Christians' Father has homes and land. He holds fortunes in his hands; precious stones, diamonds, silver, and gold. He has plenty in his vaults and many more beautiful, glorious things. Nevertheless, those words must be believed, not sung ignorantly like parrots. Nor should the supplicants be the only intended beneficiaries of the prayers. Prosperity must be available to everybody.

Sectarianism: What Cause Does it Serve?

Another annoying side effect of biblical literalism in Haiti and the world over is the sporing of a multiplicity of sects and cults, all of which may interfere with simplicity of life. If someone were to write down the names of all the Christian sects, it would be a very long list, one that includes the many different churches and temples in this world. Each name clings to a new claim to fame. Each new denomination boasts of a better perspective on the newly revealed real truth, or suggests one truth being better than the others. And indeed, each one is different.

Some of the denominations nurse their differences. They express their 'authenticity' by what they eat or the way they dress or how they worship and when they worship. Christian doctrines, dogmas, and mores are diverse, yet all are allegedly based upon the Bible. These ideas, beliefs, revelations, and so-called true-ways burden people. These habits of diet, and dress can impair these believers' quality of life. Many times, these effects manifest in disruptive ways. One tragedy bears the name of David Koresh and Branch Davidian for the ranch that burned in 1993, killing 80 people. In November 1978, there was the Jonestown massacre of the Peoples Temple of California resulting in 914 adults and children dead, including one U.S. congressman and his escort in the jungle of Guyana. These are illustrations of the extreme.

Life is not made easier in day-to-day activities in which so-called religious beliefs stubbornly oppose common sense. In medicine, specifically surgery, when a patient's hemoglobin (red blood cell pigment) level is 2.7 and his or her whole body screams for help, it's a tragedy for the actual patient when his or her fellow biblical literalists form a cordon of resistance around the hospital bed saying no to blood transfusion - even if they're praising God and the goodness of his creation while they're doing it. How can bleeding to death be God's will?

Unfortunately, to some, if it was God's will for Jesus to die on a cross for the purpose of the remission of everyone's sins, then its God's will for the pregnant woman too. Isn't that selling Jesus for purposes other than the gospel? Is it to the credit of God's love when an obstinate believer keeps his over forty-two weeks pregnant wife at home for two days after her water breaks because he was waiting for a sign from God before taking her to the hospital?

In matters of faith and spirituality, people sometimes create their own misfortunes, call them miracles, and find a way to be at peace with themselves. One devout college student found herself pregnant, unmarried, and in the first semester of her graduate studies. She went to her knees in prayer, and fasted for days, refusing both food and water. When the baby died, she called it God's miracle. Medical knowledge holds that extreme starvation ketonemia may cause fetal death in utero.

These irresponsible interpretations of Scriptures happened in twenty-first century America! Is it also true that members of churches who die testing their faith by exposing themselves to rattlesnake venom never really had faith in the first place? People have died in terrible pain and suffering to vindicate Mark 16:18:

> They will pick up snakes with their hands; and when they drink deadly poison, it will not hurt them at all; they will place their hands on sick people, and they will get well.

Yes, biblical literalism may kill or cause mayhem and surely people, in their search of the divine, often err. Blaise Pascal says it better: "Man is neither angel nor beast, but, whenever he tries to be angel, he turns beast."

Cultural biases and personal preferences are often mistaken for attributes of spirituality or holiness. Some sects, intent on restricting body exposure in the name of Christian principles, impose a dress code of long dresses, long skirts, and long sleeves attached to clothes that hide everything for all weather conditions. Some believers could never find that while such an outfit was suitable or even necessary in the North, where the weather is freezing cold, it is wrong and impractical in Miami.

Regarding the prohibition against jewelry wearing that many Christians live under, sometimes cynicism prevails. Sunday school teacher Celine Lacroix Jacob tells a story set in Cleveland, Tennessee. During a meeting, a member of the leadership of the Church of God made a motion that if Christians were discouraged from wearing jewelry, there would be more money to donate to the Church. Likewise, there was a time in the Anderson, Indiana-based Church of God when necktie wearing men, and bra-wearing women, were judged as ungodly. A woman was reprimanded by a Committee of Discipline and was almost excommunicated for attending church in a bra. In private Christian schools all over South Florida, student handbooks list bras as an essential part of a young lady's attire.

Imposing a dress code on people for the sake of spirituality and holiness is petty dictatorship. To excommunicate those who are guilty of non-compliance is a misappropriation of God's established covenant with his children. Jesus instituted communion, but he never denied it to even Judas Iscariot, no matter what one might think of the latter. Excommunication betrays the intention of someone in position of authority and power to inflict misery and shame. It's a tool of intimidation and blackmail. In the hands of the powerful, it's been used against insecure heads of state and other impressionable souls: people brainwashed into believing that only intermediaries can lead them to God. Other times, it is the punisher's personal preference or ignorance that motivates such decrees. For example, a young woman with straightened hair fell ill with pneumonia. Her pastor said he knew that was going to happen because she'd ironed her hair after he'd told her not to and he'd prayed that she would get sick.

No, no, a thousand times no! This is not what imitators of Christ do to people. People who brutalize others, even socially and in words, have, in their intentions, battery or misuse of self-adjudicating power. They are misusing the privilege of being close to someone, pushing them into the dirt, and kicking them while they're down. It's astonishing that people who claim to care so much for the spirit of the Bible in addition to the world can forget Isaiah's prophecy in which it is written, "A bruised reed he will not break: a flickering candle he will not snuff out." Perhaps they do take that into account, but in a cynical spirit rather than a holy one, applying it to hiking and candlelight dinners. Anyway, these people, the piety police, get close enough to a person to know their private business. When a person's personal conduct deviates from the dictates of the self-appointed piety cop, there is hell-on-earth to pay. In 2002, one Haitian pastor reportedly said, "It is unchristian for women to wear pants. Whenever I see a woman in pants, she reminds me of something I was happy to have forgotten." It's enough to make a person say, "Stupid. It's all in your crazy mind because you refuse to get used to it." What is acceptable to some people in terms of dress has less to do with holiness than upbringing.

There is a church of God in South Florida that is very inclusive, meaning, it welcomes people of all walks of life and quite literally so. However, once in a while the demons of personal preference and cultural bias are given voice in the body. For example, a group of young musicians from Jamaica performed there, only to face criticism from a very few members of the congregation for being too casual. Some found it unspiritual that "the shirts were not tucked inside the pants." These congregants claimed that their dress code was not respected. Other members found it undesirable that female members of the board served communion in short sleeves. But what is spirituality? What is holiness? Some kind of dignity achieved by following a particular dress code? Is it achieved by following a prescribed diet?

The answer is an emphatic, "no." If spirituality or holiness were so defined, how many would have accepted communion from Christ at the last supper? It is written that He removed his garment and wrapped Himself in a towel. In other words, Jesus exposed Himself to his disciples. What was He wearing, this holy man on the cross on that Good Friday? On that first Good Friday, who were the best dressed? Most likely the High Priest and his fellow members of the Sanhedrin.

Dress codes are just what they are: dress codes. From the "Garden of Eden" to Sundays in church, people has dressed up for a variety of reasons: 1) embarrassment or modesty; 2) protection against the elements; and 3) pride. It is only a natural instinct not yet named, as commendable as it may be, that leads us to accept, adopt, or impose dress codes. Fashion and culture have much to do with the prescription. Please consider this truth: God doesn't love a person more when they're in a tuxedo or fancy gown or less when, defenses down, they are naked. God loves you just as you are.

Dressing up has little to do with spirituality, holiness, godliness, or even dignity. Gandhi epitomized it when he shed his lawyerly wardrobe for his diaper-like loin-cloth (the dhoti). Jesus, in all likelihood, dressed cleanly and simply. According to scripture and anecdote, Jesus did not advocate any particular code or fashion. He did not come to chain people. Instead, he stated, "My yoke is easy and my burden is light." A Florida pastor, having led a culturally diverse Church of God congregation for several years, chose not to offer a strong opinion on the suitability of swimsuits. He said, "I remember that my mother would not have wanted to be caught dead on the beach in a bikini - but I also remember she would not have wanted to sit down in church near a black person."

Therefore, let believers, being mindful of Christ, give breathing space to everyone. Don't let cultural biases and personal preferences cause frustration and sadness in our brothers and sisters. If Paul stated correctly that all things concurred for the good of those who loved God, why let cultural biases and personal preferences oppress believers?

There is no condemnation for those who are in Christ. Let us not curse what the Lord has blessed. Let us not have any hang-ups about what to eat, what to drink, and what to wear, for God so loved the world God gave it Christ who came to set it free. Nothing available to people should be cursed. Not even bacteria, which are so unwelcome and dangerous in the bloodstream, are outside the beautiful tapestry of creation. Some bacteria live in the bowels and are helping agents in the transformation and processing of unabsorbed food. Some, like E. coli, which lives in the large intestine, have been enabled by genetic engineering to make useful medicines like insulin. And what would the Essenes make of that? They were a sect whose doctrines were very close to that of Christian dogmas, except for their disbelief in the resurrection. They took such a dim view of human physiology that they prohibited defecating on Saturdays (Rivkin, 1984). But tangents aside, all things concur for the good of those who love God.

Believers must reclaim their prerogative to be intelligent, and like the divine, strive for perfection, which is their destiny in Christ. That's the will of the Father - to be perfect like their Heavenly Father is perfect. In that journey toward the destiny of perfection, it's much like Paul, the man from Tarsus, said, "All is permitted, but all is not useful."

More Positives About Saint-Paul

All criticisms considered, demystification of his mythological connotations aside, Saint Paul was a great human being. Paul offered the Church his own take on Christianity, flavored by his personal philosophy, colored by his Jewish culture, and drawn on the backdrop of his training as a Pharisee. Though it may be true that Paul's only physical encounter with Jesus was on the road to Damascus, he was an exceptional, unwavering defender of the Faith, an extraordinary Christian. His powerful intellect put the other disciples at disadvantage. Paul deserved to be the replacement Apostle, and in a way he was God's personal selection (as opposed to Mathias, the other disciples' choice to replace Judas). While Mathias remained a non-entity, Paul went on to become a shining star in the launching of Christianity. To understand Paul, however, the person reading the Bible must be able to see the three dimensions in the man:

- The intellectual
- The militant Pharisee
- The zealousness of a new convert.

What saved this true mosaic of personalities in the man were the tenderness of the sincere Christian and the exemplary humility in the doctrinarian. Paul is the only one to confess that he sometimes rendered personal opinions. He demonstrated that he was an astute intellectual when he described "his thorn in the flesh" without being specific. This clever description only allows for the reader's speculation of what that ailment could be, but Paul kept this information privileged and only known to him.

Paul is admirable in a myriad of other ways. The problem is not with Paul: it is with the biblical literalist who insists that everything Paul wrote or said was God's undiluted opinion. Nothing man does escapes the censorship of the "I." *Tout ce que l'on fait, est personalisé par le moi* (translation: everything I do pertains to the "I", the ego). And Paul's writings or utterances are no exceptions. The ego is complex. Even under the influence of the Holy Spirit, a Jesus will react differently than a Peter or a Paul in similar situations. In Martha's and Mary's home, at Lazarus's death, one might see Peter angry at the sisters' incredulity (they did not expect the miracle that occurred and were somehow mad at Jesus for not being there at the time of Lazarus's illness). Where Jesus' disappointment in the sisters' lack of faith moved him to compassionate tears, Peter might have cursed them (like he did Ananias and Sapphira).

Jesus and Peter are different people, but the way Peter's words have been exalted, it's a wonder that all believers are aware of this. Paul is great when he attempts to think outside of his cultural biases and speaks under the influence of the Holy Spirit. "Husbands, love your wives like Christ has loved the Church (we do not know if he ever married or not or chose never to speak of his wife). In 1st Corinthians 6:15, the intellectual explores the merit of not trivializing the sexual act, and, perhaps of avoiding not making it a spiritual experience. In 1st

Corinthians 10:23, Paul removes himself from his cultural religiosity and aligns his formidable intellect with the Holy Spirit. He writes:

> Everything is permissible, but not everything is constructive. Nobody should seek his own good, but the good of others (the position of Abraham, Solomon, and Jesus). Eat anything sold in the meat market without raising questions of conscience, for the earth is the Lord's, and everything in it. If some unbeliever invites you to a meal and you want to go, eat whatever is put before you without raising question of conscience. But if anyone says to you, "This has been offered in sacrifice," then do not eat it, both for the sake of the man who told you and for conscience's sake - the other man's conscience, I mean, not yours. For why should my freedom be judged by another's conscience? If I take part in the meal with thankfulness, why am I denounced because of something I thank God? So whether you eat or drink or whatever you do, do it for the glory of God. Do not cause anyone to stumble, whether Jews, Greeks, or the Church of God - even as I try to please everybody in every way. For I am not seeking my own good but the good of many, so that they may be saved. Follow my example, as I follow the example of Christ.

What an extraordinary sermon. Many a sect or cult would be wise to study it! This teaching encapsulates what the Haitian Church, even that of the world, would be wise to employ. There are too many interdictions justified by or based upon the Bible. Worse, people who swear by those hang-ups refuse to admit they only abide by some of the words and principles in the Bible. No one person or one sect can abide by the whole Bible, and those who claim they do are fooling themselves, but they're not fooling God. Consider, for example, the man who worships on Saturdays but doesn't feel obligated to have himself circumcised; the believer who preaches that every word of the Sacred Book is inspired but won't heed St. Paul's admonition to obey authorities and refuses to salute the flag, go to war to defend his country, and/or won't pay taxes; the devotee who won't touch pork yet injects insulin extracted or refined from pork insulin, etc.

One may as well wonder how a judge, who believes so much in the Ten Commandments that he is willing to cause a riot by refusing to remove the Decalogue from his court, can abide by "Thou shall not kill"? A judge, in accordance with his duties, must apply capital punishment when required to do so. And what about not disobeying the Commandment which states, "Thou shall not commit idolatry / you shall not not make for yourself a graven image." Quite unarguably, a blanket application of the letter would sink the art industry and cripple the photography industry, resulting in untold sad consequences for teaching and advances in medicine such as x-rays, CT-scans, and MRI's to say the least.[8]

If the self-proclaimed followers of Jesus have a sacred duty, it isn't to pick at people for not living the way they think Jesus would. They ought to emulate Jesus by doing exactly what he did or after weighing the usefulness of certain principles in terms of the good of humanity, do what he did not have time do such as during his short ministry among his people the Jews. That should be the golden rule for Christians.

Telling people what to eat, what to wear, or how to style their hair has no actual spiritual weight. It is a dispiriting exercise of authority, a flagrant abuse of power. Likewise, refusing to celebrate a wedding in broad daylight because the bride is pregnant is a drill in dictatorship, as is imposing a dress code on preachers or those serving communion (except for the sake of respecting culture, since going unintelligently against culture is unwise, disruptive, and often counterproductive).

Christians should avoid putting people in chains (actual and figurative), breaking their spirits, and ostracizing them in an effort to make those people behave in certain ways. There exist places of worship where a woman who is menstruating is invited to leave. Compare that to Jesus who healed and honored a woman who suffered from chronic vaginal bleeding and had dared to touch Him in the middle of a large crowd!

It's fair to say that humans have forged chains of bondage to enslave people whom they should love and strive to set free. People commit the crime and justify the sin by their interpretation of the Bible. Inspired, Saint Paul has clearly expressed sentiments that contradict these attempts at bondage:

> "Everything is permissible" - but not everything is beneficial (1st Corinthians 10: 23).

---

[8] In one Pentecostal church in the late fifties, in Port-au-Prince, members refused to have their pictures affixed on membership cards in compliance with their understanding of second commandment.

> So whether you eat or drink or whatever you do, do it all for the glory of God (1st Corinthians 10:31).
>
> Do not cause anyone to stumble, whether Jews, Greeks or the church of God (1st Corinthians 10:32)
>
> Therefore, there is now no condemnation for those who are in Christ Jesus... (Romans 8:1)

That is what love is all about. Loving one's neighbor is to love them as they are. Trying to impose personal preferences or social-religious-political convictions on others, even when the imposer is correct, is to commit the sins of impatience and self-righteousness. It is evil. Believers must all be careful not to lose patience with people. Taking heed of Jesus' phrase, "The truth shall set us free," will rescue the great religion. For the past 2000 years, Christianity, in elevating the parable of the "narrow gate" to doctrine level and preaching its own perceived or fabricated truth, has chased many away from God rather than keeping them in the fold.

In dialogue, exchanges are better than violence; democracy is better than dictatorship; evolution is better than revolution. Turning from blind fundamentalism and embracing God-loving liberalism will rescue historical Christianity from its self-imposed death sentence. Individual believers can be hard on themselves if they must; but the need to be gentle with others remains. The need for repentance is so obvious that Bishop John Shelby Spong found it an appropriate title for his book, *Why Christianity Must Change or Die*.

Preachers would also be wise not to favor the appearance of piety over the real thing. Some food for thought: a pastor was serving communion. A young man wearing a hat approached the altar to be served. The pastor, with 1st Corinthians 11: 3-16 on his mind, passed over the young man and went to serve the next person in line. The young man understood the silent rebuke and without protest returned to his seat. The pastor, not satisfied that his snub had been taken in the spirit it was intended, made sure to find the young man at the end of the service. Meeting the guy at the exit door, the pastor said, "How dare you present yourself to the altar of communion with your head covered? Aren't you a man?" Before saying a word, the young man smiled then removed his hat. His hairless scalp was mottled with bruises. He said to the pastor, "I am a cancer patient and what you see on my head are the ravages of therapy. The doctors have declared my case terminal. I have but a few days left to live. Perhaps next week I'll be dead. Today I wanted to receive communion as my last act in church."

Folks, this is it: looks can be deceiving. Never should the way a person dresses be equated with their respect and love for God. The reason people are so intent on imposing ways of behaving on other people, against their personal choice, taste, and need is because we're not kind enough, not tolerant enough, and not loving enough to allow people to look different, to be different. We feel threatened or upset by anything new or outstanding.

The same may be said about decisions regarding what people should or should not eat and drink. We often make cultural choices and let them stand in the way of our getting along with others. Even though many of us think we eat according to the Pentateuch, some of those of us that do seem to ignore that parts of so-called Mosaic law could have been executive decrees aimed at protecting the people of the nascent nation of Israel from food poisoning at a time when screening and treating ill animals and preserving large quantities of food efficiently and safely was nonexistent. Is it so hard to realize that Moses wore two hats and that his was a double leadership: religious and political?

At this point, it makes sense to pause and address a delicate issue: there is, apparently, a big price being paid by Jews and Christians for the sake of a forced connection. Jesus' life and his teachings indicate that He came to show the world the way to God. He laid His life down and died on the cross out of love for people - Jews and gentiles. He would have gotten killed anywhere because the world was not ready for His message of selfless love.

Those who want to fault today's Jews because of the ones who said, "Crucify him" some 2000 years ago, and thanks to the duplicity and cunning of the High Priest Caiphas, ignore the fact that when Christianity began, its membership was 100% Jewish (Chilton, 2002). In a clear example of the pitfalls of refusing to use God-given intellect with precision, they've managed to demonize Jews over the course of two thousand years based upon what they thought they read when they studied religious scripture. Are they aware that Jesus was a Jew? That his mother happened to be a Jew may be irrelevant, aside from indications that Jews are dearly beloved children of God and Jews educated Jesus. It should have proved also that girls and women are worth much more than women-hating men of authority wish to concede. Or perhaps, the dispute in Jesus' paternity is one of God's ways of demonstrating that true paternity is more than biological.

Nevertheless Haitians and all true Christians need to know that historical Christianity, rather than focusing on Christ and Christ alone and spreading His message of redeeming love, has sought to impose a Jesus of its own perception on the world in general and Jews in particular. Perhaps that's why the Church spent more time trying to prove that Jesus was God and the Messiah rather than demonstrating that through Jesus, God is Love and that Jesus' Sermon on the Mount, his advice and clearly expressed philosophy, contain everything necessary for a thriving, happy and prosperous world. The strict command "If someone wants to follow me, let him carry the cross" is better interpreted as "If one wants to follow me, let him act responsibly" not as "We should agree to be poor and miserable." Striving for a better world is not synonymous with being materialistic.

There is sometimes huge difference between doing something good and doing what is best. It is written, "Obedience is better than sacrifice." Must 'obedient to what' be asked? Remember Jesus' words to John the Baptist when John was doubting that Jesus was the One? The message Jesus sent was that the lame were walking, the blind had seen, and the good news was being preached to the poor (Luke 7:22). In other words, Jesus' message to John was, "Tell him we have answered the Father's call; we have been obedient. God almighty does not need coaching or patronizing. God is fully aware that believers do not have Divine patience and know-how. Yes, sacrifice may be good but obedience is much better.

Aware that believers are selfish, self-righteous, and prone to violence, God manages to care more about efforts put into idealizing and emulating Jesus rather than believers punishing believers. But certain Christianities, acting as God's war hammers, resort to mental acrobatics that only succeeded in tying the historical Jesus to prophecies of a Jewish Messiah. As a result, many Christians have come to embrace both good and bad cultural artifacts of the Old Testament. However, Jewish interpretations of the Bible vary from Christian ones. Does this suggest that Christians are more God-loving than Jews? Hardly. The true Judeo-Christian connection is not necessarily in the letter of the Old Testament or Saint Paul's opinions, but in chemistry at a higher level of spirituality and understanding of God and humanity.

9

Salvation

What thus far has been presented to you, dear reader, has been a review of Haiti at its birth and a harsh but realistic consideration of Haitian international relations. Haiti has been molded by a warped socio-religious consciousness. In light of the mind-crippling legacy of murderous slavery and tainted Christianity detailed in this book, it is fitting to share a worthwhile dream - a dream of good triumphing. Take heart for Christ has overcome the world and truth shall set all people free.

This dream must live. Haiti's behavior in the material world, its political choices, its vision, and its history must be rooted in a consciousness that springs from a dynamic understanding and respect for God and humanity. Haiti, and other nations that dream of liberty, justice, brotherhood, and happiness, can encourage individuals, under God, to enjoy prosperity and equality.

The Haitian adventure once compelled world thinkers to acknowledge that freedom is a non-negotiable, God-given right. Slavery was the world's worst example of man's cruelty to man. Haiti's 1804 liberation from the colonial powers of France took place over 200 years ago. Although the slave revolt of Santo Domingo resulted in the only successful slave revolt on record, the grand beginning has not produced a glorious legacy. What will be the next claim to fame? Let's be active participants in helping reconcile the world with true, Christ-driven Christianity, demonstrated in words and deeds, as opposed to ego-driven "Constantinian, Imperial Christianity," which is sick and on life-support because it's corrupt and blood-soaked. That dream deserves a strategy to make for a realistic, reachable goal that will be achieved through the application of sound, proven methods and techniques. And God shall provide.

The recipe for the kickoff is quite simple:

- Prayer
- Awakening for the whole of Haitian and American religious leadership
- Renunciation of violence, abandonment of division, and the practice of acceptance and forgiveness in its place.
- Haitians ought to worship God in spirit and truth. Their actions ought to be oriented to God's kingdom.
- In conclusion, enlightened believers shall come forth and write the blueprint for the new political leadership.

To accomplish such, Haitians need prayer. The time is right. Haiti today is again the object of the world's attention. And God is watching and willing. It's time to take God up on the promise, "If my people, which I called by my name, shall humble themselves, and pray, and seek my face, and turn from their wicked ways, then I will hear from heaven, and will forgive their sin, and will heal their land (2nd Chronicles 7:14)." No need to reinvent prayer to God. Examples are plentiful in the Bible, one of which is the Lord's Prayer, "Our father who art in Heaven, hallowed be thy name. Thy kingdom come, thy will be done..." Every sentence in that prayer must be uttered with conviction - not only on behalf of the supplicant - but the whole nation. If Haitians would pray that way, their faith would carry enough power to lift up Haiti. Believers who love Haiti need the fervent and loving prayer of Solomon, the compassionate intercession of Abraham before God. Since we cannot yet count on the political leadership to lead us in that quest, let the move start where it really matters: in the people. Every day and every night, may every Haitian find a few seconds to think and say something good about Haiti and thank God for it. Such an attitude of constant mindfulness of God will unite its believers in love and will open the way for the blessings. We do not need a confrontational pilgrimage to Bwa Kayiman to exorcise a tree. The power of prayer defies space and time. One positive spiritual resonance originating anywhere in the universe, be it in Miami, Ottawa, Paris, or Dhaka, can shake Port-au-Prince. And the more we are in it together, the faster and better the result. God is that powerful. Remember Einstein's equation? Masura Emoto suggests that the energy of prayer with genuine love and gratitude is in e=mc², except that here "c" stands for consciousness instead of the speed of light.

The religious leadership, en bloc, must wake up. Preachers must reinvent themselves and seek the truth and preach only the truth. Jesus' prophecy, "You shall know the truth and the truth shall set you free" must be fulfilled. That means the era of lies, embellishments, deceits, and the fabrication and destruction of evidence is over. Seeking the truth also means kicking intellectual laziness out of its comfort zone and embracing hard work. Focusing on true spirituality, the religious leadership will find a definition of religion that is likely to reconcile their nation. Indeed, religion can become a force that rallies rather than divides. Religion can build bridges rather than create walls between people. And God knows how badly bridges for the reconciliation of all of the Americas' children are needed. That unity in spirit is a necessary primer (*un mordançage spiritual indispensable*), and, despite hideous stories to the contrary, politics and religion can work in partnership for the good of people. In the case of Haiti and America, that godly partnership is a must. Histories indicate that these partnerships, across the board, have not always been praiseworthy. That too can and must change.

According to Joseph Tragert (2003), there was a time, in Mesopotamia when people lived with no government and no priests. They were not needed. In that area - believed to be near the so-called lost Garden of Eden, between the Tigris and the Euphrates - life was not bad at all because there existed everything necessary for human sustenance (provided they worked). It so happened that some of the residents of that land pushed themselves to be more productive than others and accumulated surpluses. Then, through trade with emerging civilizations in the Mediterranean, North Africa, and the Far East, they developed wealth and wealth conveyed to some the status of "strong men." These strong men also had the means to provide defense for themselves and others against neighboring thieves and marauders. The ancient people who lived in this area gradually evolved from a process of clan and patriarchal decision-making to appointing a king who ruled them. How did it happen? Food surpluses enabled a ruling class, its bureaucracy and army to be supported by other people's work. The powerful elites of the ruling class, bureaucracy and army gradually solidified their authority by becoming kings, claiming divine lineage, and establishing administrators.

The evolution of the divinely justified king, supported by a bureaucracy and propped up by an army, who ruled over an increasingly complex social and economic structure, accompanies the development of the pre-Sumerian city-states in Mesopotamia. The king enriched a priest-class bureaucracy and military class, so that they would support him and remain loyal to him (Tragert, 2003).

It started with the "strong man," made strong because he managed to be more productive than his neighbors and because he learned the secret of concentrating the means of production and defense, and used his advantages to make everybody else subservient to his whims and will. Preachers entered the game as cheerleaders to rubber-stamp the decisions and decrees of "the powers-that-be."

Preachers were described as having declared that only some people were divine. These people were either "strong men" (meaning warlords or kings) or had been made strong by God's favoritism, instead of seeing the divine in every human being. Preachers of the religious leadership, it's time to reclaim the power God gave you. It's time to acknowledge the divine inside every human being. Don't let warlords credential you anymore. Someone dear to you came years ago and proposed a new world order. Jesus the Christ asked Simon Peter if Simon Peter loved him. If Simon Peter did, Jesus expected Simon Peter to feed Jesus' sheep. Jesus wants the power to come from the base - a base that's a well-prepared body, cleaned up in preparation for the new dress.

After Jesus asked if Simon Peter loved him, Jesus added, "Who among you wants to be chief, let him be the servant...When you do this to the least of these you do it to me." Preachers, that's your call. Do not go on a self-righteousness trip, dividing and conquering the faithful. Instead, but work hard to make believers one in God - in truth and spirit. What does that mean? Preachers of the Christian faith must stop insisting that their particular sects are best. For Haiti, too much time has been wasted, and Christians have been part of the problem rather than the solution. Whether they be Pentecostal, Baptist, Jehovah's Witness, Roman Catholic, Seventh Day Adventist, Methodist, or Episcopalian, it's time for church leaders to show respect and allegiance to the common denominator in the fraction: God, the loving Omnipresence. All together, start building the bridges of unity, for God's sake. And for the sake of the world.

In this, the twenty-first century, a well-grounded believer must be able to feel at ease, at least for a week, belonging to any religion that loves God. That's the way toward Haiti's salvation. Let's not judge and condemn any sect or faith for not sharing our liturgy, doctrines, and dogmas. Instead, let's be patient with one another as God has not finished with any of us yet. Let us stop cultivating drift and dissension in God's name.

Who knows how much believers have lost in trying to determine if Haitian Christians are superior or more in the right than Muslims, Buddhist, Hindus, and others. Haitians are 97% Christians and Vodouists, yet the sad reality may be, if Haitians would look at a fellow Haitians with Buddhist eyes, they'd perceive that every human being is an expression of God. With eyes like that, perhaps people would not be so quick to beat, torture, and kill their brothers and sisters or watch them go hungry and unsheltered. If our people had perfected the sense of the Sacred so dear to the Hindus, our dead loved- ones would be resting in peace - wherever they are. People wouldn't fear someone coming in the night to pull their dearly departed from their graves and make them into zombies, or breaking into the tomb, stealing the coffin, and dumping the body on the ground on the very night of the burial.

Haiti's Christianity has been unable to suppress these practices. Perhaps Haiti's Christians have taken the wrong approach. It is time to be eclectic, not sectarian. If we humans care so much for our children, why wouldn't God care for everybody? Especially those who seek God with all their hearts and call on God's name? We are all God's children and we can be one in Him. This also applies to Vodou adepts that reject murderous witchcraft and refrain from boasting that they are the masters of creation. The question whether man is god would no longer be so troubling and divisive if people would remember humility's truth. A person may be a god, but they are not God Almighty. While a flame is a living fire, a person is candlelight (not the Source of light). In John 10:32-34, Jesus, admonishing those who wanted to stone Him, acknowledged the divinity of man ("Is it not written in your laws, I said, ye are gods?") If Vodou placed more stress on our duty as children of God to love one another; if Vodou insisted that its faithful pursued oneness in Christ in actions, perhaps Vodou would launch all its adherents to higher spirituality.

Inside the Temple Jesus declared that the spirit of the Lord was on him and it had empowered him. The Master may have stood up to acknowledge a crisis of possession by the Holy Spirit; a crisis of possession that allowed him to empower His disciples and fueled those famous miracles: walking on water, halting stormwinds, healing sick people, and raising the dead. Alas, Vodouists, much like traditional Christians, appear intent on justifying their religion and excusing their short-comings. They resemble one another in their self-righteousness. They too refuse to clean their house; they refuse to admit they have been wrong. That too would take kissing their brains 'hello'.

The Vodou Religion Must Come Clean!

Yes, a major cleaning of the house for the Haitian-African religion is in order. While acknowledging the positive in Vodou, we must stand firm demanding corrections or else Vodou and Vodouists shall be dismissed as irrelevant and unproductive. Enough of the ugly side of Vodou-based problem-solving! Enough of the promotion of a culture of fear in which the other is too often perceived as the enemy next-door. The pitfall of most religions is their determination to overpower the will of others - to control mind, body, and behaviors - and in overestimating their limited power. Instead, Vodou should be used to liberate people (the true meaning of the Bwa Kayiman ceremony). Let those with some special gifts help, heal, and liberate rather than hold others in debt or in bondage. Let Vodou take its adepts out of this perpetual survival mode. Free them up to live life to the fullest, without fear of tomorrow, fear of one's neighbor, fear of illness, fear of unemployment, fear of death, or fear of never succeeding beyond basic survival mode (*survivre n'est pas vivre*). The Vodou religion can succeed by promoting togetherness, and by demanding functional literacy, health care, and job security. It must seek to open minds by encouraging all its believers to embrace science and technology. Finally, Vodou must put pressure on elected officials to work for the common good. In doing so its leaders will be agents for change who know their limitations in the physical world and defer to government and collective actions for problem solving. In fact, Vodou masters should be at the forefront, pressing for government to serve the people rather than con them. The Vodou moral code should be known to all, and all guilty parties held accountable.

Vodou should become a dynamic religion that sees in zombification and murderous witchcraft obsolete devices of a desperate past. Having been pushed down to the bottom rung of the ladder for so long, having been kept for so long away from school and modernity, Vodou should acknowledge its lack of progress and its past mistakes and make amends. Ignorance and mediocrity should yield to enlightenment. Then, because the other religions in an exercise of self-righteousness refuse critique, Vodou will jump ahead as an even more wonderful platform for human spirituality. Acknowledging the Great-Master, King of the Universe in all one does helps those who embrace mysteries to enjoy closeness with God and many of the questionable intermediaries will be needed no more.

Religious observances are dresses. Dresses reveal the body shape, fitness, and the grooming habits of their wearers. In that spirit, the question about religions in Haiti should not be which one is best, but why is it that in Haiti, nothing seems to work? Why is there neither constructive religious fervor nor effective political revolution? Why neither dictatorship nor democracy nor occupation?

Catholicism has positive values that have up-lifted other nations, but in Haiti, what is the yield? A foolish variant of Liberation Theology. The Catholic Church appeared, not too long ago, as having favored only the values of the Haitian elite. Protestantism made a triumphant entrance in Haiti among the poor, winning over many of them, but Protestantism, too, appears to deny the disadvantaged any aspiration to better days. The prayer to God that gave Haitians their victory against Napoléon originated from a Vodou ceremony but in the centuries following that victory, Vodou and Vodou priests have often been agents for political oppression and personal vengeance too many times. How much did they differ from their Christian counterparts?

A Haitian expatriate, "Doctor Ell" (name changed to protect privacy), tells the following story: one afternoon he was asked to make a house call. The jeep that picked him up drove cross-country for hours. By ten that same evening the doctor arrived at his destination. From inside a poorly lit room, a familiar voice welcomed him. "Doc," said the voice. "I know you are shocked, but this is indeed me. Do what you are asked to do and then go home. I'll be all right." The man speaking to the doctor, the supposed patient apparently now sick with malaria, had been buried three months prior. Doc Ell had been present at his funeral and burial. The man was now a zombie. He had been poisoned, buried, dug up and then put to work as an obedient slave. This suggests that the Haitian victims of white supremacy may have accomplished in slavery something that white men could not: the creation of an obedient slave. The oppressed had taken on characteristics of their oppressors. Yes indeed, children often manifest the vices and weaknesses of the rejected parent (adoptive or biological).

Haitian society must eradicate such crimes. If Haitians are to call one another a civilized people, if Haitians are to enjoy the full blessings due children of God, that ugliness condoned by culture must be removed forever. That practice of robbing someone of their life is no good: it must go. It's as if the white slavers left Haiti, but black slavery has remained. That is evil, the same kind of evil demonstrated by the pastor who had the authority and audacity to punch a helpless child's head until that child's eardrums burst. It's as foul as framing another man, as evil as torturing political dissidents, and as ugly as redefining torture so that bodily harm can be brought to bear upon helpless prisoners. All these stem from the same general root of wickedness as it thrives in social-Darwinist, selective-literalist, false-piety-riddled societies.

Long Live Togetherness! Let Grace Rule!

Haiti's many constitutions are full of prohibitions. Haitians should instead have constitutional prohibitions against anyone running for public office who has shed Haitian blood, whether they've done it in person or through third parties, or ever showed contempt for human life. Haitians, wherever they live, should bestow leadership recognition only on the most enlightened and loving of souls. If Haiti were a country of justice and wisdom, the whole world could be even more blessed. We are one. Where one suffers, all suffer. The word Haitian would resonate wonderfully with good people for having endured the pain and suffering of slavery and spinning those experiences into love. Doing so would keep the whole nation in a constant state of prayer, what some Buddhists call being in a constant mindfulness of God. Haitians need a new vision of the Haitian nation, and they must pursue it adamantly. We need a new definition of nationalism and national sovereignty, operational and inclusive. The new political leadership must catalyze togetherness rather than elevate any individual to Messiah.

Haiti requires a collective leadership that includes masses, bourgeois, blacks, mulâtres, and everyone else. Time for the demons of divisions to be removed! Haiti was not created to be exclusively a nation of bitter survivors. Just look back. At the beginning it was Léger Félicité Sonthonax, a white Girondin-Jacobin, who empowered the enslaved. Sonthonax should be revered instead of being dismissed as a demagogue. He was a spiritual son of Haiti but some Haitians resent him. Before Toussaint Louverture became the master of the island, Sonthonax distributed arms to the enslaved Africans. Sonthonax told them, "Whoever shall try to take these away from you will want to make you slaves again." Long before Dessalines declared, "Et les pauvres nègres dont les pères sont en Afrique ils n'auront donc rien?" (What about the black men whose fathers are in Africa? Shall they get nothing?) Sonthonax declared, "The land of Saint-Domingue belongs to the blacks. They have acquired it with their sweat and blood." Perhaps people don't know that Toussaint was skeptical of the French Revolution. He considered Sonthonax, and all the French revolutionaries, to be un-Christian and vulgar regicides. Toussaint said the world had always been ruled by a king and that he could not live under any other form of government.

In Les Révolutions de Paris # 66, October 16 1790, Sonthonax wrote:

> What do I hear, the Negroes will never be free? They will be; in spite of their tyrants; yet, their freedom will be paid in blood, and their barbarous oppressors shall receive their just punishment for having resisted the demand of Nature and Humanity.

For the final erection of the true Haitian Citadel - the one that will never rot - the magic formula, the "Holy Grail," should be how to get the Louvertures and the Sonthonaxes to love one another, swear allegiance to one another, and to work together for the salvation of the black man and the world. Quite recently a wealthy Haitian, of Palestinian origin, Antoine Izmery (a man misunderstood by his fellow Palestinians, Arabs or whites, let alone by Aristide himself), was murdered while working toward the restoration of Aristide to the presidency. He spent his fortune and gave his life on behalf of the Haitian masses that he loved so passionately. There exist Aristide haters, who would rather see Aristide serve three consecutive presidential terms rather than accept the presidency of a light-skinned person (even someone like slain radio personality, activist, and the people agronomist Jean Dominique). Yet it is doubtful that Haiti was created to be a country exclusively for blacks or whites or mulâtres. God's plan may have been for the Europeans, Africans, Arawaks and Tainos to learn from one another, in Haiti as elsewhere. The short-lived but wonderful Louverturian experiment showed that blacks, whites, mulâtres, former slave owners, and former slaves can work together and be productive. Noirisme or mulatrisme was not the founding fathers' vision for Haiti. The beautiful philosophical doctrine of Négritude is the mountain that gave birth to a mouse. Dry, martial, sterile nationalism is no nationalism at all; it is a shameful indulgence in discrimination that tempted out-of-breath politicians to lead Haiti in self-destruction. Likewise, national sovereignty should be an investment in the individual Haitian that fosters a constant feeling of belonging, an undying sentiment that as a Haitian, one is always important in the eyes of fellow Haitians. When Haitians invest in other Haitians of all shades and speech, they co-create long-lasting loyalty and collective pride. A hollow yet noisy national pride has spoilt the Haitian collective consciousness. This myth of sovereignty has caused countless Haitians to go hungry and without decent housing or adequate health care. Haitians who could not tolerate the Darwinian rigors of life in Haiti took to the sea. Others ran or flew away when not simply expelled, thus becoming de facto expatriates.

The enmity between Haitians of the Diaspora and Haitian politicians would have been irrelevant to Toussaint Louverture. In the service of Haiti, Toussaint was a citizen of the world. The military legend transformed himself into a Spanish warrior, an anglophile when flirting with the British Crown, while seriously courting France. Toussaint's peregrinations were only a means to an end: to set all blacks free. One of Toussaint's points of contention with Sonthonax was that Toussaint hinted at the possibility of a move toward the United States. Sonthonax distrusted American slave owners in addition to despising the French bourgeoisie. When Sonthonax voiced his doubts, Toussaint accused him of being willing to kill all the whites.

Among Haiti's founding fathers, Boukman was Jamaican and King Christophe came from Grenada. Haitianity transcends geography, color, and ethnicity. The land of Haiti should be the official tabernacle to all Haitians. Haitians must stop cheap rivalry and renounce violence, even violence in words and body language.

A small history book used in Haitian preparatory schools reads, "Never has any soil been as bloodied as ours" (*Jamais sol n'a été plus abreuvé de sang que le nôtre*). Violence begets violence, but after Haitians rightfully used it to break the chains of slavery, violence became useless to Haitians. Let violence be thrown away. Let all Haitians embrace forgiveness.

To borrow from Jose Martí, hate is not constructive. Let's do away with revenge and declare violence an enemy to Haitianity. Let us learn to see and admire the divine everywhere, and may we be grateful toward life. Most importantly, let us train ourselves to be sensitive to the pain of the mistreated so we can learn to treat everybody fairly.

Compassion is divine.

And on that note, it has been reported that some Indigenous hunters shoot to kill. When the animal hit is not dead, the hunter, mindful of the prey's suffering, kneels near the wounded animal and asks for forgiveness. "You see," the hunter may say, "I do this because I don't have a choice, I'm doing it for survival. Please forgive me." These words are indicative of respect for life. Ending the animal's suffering becomes an act of mercy. Some might find that attitude ridiculous, but it is a gesture of kindness that Haitians would be wise to emulate. Far too often, Haitians show recklessness in the disposition of life.

In many ways, Haitians are rugged individualists. Haiti is a place where the maxim of "survival of the fittest" is lived out every day (it is also neatly accompanied by survival of the well-connected). Wherever it reigns over habit, Darwinism invites people to favor brutality (*Homo homini lupus*) over compassion. Christian believers are not exempt from this, even though God favors mercy for the weak and disenfranchised. Jesus said, "Blessed are the meek for they will inherit the earth (Matthew 5:5)." (*Heureux les débonnaires car ils hériteront la terre*)

Strength, endurance, and toughness freed Haitians from colonial bondage, but Haitians have not escaped bondage from unrelenting toughness. It is time to soften up! Let Haitians abhor cynicism, torture chambers in their barracks, and penitentiaries. At the same time, we must ban beatings. May Haitians only have contempt for self-important and power-crazy politicians who resort to crimes committed under cover of correctness to advance their self-centered agendas.

When Haitian believers change their ways, real leaders instead of the power leeches will emerge from their ranks. Men and women will accept positions of power only to improve Haiti's reality and thus its image, moving the nation in a positive direction. Such people will define power rather than be defined by it. These fine leaders will not seek to remain in power for life, either officially or "behind the scenes," but will gracefully exit upon the end of their terms, unafraid of rejoining the ranks of private citizens, as did Nelson Mandela, George Washington (who refused to be made king), Haiti's Nissage Saget (who retired voluntarily to his beloved St. Marc), or Charles de Gaulle (who showed toughness when he had to but gracefully withdrew from politics when he perceived he was no longer in the will of the French nation). Democracy is tough, and it is best suited for the strong, not for the faint of heart. Winston Churchill described it as, "The worst form of government, except for all the others." Yet, in a country where many gifted and educated brains wish for what is best for all, democratic plurality has more charms than dictatorship.

Worship in spirit and truth and be kingdom-oriented. We must turn away from religious fundamentalism, embrace God, and worship Him in spirit and truth. Jesus was put on the cross by hard-liners and fanatics with set opinions of God and God's will. Those hardliners were closed-minded, but Jesus spoke the truth. He did not compose a liturgy. He neither created dogmas nor upheld doctrines. If anything, Jesus challenged them. In trying to be like Christ, believers ought to be better informed and much more open-minded. The duty of preachers is to extract the message God smuggled into the Bible, not to hide behind the imperfections of the letters, words, and thoughts to create enslaving, self-serving rules and regulations.

Getting the juice out of literary fruit is no simple task. There is no room for intellectual laziness or dilettantism. It is so easy for people to sit down, study the Bible, and come away from it calling good evil and evil good. Openness to the spirit, a willingness to be harder on self than on others, united with reliance on the mindfulness of God, is absolutely necessary. The Holy Spirit works best when will and effort submit to the call of the Holy. Be mindful of what happens to the subconscious when a person is made to believe that every word in the Bible, even the mistakes of translations, is God-inspired. An understanding driven by 1st Kings 13 may inspire a pastor to plot against another. Reading about what one man of God did to another, effectively causing the other pastor to fall and lose his ministry, may read like the biblical thing to do. Following Luke 16 may excuse prevarication, pilfering, and embezzlement. The parable of the dishonest servant who, knowing he was about to be dismissed from his master's service, cancelled the debts of his master's biggest debtors, may encourage biblical literalists to accept professional dishonesty in themselves or in public affairs. Believers must seek the truth and preach the truth. That's the will of God. The truth shall set us free.

Let there also be a more dynamic interpretation of the sacraments and rituals. The symbolism in foot washing, for instance, should foster humility in Christian interaction. No task should be considered too menial if it is a way of helping a neighbor in need. For what good is it when the church foot washer is the same person who channels the dirty water from his home into his neighbor's yard? Or, when a great Christian nation dumps its toxic waste on a smaller, impoverished one, even if that Christian country benefits from the complicity of some native renegades or money-hungry pragmatists? Likewise, the bloodstain on the doorposts for Passover should be interpreted as the distinct sign of care and cleanliness that one should sense while visiting a Christian neighborhood - an indication that Christians care for one another's health and welfare. A Christian act is to remove the garbage from the front of the neighbor's house instead of dumping it there, graciously picking up non-biodegradable trash from the canal rather than adding to the mess. We could go on and on with these dynamic, kingdom-oriented interpretations of the Sacred Word to the greatest benefit of our nations.

Believers must renounce convenient (selective) biblical literalism, the root of Christian fundamentalism, lest they become distraught fanatics. Sayings like, "Spare the rod, spoil the child" must be taken with a grain of salt - even if it can be demonstrated that they are drawn from the Bible. Why? To legitimize violence against children, even when it's called "spanking" and said to be for the children's ultimate good, may go against Jesus' recommendation. Inflicting violence against children, no matter how well meant, sets them up to become citizens insensitive to the suffering of others. Examples include heads of state who permit torture and assassination on the pretext of the country's welfare and weekday executioners who transform into Bible-toting Christians on Sundays. Let Christians stop training children to view violence as a noble manner of problem-solving.

Let's acknowledge an idea: in the Bible, certain opinions are culturally biased. Some biblical opinions could also harbor violence toward the mind, an example of which is the ignoble attempt to impose one's mindset on others. Terrorism may also be intellectual. Could it be that people who attack free thinking and who force their views of God's laws upon others are intellectual terrorists? Consider, for example, preachers who impose dress codes on the basis of a letter written by a person of different cultural convictions who lived thousands of years ago. Such is the demand that men must not cover their heads because they are the image of the glory of God (never mind that no one has ever seen God, according to the Bible) while women must cover their heads because they are the glory of man.

When church thinkers declare, "It is bad for women to speak in Church," they are not giving respect to God so much as they are elevating the culture and experience of Saul of Tarsus to the level of divine decree. To impose those statements upon people living nearly two thousand years after those declarations is not necessarily adhering to the timeless will of God. Naively and with no discernment swallowing those pronouncements is likely to subvert the respect and freedom offered to God's children through Christ and the Holy Spirit.

Preachers should avoid projecting themselves as uncompromising representatives of an idealized, poorly understood, ancient culture. Now is the time for eclecticism, not sectarianism. Consider bees as inspiration. They gather nectar from many different sources to make honey. The truth is not in the extremes but somewhere in the middle. If people reject uninformed fundamentalism and focus on spirituality, they could open the way for fellowship where mutual respect and desire for truth enable receptivity to dialogue and blind self-righteousness can cease. Preaching by example could make proselytism unnecessary. Preachers of division take issue with ecumenism, demanding that goats be separated from sheep, but they forget that God will separate them when ready. According to the Bible, an altar to Baal was built in proximity to an altar built to the Lord (1st Kings 18:22-39). A prophet of God had challenged the priests of Baal to prove that their Baal was greater than the Lord. The believers' task is to make room for God and to open the doors to Him. That done, God's will - salvation for everyone - shall prevail.

Believers and respecters of God need not go on rampages, knock heads, break bones, or ruin reputations in the name of God's will. Our mere presence serves as salt of the earth or as reality checks when in humility we choose to make a difference in the quiet spaces of our lives. It is said, for instance, that Toussaint Louverture, arguably an enlightened Christian, was present at Bwa Kayiman. According to a well-informed source, Louverture's presence may have saved Haitians from a worse karma. Supposedly, Louverture stood in the circle where a password was being communicated, mouth-to-ear between the celebrants. When Louverture's turn to share the password came, he changed it and, as a result, a pig - instead of a white man - was sacrificed.

Eclectics, not fundamentalists, will bring people together. Who, besides God, has a monopoly on truth? Jesus cares more that God's children love one another, not that believers hammer the Muslims, the Buddhists, the Hindus, the pagans, and others out of respect for truth. "Father," Jesus prayed, "make them one." That is God's will. That is the Lord's dream. To consider Jesus' authority in biblical terms, in Paul's first letter to Timothy (2:5) it is written, "For there is one God and one mediator between God and men, the man Christ Jesus." Indeed, it is reported that Jesus said, "I am the way, the truth, and the life." What if Jesus really meant, "Do it my way. It is the way to the truth and the life" or "The Christ in me, which I came to bring out in all of you, is the way, the truth and the life"? From the mouth of the person reporting Jesus' words to the pen of the scribe taking the dictation, there was distance, illiteracy, time for alterations. It would matter less that fellow Christians believe that there is no other way for salvation except through Jesus than they accept the faith of those who want to emulate or idealize Jesus and love them sincerely as Jesus Himself commands.

God so loves the world and he cares so much for His children that it's hard to imagine Him favoring only a minority of them or that He only once sought to manifest Himself among men. Until the opposite has been proved, believers should not discriminate against those who love and seek God with all their hearts but worship differently. A new awareness is needed in Haiti (and in the world) for transformative, redemptive reconciliation to take place. When Haitian Christians (and all people) are all kingdom-oriented, then all shall be called children of God.

A verse tragically misinterpreted by Haitian biblical literalists is, "But seek first the kingdom of God and His righteousness, and all these things will be given to you as well." It has been taken to mean that Christians should distance themselves from the material world. It often serves as an excuse for men and women to neglect their responsibilities to themselves, their children, family members, and friends. Too often, this verse is interpreted as an injunction to crucify the flesh, to despise the world and its attractions. Falling prey to a deathly, sorrowing, bitter set of ideas, like some believers, too many Christians are so heavenly minded that they have become earthly inefficient. They have wasted precious time that could have been used to serve God's will and His plan for His children. We must commit ourselves to improving our sad realities for the advancement of His kingdom on earth.

To stay kingdom-oriented, one must cultivate transparency in attitude, actions, and prayer. It's a commitment to be in the service of good versus evil: to offer the world "a foretaste of glory divine" as "heralds and apostles" of the kingdom to come. To do otherwise is to be in contradiction with oneself and one's God.

On earth, Christians must be bearers of good news, servant catalysts for the good of others, children worthy of the Father, tools in His hands for the Great Construction. A kingdom-oriented believer does not indulge in deceit and deception but is, instead, sensitive to the suffering of others. A kingdom-oriented believer blesses rather than curses and is not a hypocrite. A kingdom-oriented person does not make himself the center of attention. He does not monopolize everything while leaving nothing for others. He does not hoard, connive, and market, crediting his faith for making him rich, while looking down on the disenfranchised and claiming that the poor are reaping the consequences of their sins. To be kingdom-oriented is to understand and live the message of Christmas as given in the French, "*Paix sur la terre aux hommes de bonne volonté,*" or "Peace on earth to men of good will." Good will means doing the best one can in the exercise of one's profession, and doing so with competence, integrity, and love, knowing that love and compassion go many miles further than dry professionalism. To be kingdom-oriented is to embrace the healing power of forgiveness. So many crimes have already been committed on earth that there is little time or energy left for well-deserved punishment or retribution. Vengeance consumes too much energy. It is a fruit with a bitter and everlasting aftertaste.

Even in the quest for justice, wisdom must be exercised because when the line between revenge and reparation is blurred, constructiveness is a casualty. God knows that people who are down cannot be in a forgiving mood. Only Jesus accomplished that. That's why God avails victims to be in a position of strength once in a while and at that moment, if the victim has the grace to forgive; the circle of injustice or violence is broken.

Breaking the cycle of injustice and violence is what Joseph did from his position of strength when confronted with his deceitful, abusive brothers (Genesis 45:5-11). He had the opportunity and authority to crush them and the people they chose to protect into the dust. They deserved it, but he pardoned them. A more recent example is that of Mandela in South Africa. As midwife to the birth of Haiti, Toussaint Louverture did it. It worked for about ten years and would have probably worked long-term in Haiti had malice not allowed Napoléon and the counterrevolutionary French bourgeoisie to have their way.

Forgiveness is pleasant in the eyes of God and opens the way for His blessings. Anytime people use their position of strength as a platform for forgiveness rather than vengeance, they emulate Jesus Christ. Oftentimes, things do not work because victims fail to realize they stand in a position of strength and the healing power of forgiveness is not given a chance. Haitians lost blessings untold when that happened with Louverture and Rigaud; Dessalines and the mulâtres of the South; between our forefathers and the French who were stranded in Haiti after Haitians won their war against Napoléon. Haitians may have lost a great deal when, after February 7 1986, no leadership arose to tell the country, "Now that we the people have a chance to be in control, let us all forgive and bind together."

More recently, the sad pattern was repeated under Aristide between the Haitians of the slums - his vengeful partisans - and the rest of Haiti. Forgiveness is divine. What do hate and grudges build?

We are kingdom-oriented when our prayers are like Abraham's, Solomon's, and Jesus Christ's. Christians have no right calling on God to curse people. Even those who displease us deserve our love and compassion. That was Jesus' recommendation in the Sermon of the Mount. Reading imprecatory verses and psalms with the intention of causing harm is not a godly act. It goes against Christ's prescription of mandatory love. According to scripture, it is possible to commit murder in one's heart.

Being kingdom-oriented requires sharing, which is not to be confused with self-neglect. A person cannot share what a person does not have. One cannot give what one does not own. Some people think they can, and some think they must. They talk about redistributing wealth among the people, dispossessing the "haves" to empower the "have-nots." That is sheer robbery, and it impoverishes everyone involved. Responsible leadership must encourage goodness and obtain an operational collective interest that inspires confidence in togetherness - not something that elevates the poor at the expense of the rich or otherwise successful. The orientation alluded to here is a change that must come from the heart.

Former President of Nicaragua Daniel Ortega[9] eventually figured it out. After losing power in Nicaragua, he confessed in an interview that he erred when he attempted to change society through armed revolution. He'd come to realize that only a change in the hearts can transform the world and that only God through Jesus can change hearts.

To be kingdom-oriented is to respect other human beings, even those who look very different from us. Our emotions with regard to everything in life, including our reaction to and interaction with peo-

---

[9] Ortega began as a Sandinista in the revolutionary threesome that included Alfonso Robelo and Violetta Chamorro. Ortega later became Nicaragua's first post-Somoza President.

ple, cover a range of sentiments ranging from love to indifference. In a regressive way, it goes like this:

- Love
- Admiration
- Friendship
- Respect
- Hate
- Contempt
- Indifference

Love and indifference hold the extremes. On top we have all the positive emotions. The negative ones lay at the bottom. By some strange co-incidence, respect holds the scale like an axis of symmetry. It goes without saying that respect is the base for all our positive sentiments. If it disappears, nothing is left to hold friendship, admiration, or love. Anything less than respect leads to hate, contempt, or indifference. In human relationships, respect is a nonnegotiable ingredient, a *sine qua non*. It is a must between leaders and followers seeking common goals. Respect for the people is key. Consider Solomon's prayer to God for wisdom:

> Your servant is here among the very people you have chosen, a great people too numerous to count in number. So give your servant a discerning heart to govern your people and to distinguish between right and wrong. For who is able to govern this great people of yours? (1st Kings 3:8-9)

Besides the humility in the supplicant who comes into the presence of the Lord like a child and who forgets about himself to think about others, there is that sense of respect for the people that permeates the whole text. What a difference there is between Solomon and so-called leaders who wish to be president to "save the people," when in actuality, they despise them and cannot wait to enrich themselves at the expense of others and send good faith dissidents to prisons! It seems that God is not kind toward the leaders who do not respect those they lead. Even when those leaders appear to have a head start on everybody they soon fail. Leaders must inspire. The best leaders are humble, strong, and loving. It is difficult to work for someone you don't respect, and it's almost impossible to respect someone you view as inferior. It is that simple. Haitians in position of authority beware! It's time that those in public services know that they are servants not rulers. That is the core of democracy. Perhaps that's why some Haitian egos struggle to accommodate it.

If it is in fact true that God resists the proud but has mercy on the humble, certainly being God's kingdom-oriented is to embrace humility.

To be kingdom-oriented is to embrace work. It is in working that one can honorably gather enough for self and for others. It is also helping when one puts his or her money to work by investing it rather than hiding it in the ground. A natural instinct is to believe that we have done enough when in reality we have not really paid for the meal; we have only tipped the waiter and quite stingily so. A kingdom-oriented professional goes the extra-mile in serving others, bending backward to allow the others to do right, to feel important, and to be useful (but not used). We must earn the comfort zone and move away from it. We must embrace work with the will to perfect our skills and techniques and to multiply talents whether we are in a liberal or a manual profession. We must never be shy about asking questions or improving knowledge. We cannot afford to sit on our laurels. We must question our motives and seek the truth. We must experiment and read and search and learn, doing so with care and wisdom. And we must pray and preach by example.

Being God's kingdom-oriented means also to be tolerant. Tolerance dispenses from the negative sentiments (hate, contempt, and indifference). Tolerance involves welcoming differences, giving others the benefit of the doubt, and not imposing one's own perspectives. When, for instance, God grants us a vision, or when through His generosity we receive a passing grade for doing "something good," we should not use our experience to write doctrines, create dogmas, and speak like expert witnesses ex-cathedra. One is not automatically an expert exorcist, or an authority in demonology for having been branded "demon-possessed" and cured. Consider this pearl from Oswald Chambers, as quoted by John Eldredge in *Wild at Heart*: "Never make a principle out of your experience; let God be as original with other people as He is with you." Likewise, when by grace, one feels liberated from hang-ups with regard to food or drink, we must not brag about it, impose it, and cause someone else with a weaker faith to fall. Leave the option of censoring and whipping to God Almighty. Let Him sanction, for ours is a duty to love, no matter what one may think of the mandate to St. Peter and his successors (Matthew 16:18:20). Many things we men do occur because we are men. For instance, Jesus instituted communion, and men's idiosyncrasy invented excommunication. Perhaps Matthew 16:19 is responsible for all the Church erring of the dark ages: "I will give you the keys of the kingdom of heaven; whatever you bind on earth will be bound in heaven, and whatever you loose on earth will be loosed in heaven." Now is the time to start on the right foot, to grab from the Bible the message most consistent with Jesus' personality and character: Do not curse, do not judge, let the enlightened Christian be intercessor like Abraham, like Solomon, not wardens on earth but liberators.

As a result of this 180-degree turn, Haitians will not repeat history and elsewhere there will be no more witch hunts, no replays of the Inquisition; no crusading invasions of Jerusalem to desecrate holy places with bloodshed; no ex-communication of heads of state; and best of all, no marriage between politics and religion where true spirituality is held hostage. When we all are God's kingdom-oriented, fellowship is a given. People will love to help one another, prejudices will be put to shame, and social/racial discrimination will die. God then will live among us, and He shall be crucified no more. And like the cells in the living body, it will truly be *"e pluribus unum,"* or "out of many is one."

Slaves and masters will be no more, for everybody shall be everybody's servant. Leadership will emulate the selfless nervous systems of our sophisticated living bodies. Leaders will be empowering, well co-coordinated, and attentive to all, even to the smallest at the lowest station. Humanity's destiny is encapsulated in the scripture: "Be perfect as your Heavenly Father is perfect." Therefore let us now begin the apprenticeship of perfection. That is God's will. Let us no longer excuse selfishness because "this is," we've convinced ourselves, "a dangerous world." Let us stop marketing the love of God as just a convenient, cheap commodity, with the assumption that God favors our war machines over patience with and compassion for his children.

To be kingdom-oriented is to distill the true message between "Do not love the world or the things that are of the world..." and "For God so loved the world he gave His son so whosoever believes shall not perish but will have everlasting life."

Eternal life starts here on earth - in the hearts of believers. Eternity is now and it is misguided hypocrisy to dream of felicity in heaven while allowing or perpetrating havoc on God's earth and mayhem on His children. And shall we pause here to wonder for a moment with you, reader, what "eternity" is? What if eternity were what we bring to it? The sum of all our wishful thinking, good and bad, a permanent crystallization of all our life hopes and desires, the state of mind resulting from our efforts, fights - beautiful and ugly - accomplishments and failures on earth and beyond. In John 14:2, Christ declares that in his Father's house there are many mansions. What if this postulate is closer to the truth than the expectation that after death one enters an admission-free Disney World or an inescapable concentration camp? What if our mission on earth were to learn, to imprint in our minds all it takes to go into eternity, where we shall proceed to be co-creators with God Almighty? What if failure to do that, failure to answer our highest calling, is rewarded by our minds being locked up in a hell that is the sum of all our fears?

Sometimes in our sleep we dream. What if dreams were the "reality" that illustrates the power of the mind? What if dreams happened in our sleep so that we may know that life goes on even without the participation of the flesh, and that the flesh, with all its sophistication, is nothing compared to the immensity of the spiritual? What if death were a spectacular passage from life as we know it to an everlasting dream-state some call "eternal life"? Perhaps we have a choice between a "nightmare for ever" (hell) and a dream of nirvana/heaven, where everything beautiful we ever wished or worked for came to us magnified and "real." If so, would those of us who have ever lived a nightmare have any motivation to choose wrong? In that vein, until the truth is known, it is advisable that no one be caught dead in the midst of a hell he or she has created, and let no one go to bed or fall asleep with his or her demons, because he or she may be locked up there forever with them, and the Lucifer of your bad dreams, the Great Satan of your wishes on other people, will be there too, ready for you. Forever and ever! Even being caught dead counting money or killing for it is going to be hell. Imagine yourself doing that in a "never-ending-dream"! Jesus said it so well, "How much does it help a man (or a woman) to have gained the world if he were to lose his soul?" And to borrow St. Paul in one single statement: "To fight the good fight, to finish the course, and to keep the faith is to manage in a way that no challenge, no glory, and no tribulation can separate us from the love of Christ."

10

Conclusion

God does not make junk: people do. Every human being, and every living creature, is precious in the eyes of God. People make junk out of other people - at least in their minds. They despise and stigmatize their fellow humans: to exploit them, to enslave them, and to convince them they are inferior. The Haitian revolution occurred because this crime against God, against humanity - the race-based slavery - had gone too far in God's eyes. That's when and why Haiti came into existence. God, in all probability, had a purpose for that new nation. The birth of Haiti was God's pilot project, established to eradicate racial discrimination. Haitians were to be heralds and examples that all people are indeed created equal and are endowed with God's mightiness of inalienable rights to "life, liberty, and the pursuit of happiness." The faithful in Haiti and the faithful in America were to work together for the purposes of God's glory. Alas, the founding fathers of both nations fell far from the mark of the high calling of God in all his children - European, African, and First Nations.

Haitians and Haiti could have been God's case demonstration of truths that had been prophesied by America's founding fathers, but Haitians failed to realize true liberty, just as the Americans of the United States did. Why? Because they did not acknowledge their brotherhood. Their ideas regarding common sense and divine endowment did not extend to all their countrymen as defined by their nations' borders and the founding fathers' and mothers' philosophies. But then, both are nations of Esaus and Jacobs.

In less than ten years under Louverture, Haiti shone brighter as a prize-jewel in the Caribbean for the whole world to see. White, black, mulâtres, former slaves, former slave owners, old Royalists, and new French revolutionaries built a balanced society. Even after Hédouville, the snake, tricked Toussaint and Rigaud into committing the original sin of brotherly hatred, God did not abandon Haiti. Right after the victory and for two hundred years, however, Haitians have remained divided. Haitians won the war against Napoléon's fierce army and then waged a bigger war amongst themselves. As slaves Haitians fought violence: as free people, Haitians embraced violence as if it were a prize wrestled from the slave-owner to proudly exercise it against their own.

Two centuries later, the parallels between Haiti and America are distressing. In Haiti, as in America, violence is present in homes, in society, and in politics. It is cherished in religion and in school. People nurse violence like their favorite children, stoking it against people, against women, against other children, and against the plants and animals. In religion, we've embraced superstitions, hatred, self-righteousness, and a biblical literalism so primitive it blinds and distances the faithful and hopeful from the true message of the love of Jesus Christ. It's time for repentance, in Haiti and all the Americas.

Again, the Church isn't the problem. Nor would the Bible be. The problem lies in the use made of the Bible and the Church to control and manipulate the wounded, the hungry, and the broken-hearted. Should the Bible be on the highest pedestal? Definitely yes. Should it take over God Almighty's throne? Absolutely no. Here is the inconvenient truth: even though there is more to Christian diversity than Protestant or Catholic, in the baldest terms: Protestants in error have deified the Bible while Catholics in error have deified Church hierarchy.

But God is great and is faithful to God's promises. Enough of our expecting the political leadership to perform our long-awaited miracles. For a people to have the political leadership they deserve, change must come from the root and from the heart. Jesus laid out a new world order: "Simon," He said, "Do you love me? Feed my sheep." Jesus also said, "Let he who wants to lead be servant... he who wants to be the greatest, start serving the littlest among you...When you do this to the least of these you do it to me." This is true revolution at hand.

The biggest and most rewarding task awaits the religious leadership, the religious leaders being those closest to the people, and the ones already with authority over the people. May those leaders be great servants. Let religions build bridges between nations and communities, instead of erecting walls between them. And without holding state or government hostages, may that leadership put the primer on the people through a true spiritual interpretation of the biblical message. The emphasis must be on interpretations that focus on God, the redeeming power of love, and on Jesus Christ - the perfect example of how man should relate to God and to one another. Jesus Christ exhorted people to forgive debts as they hoped to have what they owed other people - and God - forgiven.

Teach the people to love, not fear! Learn to walk and breathe in love, not fear. Set them free by telling them the truth. Do not be afraid of challenging old concepts that insult intelligence. Let us not be afraid of asking questions. God is not a God of blackmail or intimidation. If we find ourselves intelligent, it is a gift from God; therefore, if we implore God to give us the Holy Spirit, our intelligence will be insulted no more. Many things we now do not understand will become crystal clear. When the enlightened people change their ways, the right political leadership will show up. Prosperity, happiness, and peace on earth will be the answer to our prayer: "Thy kingdom come, thy will be done." Then, as the late Dr. Beauvoir Edmond stated a few weeks before he passed on, *"Et le pays redeviendra vert."* (And Haiti will be green again.) Therefore, for Haiti's sake and for the sake of the world God loves so much, let all believers be God's kingdom-oriented.

There are people who look at today's world and say, "We have a great civilization. The victims of the past (people of African extraction living in the Americas) are better off than their brethren who were never enslaved." People who deny the shaping of the present by the past ignore the things of the present that mirror the hideous past. They will not approve of a President's apology for the sin of slavery. They oppose commissions of truth and reconciliation. They demonize victims they cannot ignore. They minimize the suffering of the survivors of injustice and the descendants of the oppressed. They tell those who complain about the present to shut up. Sometimes they couch "shut up" in more pleasant terms. They might say, "Things are much better now than they used to be," and "You're better off here than you would be in the Sudan or Liberia."

Because something works does not mean it was right or necessary. Because something seems to work does not mean it was God's plan. Quite simply, God is too great to be outdone. God's forgiveness and patience should not be construed as approval of our sins. Because slavery built the economy of the nineteenth century, thus resulting in this status-quo, does not make slavery right. There could have been a better way to bring electricity and modern literacy to Africa and the "New World" without resorting to greedy theft. Then there would have been no need to keep rationalizing the hideous past as historically necessary. The facts would speak for themselves. The violence enacted then and now stands as a measure of the people of the Book's faith in the greatness of God.

Last, but not least, Jesus Christ exhorted people to forgive others' debts as they hoped to have what they owed other people - and God - forgiven. Let the believers of the wealthiest nations of the world - those whose countries and countrymen are owed the most monetarily by the poorest nations of the world - demand that the debts of the debtors be forgiven. This is a most practical application of the core principle of Christianity - just as it is in the only prayer scripture records as being taught by Christ - the Lord's Prayer. The debtor nation of Haiti is crippled by what it owes the United States and other countries (Damu, 2003). Let those countries that call themselves Christian cancel those debts. If the people of those countries want their countrymen to be forgiven their evils, those people should demand debt forgiveness. Indeed, for over two thousand years, so much harm has been done and so many crimes have been committed in the name of God (and civilization). Why is it unreasonable now to do right in God's name?

An inspiring change of attitude should be demanded of Haiti's leadership. The ugliness displayed when executives insulted an expatriate Haitian seeking the presidency while throwing flowers at the feet of a foreign secretary of state illustrates the contradictions of politicians in whom narrow nationalism and selective xenophilia drive symbolic cannibalism. Only cynicism or stupidity would lead anyone to brand a native-born Haitian who holds American citizenship a foreigner just because they don't want him as president. Why doesn't it matter that this man supported health care, drinkable water, food, and schools for Haiti's peasant children? It is a malicious form of intellectual violence, and those guilty of this abuse of human rights deserve to be called the new breed of intellectual terrorists, unworthy to be leaders in a democratic society.

Conclusion

Are those expert obstructionists afraid that the new horde of nation builders consist only of those who have been close observers of the statesmanship, the intellect, and universality of Pierre Elliott Trudeau; the boldness and verticality of Gerald Ford; the indefatigable humanism and frugality in government of spending of Jimmy Carter; the political savvy of Ronald Reagan; the composure of George Herbert Walker Bush, and the brilliance of the Clintons? These qualities should be demanded and treasured by the new political leadership. *C'est ce dont le réservoir Haïtien devrait faire le plein pour que l'eau enfin, en ce pays, soit potable.* Haiti must no longer be a country in which a government official uses the government car for his private business or have a quota of gasoline from the government that he distributes to his friends. Surely the Diaspora, which counts among its members Haitians who have served in the greatest armed forces on earth, would support an honorable Haitian army. Perhaps the problem some Haitian politicians have with political aspirants of the Diaspora is that leadership emanating from the Haitian Diaspora rejects the existence of soldiers or police officers who protect the interests of the "haves" at the expense of the "have-nots."

Many members of the Haitian Diaspora have prospered in countries where the phrases "government ethics" and "military intelligence" aren't jokes. Haitians who have never lived outside of Haiti are aware and inspired by these realities too. They might welcome wider pools of political candidates just to secure for their country those attributes and qualities. Having a double-nationality does not un-Haitianize a true Haitian. The confusion between the rights any person has to legal recognition of their nationality and the rights and privileges associated with legal citizenship hamper Haitian politics. Presidential debates should not focus upon who gets to be president based upon the number of passports they possess.

In Haitian politics, when someone is accused of rejecting their Haitian identity because they have dual-citizenship, the accusers may be planning a swindle. François Duvalier and Lorimer Denis branded that sort of attitude "crabs alive in a basket." If necessary to avoid conflicts of interest, let the Haitian Constitution demand that no Haitian president be sworn in who has not renounced all other citizenships. No more was demanded of Canada's foreign born 27th Governor General, Haiti's Michaëlle Jean.

Those who might call this proposition "utopian" must realize that what is indeed killing Haiti is too much realism and too much pragmatism that blinds them to only struggle for the short term. The pertinent question should be, "What does the future hold? What is the legacy for the next generation?"

The change of attitude in the leaders must also establish the groundwork for further development. We should learn from the other island nations and insure that progress won't be a burden on the backs of the people. Rather than lowering rent on homes it does not own, government officials should declare that they are going to learn to fish with the people and for the people; build with the people and for the people; and farm with the people and for the people.

The country's leadership should embark on creating a working constitution that has the strength and flexibility of the constitutions of the best countries of the world. Perhaps more than elections, a working constitution is an absolute necessity. Haiti needs a good, time-tested fundamental charter. Most previous attempts have been intellectual exercises in surrealism. The present constitution reflects the insecurities and obsessions of the post-Duvalier era. Haitians need a constitution that calls for unity and sets the framework for unity. Too many Haitian constitutions stand like decrepit homes, health hazards that hide politicians ready to shoot in the back or punch in the kidneys.

As for the proud and the covert members of the Haitian Diaspora, they comprise a pool of good will, competence, science, and technology. They should continue to set an example that American believers cannot ignore. Among them are retirees and semi-retirees - accomplished people who acquired admirable skills and abilities in the pursuit of professional and personal excellence. Let them come and serve their native country. Let them donate their valuable abilities and knowledge to Haiti - without seeking profit. Let them serve Haiti at their expense. Those who do so will not have donated their talents for nothing. They will do so to save Haiti and that will be like giving option to life anew to their children and grandchildren. They will open the eyes of others whom God has gifted to the possibility of saving the world.

Finally, to those who are guilty of wrongdoing, let this be said: The cynical games of robbing, kidnapping, and maiming must stop. The upper hand and the last laugh belong to the forces of good. No matter how justified your rage, your joy in the misery of others will be short-lived. Victims and perpetrators must break the cycle of violence. Together we have failed to save Haiti, and together, we must now save

Haiti. The country needs to cool down for the healing to occur and for the "rebuilding together" to begin.

Then blessed be he or she who comes in the name of the Lord!

Epilogue

During the writing of this book, important elections occurred in Haiti and in the United States of America. It is disappointing that in some terrible respects, irregularities characterized each one. Is it impossible that some leaders invented artifacts that enabled their candidate of choice, no matter how terribly unpopular, to assume leadership of their countries? To that end, rules and regulations may have been selectively enforced for purposes other than freedom and justice for all.

If it is true that democracy can survive anything except democrats, if it is true that practically speaking, democracy is wrong for a republic, then maybe Haitians and Americans have the government they deserve. If one believes that the citizens of a "first" among nations are not ready for true democracy, then maybe popular elections are inappropriate.

In the case of Haiti, however, it is not proven that average citizens, even illiterate ones, lack common sense. Arguably, the common folk demonstrate a better grasp of the concepts of country, nation, community and government than the so-called elite. Indeed, the Haitian masses crave for one thing: the sentiment of their importance. They want to belong. They wish to be acknowledged. Over a century ago, the saying "power to the most capable" came under popular criticism. People should be cautious in trusting those who call themselves the most capable. What a good republic needs from the greatest among them is to demonstrate that the majority respect the rights of the minorities. Shamefully, the reverse is traditional: power in the hands of special interest groups who hide their contempt for the majority while pretending to be a part of it.

The 1987 Haitian constitution and the resulting (or improvised) electoral laws are evidence that some Haitian intellectuals are distracted from problem-solving by self-aggrandizement. Making the access gate to the presidency as narrow as the eye of a needle does not make a country great. Rather, it is by honoring the people whose contributions make things like public education and traversable roads possible. Thank God there are citizens wise enough to ask, "Did you do me such a big favor that I should name my kid after you?"[10]

The parallels between Haiti's failures, the failure of the religious faith, the failure of the mulâtres, the disenfranchised well-to-do, and the blacks enjoying the benefits of class privilege corresponds all to baldly with America. It is written, the first shall be last and the last shall be first. Why let that happen here? For too long Haitians of means misbehaved at home, benefiting from racism in some respects while suffering because of it in others. Americans would do well to consider that while their country is a target of hatred, fear, and envy from those abroad, there are those at home who have less interest in making America great than in benefiting from selling out the highest aims of liberty, equality, and justice for all.

Yet may we have faith that God Eternal has the plan.

---

[10] In Kréol : Ki sa Koukou té jwen-n nan men Frizé
Pou'l t-a rélé pititt li Frizélia.

Acknowledgements

Senator Hillary Rodham Clinton wrote *It Takes a Village to Raise a Child*. I must add that it takes a lot of people to write a book.

My most sincere thanks go to my family, immediate and distant. This book is the work of the family's creative writer, my daughter Ruthy. She has proven that she can look at an idea buried in hard concrete, chisel it out, lift it up, breathe life into it, and reshape it to perfection with the patience and fearlessness of a sculptor. My wife Rita was our impartial referee in moments of co-writer clashes, generous in her praises, yet never hesitant to give the necessary unbiased opinion. Jean-Luc, my son, the soon-to-be Doctor Charlot, a man of powerful intellect, provided much needed encouragement and constructive criticism in the few short moments he was able to glance at the manuscript.

To all my sisters in Atlanta and Miami, and my many cousins scattered throughout Canada, the United States, and Haiti, I say thank you. When I finally decided to write, sensing the difficulty and enormity of the task, the drive and the fear being equally overwhelming, I panicked and felt the need to call for spiritual assistance. All my relations, mostly Pentecostal Christians and Seventh-Day Adventists, and many of them preachers, agreed to pray and fast with me for forty days. Here it is: the book your love unconditional helped me write.

My long time friend and pastor Dr. C. Daniel Harden deserves all my gratefulness for kindly previewing the book. He read the manuscript, made corrections, verified with me the biblical quotes, and helped me avoid historical blunders in writing about Christianity. At times, my personal theology made him uncomfortable. But when I confessed that I'd written this after listening to his sermons for twenty-two years, he said he could only be proud of me. He also warned me against any illusion that my deep-seated, fully-expressed, and unwavering God-loving liberalism may resonate well with the conservative church of today and not to expect any endorsement. The pertinent question: Is the Church frozen in the same self-defeating, stubborn attitude of the Lavalasse people and the Vodouists; that of wanting to "have the last word" rather than looking for and honor "the truth"?

My sister, Reverend Pastor Marthe Charlot, has been instrumental in finding the right scripture quotes at the right time and in the right context. She never tired of me calling her any time, day or night. Whatever the question I asked, specific or tangential, she went the extra mile to find me the answer. For instance I might say, "Sister Pass, I vaguely remember a passage where Jesus appeared to have acknowledged man's divine nature, that, in answer to a question from the crowd, he did not rule out that we are gods. Can you help?" She would only say, "Oh, give me five minutes." Then in less time, the telephone would ring and she would be on the line with her answer.

One other major blessing was having my childhood Sunday school teacher, Céline Lacroix Jacobs, as a sounding board. Forever young, and gifted with the most fantastic memory, she - is in her own rights - the Haitian Church of God historian. She supported me, encouraged me, and she told me the following: "Listen, God has special calls for each one of us. If yours is to speak up, go for it. No one can then accuse you and be right."

Hertha Bovery, a true friend since my years as a medical resident in Boston, Massachusetts, urged me to write. One day we were on the phone exchanging ideas about our Haitian heroes of the Independence when she said, "Why don't you write? Your ideas and interpretation of history are so interesting. People should read what you are telling me." An excellent proofreader, she provided much needed strong, yet constructive, criticism. She turned out to be my toughest debater in defense of her Roman Catholic religion. So, Hertha, in a big way, you have set the monster free. Now you have to teach me how to dodge the bullets from the enemies of freethinking.

Professor Everett Long, my piano accompanist for the saxophone, was the first to tell me this was an excellent book after reading the first draft. Thank you, Brother Everett, for advising me to avoid name-calling and not to show anger, lest the readers feel targeted and take offense. I've tried all along to heed your excellent recommendation.

Acknowledgements

A special thank to Pierre Michel Elysée, an agronomist with a special knowledge of Haiti and Haitians. He made helpful suggestions for the section on Vodou.

One other person in Miami cautioned me to be more polite and more conciliatory. It is with him I proudly share the Charlot name. "Drop the hammer," he told me. He also said, "No one must write the way he or she speaks." Soon, indeed, I watched on CNN a presidential speechwriter share his secret for successful writing: "Never speak the way you write, nor write the way you speak." Thank you, Albert Charlot. You're a great mind. You made me stretch and you forced me to heed the great critic's prescription, *"Vingt fois sur le métier remettez votre ouvrage. Polissez-le sans-cesse et le repolissez."*

Fritz Mardy, my friend of half a century, assisted me with his unflinching, no-nonsense mathematician's way of reasoning over a problem, be it religious or political. Fritz, thank you for your support, and thanks for your predictions about this book. Thank you for expressing confidence in a classmate's ability, and for never losing what made you one of the best mathematicians of our class at the Lycée Philippe Guerrier. But I am sorry: you are no atheist. Even if you'd been accused of, or at times have fantasized about being one. Not in my book! You're just an intelligent, loving, restless questioner who sometimes asks embarrassing but pertinent questions.

Two persons I must mention gave me the boost to carry on. My friend and fellow colleague of many, many years, Dr. George Battle, and his wife Elizabeth.

Reverend Fritz Bazin gave several inspiring sermons on Haitian radio programs. These sermons inspired my boldness in biblical interpretation. He kindly agreed to preview the manuscript.

Gérard Gène of Montreal got me most of the information I needed on Napoléon and Joséphine. Gerard was instrumental in the search for the right publisher. Thank you Gérard, *"Zanmi lwen cé lajan séré.* (A friend from a distance is money in the bank.)

Thanks to my daughter's love of perfection we both were humble enough to submit our text to a professional editor. Mr. Leonard D. Nash, you did a wonderful job. And I'm so happy that you don't mind that your name be in this book and this acknowledgment.

For my love of the saxophone I owe the friendship of Carl Fontaine. Thank you Professor Carl for your words of encouragement, and your strong recommendation that I read J. A. Rodgers's *World's Great Men of Color*. Reading the two volumes confirmed that racial prejudice, color bias, and sex discrimination are stupid mistakes.

Finally, this book is a tribute to my former Haitian teachers, most of them sadly no longer of this world. Those great minds of the Lycée Toussaint Louverture in Port-au-Prince, and Philippe Guerrier des Cayes gave their best. Those poorly paid, misunderstood teachers demonstrated that education raises a man to his full dignity. Their teachings instilled a certain sense of pride and responsibility for being Haitians no matter the apparent destitution and the feeling of helplessness. In planting the seeds of hope, they nurtured the dream that will bring about our beloved Haiti's resurrection.

—Jean-Baptiste L. Charlot, MD

This has been an extraordinary, seasoning experience. I have learned more about privilege, "oppression Olympics", fortitude, assimilation, acculturation, team-building, and co-operative economics than I before thought possible.

Kelley Walters, Saima Hossain, Giggles K. Anderson, Ife M.O. Jacobs and Anne Campbell have been my angels and shining stars. They are the people whose strong minds and penetrating insight have sharpened my own like iron sharpens iron. A girl needs her girlfriends and they have always come through in terms of discussions regarding life, privilege, religion, faith, the universe, and being one's best version of herself. In terms of friendship and good sense, I must also thank Christopher Chinn for not only being armed as well as braingerous but also for his facility in supporting the besieged.

Additionally I must thank Dr. Nestor Javech for putting my leg back together again, Will Gutierez and Armando Mello, and the good people at Polestar Pilates for helping me get my groove back, and Grupo Ondas for providing me with the greatest physical challenge of my adult life. Were it not for the tests and opportunities afforded by my time with Grupo Ondas, I would not have such flexibility with dancing: be it intellectual, physical, or spiritual. Axe.

Also, I must thank Leonard Nash, for his extensive critiques and edits.

Nearly last, but not least, I must thank Andrea LaRosa for the loan of *The Politics of Denial*. Without it, and the many conversations we shared regarding it, I may never have stumbled upon the possibilities of shared misery and the mechanisms of cultural survival that manage and promote it.

To Tara Xavier Hepburn, I am ever grateful for friendship, support, macaroni-and-cheese, the gathering of jokes, the sharing of stories, and the joys of wingspan. Real irony can hurt, but it also illuminates. And flying is for the free. I look forward to the next round of celebrations, tripping the light joyous at the party eternal.

—Ruthy Charlot, MS

References

Armstrong, K. (2001). *The Battle for God*. New York: Ballantine Publishing Group.

Augustin, J. (1999). *Le Voudou Libérateur: et si le vodou était une valeur!* Montreal: Éditions Tamboula.

Bell, M. (1994). *All Souls Rising*. New York: Pantheon Books.

Benstein, R. B. (2002). *The Wisdom of John and Abigail Adams*. New York: Metro Books.

Bonaparte, N. (1986). *Napoléon's Memoirs*. New York: Learning Links.

Carter, J. (1998). *Living Faith*. New York: Three Rivers Press.

Carter, J. (2002). *The Personal Beliefs of Jimmy Carter: Winner of the 2002 Nobel Peace Prize*. New York, Three Rivers Press.

Carter, J. (2005). *Our Endangered Values: America's Moral Crisis*. New York: Simon & Schuster.

Chilton, B. (2002). *Rabbi Jesus: An Intimate Biography*. New York: Image Books.

Chomsky, N. (2003). *Hegemony or Survival*. New York: Metropolitan Books.

Damu, Jean. (2005). How the U.S. impoverished Haiti. *The Black Commentator*. Vol. 56.

Davis, K. C. (1999). *Don't Know Much About the Bible: Everything You Need to Know About the Good Book but Never Learned.* New York: HarperCollins Publishers.

Dawson, J. (1994). *Healing America's Wounds.* Ventura, California: Regal Books.

Deloria. V. (1974). *Behind the Trail of Broken Treaties: an Indian Declaration of Independence.* New York: Delacorte Press.

Deloria, V. (1994). *God Is Red: A Native View of Religion.* Golden, Colorado: Fulcrum Publishing.

Donald, D. (1970). *Charles Sumner and the Rights of Man.* New York: Knopf.

Dorestant, N. (1998). A Look at Haitian History from a Haitian Perspective. Retrieved May 27, 2005, from http://www.geocities.com/CapeCanaveral/9972/haitipai.htm

Dunkel, G., & Flounders, S. (Eds.). (2004). *Haiti: A Slave Revolution: 200 Years After 1804.* New York, International Action Center.

Ehrman, B. D. (2005). *Misquoting Jesus: The Story Behind Who Changed the Bible and Why.* New York: HarperCollins.

Eldredge, J. (2006). *Wild at Heart: Discovering the Secret of a Man's Soul.* Nashville, TN: Thomas Nelson, Inc.

Ellerbe, H. (1995). *The Dark Side of Christian History.* Berkeley, CA: Morningstar Books.

Gardner, L. (2002). *Blood Line of the Holy Grail: The Hidden Lineage of Jesus Revealed.* Beverly, MA: Fair Winds Press, Inc.

Graham, L.O. (1999). *Our Kind of People: Inside America's Black Upper Class.* New York: HarperCollins.

Harris, S. (2004). *The End of Faith: Religion, Terror, and the Future of Reason.* New York: W.W. Norton & Company, Inc.

Hawking, S. (1998). *A Brief History of Time 10th ed.* New York: Bantam Books.

Anonymous. (1912, June 16). The hermit of Ferney: Voltaire as a victim of his own garrulity when studied as a man rather than as a writer. The New York Times. retrieved December 16, 2007 from http://query.nytimes.com/

Jalsevac, P. (2004). *The Inherent Racism of Population Control.* Retrieved December 8, 2006 from (http://www.ifrl.org/IFRLDailyNews/040519/1/)

James, C.L.R. (1989). *The Black Jacobins.* New York: Vintage Books.

Johansen, B.E. (1996). *Native American Political Systems and the Evolution of Democracy: An Annotated Bibliography.* Westport, CT: Greenwood Press.

Johnston, D. & Sampson, C. (1995). *Religion, the Missing Dimension of Statecraft.* New York: Oxford University Press.

Jung, C. G. (1968). *Man and His Symbols.* New York: Dell.

Kaltreider, K. (1998). *American Indian Prophecies.* Carlsbad, CA: Hay House.

Lockwood, C.J. (2005). The courage of contraceptive 'convictions': Griswold v Crawford. *Contemporary OB/GYN*, 50(10), 8-11.

Madiou, T. (1987). *Histoire D'Haïti (Vol 3-4).* Port-au-Prince, Haïti: Editions Henri Deschamps.

Millburn, M.A. & Conrad, S.D. (1998). *The Politics of Denial.* Boston, MA: MIT Press.

Miller, A. (1997). *The Drama of the Gifted Child.* New York: Perennial Books.

McWhorter, J. H. (2000). *Losing the Race: Self-Sabotage in Black America.* : Free Press.

Moore, M. (2002). *Stupid White Men.* New York: Penguin Books.

Ohadike, D.C. (2002). *Pan African cultures of resistance A history of liberation struggles in Africa and the diaspora.* Binghamton, NY: Global Publications, Binghamton University.

Ortega y Gasset, J. (1994). *The Revolt of the Masses.* New York: WW Norton & Company.

Parton, J. (1881). *Life of Voltaire.* Boston: Houghton, Mifflin and Company.

Pieterse, J. N. (1992). *White on Black.* New Haven, CT: Yale University Press.

Rice, C. (2005). USA Secretary of States, visiting Haiti, September 2005

Rivkin, E. (1984). *What Crucified Jesus?* New York: UAHC Press.

Roberts, C. (2004). *Founding Mothers: The Women Who Raised Our Nation.* New York: William Morrow.

Rogers, J. A. (1996). *World's Great Men of Color* (Vol. 1). New York: Touchstone Books.

Saul, J. R. (1992). *Voltaire's Bastards: the Dictatorship of Reason in the West.* New York: Vintage Books.

Snelling J. (1991). *The Buddhist Handbook.* Rochester, VT: Inner Traditions International, Ltd.

Spong, J. S. (1992). *Rescuing the Bible from Fundamentalism: A Bishop Rethinks the Meaning of Scripture.* New York: HarperOne.

Spong, J. S. (1999). *Why Christianity Must Change or Die: A Bishop Speaks to Believers in Exile.* New York: HarperOne.

Tragert, J. (2003). *The Complete Idiot's Guide to Iraq.* Indianapolis, IN: Alpha Books.

Voltaire, F.M.A. & Redman, B.R. (1977). *The Portable Voltaire.* New York: Penguin Books.

Wesley, C. "The U.S. Debt to Haiti". Retrieved http://www.schillerinstitute.org/educ/hist/toussaint.html retrieved April 16, 2004

West, C. (2005). *Democracy Matters: Winning the Fight Against Imperialism.* Penguin Books.

West, C. (1989). *The American Evasion of Philosophy: A Genealogy of Pragmatism. Madison, WI:* University of Wisconsin Press.

Wooster, H. (1994). *Faith At the Ramparts: The Philippine Catholic Church and the 1986 Revolution.* In D. Johnson & C. Sampson (Eds.), *Religion, the Missing Dimension of Statecraft.* New York: Oxford Press.

Wyatt, G.E. (1997). *Stolen Women.* New York: Wiley.

To order

Saving Haiti / Saving the World

Go to: www. lulu.com or

Consult our web site: www.savinghaiti.net

On www.savinghaiti.net you may also preview the book, listen to beautiful Haitian tunes, or to radio interviews by one of the authors and/or freely participate in the Free Thinker Forum.

For contact, write to: Saving Haiti / Saving the World
                                Packmail Center of America
                                13015 SW, 89 Place, #163
                                Miami, FL, 33176
                                Tel: 305 454 7920